PRESSURE COOKING

IDA BAILEY ALLEN

Pressure Cooking

Garden City Publishing Co., Inc.

GARDEN CITY, NEW YORK

Acknowledgments

I WISH TO THANK SINCERELY THE FOLLOWING ORGANI-
zations for supplying the illustrations which appear in this
book.

American Broadcasting Company, Television Division,
for photograph of *Ida Bailey Allen and the Chef* in their
video show covering New York, Philadelphia and Schenectady.

Parade Publications, Inc., for permission to use
Pressure Cooking in the Air, from one of my former pic-
ture-food pages; Photographer Tad Horton.

The American Spice Trade Association for the photograph, *Treat Turkey Like Any Other Beast—Cut It Up.*

The National Association of Margarine Manufacturers
for photographs of *Pressured Crab Gumbo* and *Green
Peas With Onion-Spice Seasoning.*

The Brazil Nut Association for the photograph of
Little Christmas Puddings Brazil Style.

The Can Manufacturers Institute for the photograph of
An Hors D'Oeuvre Supper Platter.

The Florida Citrus Commission for the photograph *A
Trio of Grape Fruit Salads.*

The American Meat Institute for photographs of
*Pressured Five-Minute Lamb Chop Platter; Stuffed Roast
of Lamb With Mushrooms; Pressured Pork Tenderloin*

With Pear Compote; Pressed Veal Buffet Style; and *How to Stuff and Truss a Shoulder of Lamb.*

The *Hotel Monthly* for *Battery of Individual Pressure-Cookers in the Palmer House,* Chicago.

Contents

PRESSURE COOKING

Ida Bailey Allen Speaking:

SEVERAL YEARS AGO I BEGAN MAKING THE PRESSURE-cooker my kitchen companion. I experimented with all makes and sizes, pressuring foods of all kinds with amazing results—finer flavor, higher nutrition, unbelievable speed.

But how was Mrs. America going to react to the pressure-cooker? I took a nation-wide trek to find out. Thousands of home-makers attended my studio broadcasts in leading cities and were glad to give their reactions. En route I talked to clubs and PTA groups; rang door bells; chatted over back fences, and even invaded Hollywood!

Everywhere I found almost incredible interest in pressure cooking. Tell us more about it. Give us more recipes. How can we get the most out of our pressure-cooker? Can it really help us to get out of the kitchen? This was what I heard from coast-to-coast.

So here it is—the book YOU requested. It is presented with the prediction that pressure cooking will be adopted as a regular procedure in the homes of America.

CHAPTER I

YOUR PRESSURE-COOKER
AND YOU

COMPLETE DINNERS READY TO EAT IN FIFTEEN MINUTES, vegetables cooked in two or three, fruits stewed in seconds! The amazing performance of the pressure-cooker has captured the imagination of homemakers everywhere who value the saving of time. Not only the seventeen million employed homemakers in the United States, who are carrying on two jobs, but also countless thousands of apron-tied home-staying women who are bringing up families and doing the housework with no outside help. For the old-time domestics and day-workers have, like the hired man, almost disappeared. It is up to the homemaker to solve her problem by increased efficiency.

Is the pressure-cooker the answer to the quick cooking of satisfactory meals? Does its performance equal the advertising claims?

In answer, let me state that, used with intelligence the pressure-cooker can turn out delicious meals in a third or less the usual time. But even more important, it can save, in addition, countless kitchen hours if used for the preparation of foods that do not constitute whole meals in themselves, but that often take up the longest time-element of the meal being prepared. Among these are cereals, dried fruits, fresh and dried vegetables, soups and soup-stock, various desserts that may be steam-cooked, as well as pureed baby foods.

Learn to know the complete possibilities of *your* pressure-cooker; make a habit of using it in every possible way, and you will agree that the advertisements understate its usefulness. 43% of the families in the U. S. own pressure-cookers.

What Is Pressure Cooking?

Pressure cooking is a system rather than a method, by which foods are cooked by super-heated live steam, at a temperature much higher than boiling point. For instance; the temperature inside an average cooker at 15 pounds pressure is 250 degrees Fahrenheit. This high heat, coupled with the fact that the pressure generated in the cooker actually drives the heat into and through the food more than twice as fast as ordinary methods, explains the rapid cooking action.

High Altitudes: Pressure-cookers operate successfully at high altitudes. American Overseas Air Lines have been using pressure-cookers in the galleys on their airliners for several years and report a satisfactory performance.*

The New Cookery

Pressure-cooking belongs definitely to the era of what I term the New Cookery, an era which recognizes the necessity of conserving food values, avoiding waste by decreasing shrinkage, speeding up cooking rates to save kitchen-hours, preserving natural flavors and producing more appetizing food.

And this New Cookery is not difficult. It can be mastered by any man or woman, young or old, interested in good food and the vital necessity of keeping the body well

---

*Allow extra time for pressure to be built up to 15 lbs. and 10% more time for processing.

nourished and in a state of good repair. The amount of effort and study required is negligible. You need merely a working knowledge of the balanced ration and necessary food elements; of simple everyday cooking methods, and the intelligent use of the pressure-cooker to *protect* and *conserve* the nutritional elements of the many foods that can be cooked with it.

Pressure-Cookers and Pressure Sauce-Pans

When I say "pressure-cooker" just what do I mean? Is this synonymous with the pressure saucepan? As far as I am concerned it is. For the method of cooking in both is the same. A saucepan is traditionally a cooking utensil with a handle at the side; the dictionary also defines it as a stew-pan. So in this book I have grouped all utensils of the pressure type as pressure-cookers.

The stores are showing many models, including those with a flexible top, with sliding-handles, spring top, elliptical top, the breathing collar closure, and the metal-to-metal seal with clamps. These pressure-cookers are made of pressed or stamped aluminum, cast aluminum metal alloy, enamelled steel, or stainless steel with a copper bottom, and are variously equipped with pressure indicators, gauges and controls. Some have pet-cocks or valves for the quick release of steam and cooling of the cooker. All have a safety device—the over-pressure plug. Choice depends on personal preference. If you are planning to buy a pressure-cooker in the near future, shop thoughtfully before you buy. Watch the demonstrator closely. Then actually handle the cooker yourself. Select the model that will be sufficiently large for your needs and that is easiest for you to operate.

In any case, be sure to buy a model made by a reliable manufacturer. I would recommend purchasing a cooker from 4 to 7 quarts capacity whatever the size of the family. This type of cooker can be used for all kinds and amounts of food. If a second cooker is needed—and I strongly recommend it—choose a 4 quart size if the family consists of more than four persons, or a 2 quart size for a family of two, or to use solely for the preparation of food for an infant or young child, or buy a pressure-fryer, top 10½".

If you can find a cooker equipped with insets or compartment pans it will prove most satisfactory. Or "dividers" are on sale for use in certain types of cookers. A divider is an aluminum gadget divided into sections or divisions which make it possible to pressure-cook several foods at the same time. Various manufacturers recommend the right kind of divider for their cooker. It is advisable to follow their suggestions. A colander cover is useful.*

Pressure Cooking Saves Nutrients and Conserves Food Values

Let me prove the truth of this statement. There is no escape of steam from a pressure-cooker as there is in most usual cooking methods. Remember how the aroma from a regulation boiled dinner fills the kitchen? This is because the evaporating steam carries with it part of the nutrients of the meat and vegetables. Actual wasted *substance* is what you smell—the valuable soluble proteins, minerals and fats.

Full food values are conserved when a pressure-cooker is used. The tough meat fibres and the gelatine in the gristle are thoroughly cooked and made tender; calcium in bones is cooked out and made available; the starch-grains in cereals are fully burst open, and so are conse-

---

*A cooker equipped with a removable collar attachment makes the cooker deeper as needed. It is useful for cooking large pieces of meat or for canning. The collar may be bought separately.

quently well-cooked and digestible. The minerals are retained in the foods, not flooded into the cooking water. And what little cooking liquid there is can be made into a sauce for vegetables, or gravy to serve with meats. As to the vitamins—that is a big story. First let me give a bit of scientific data, then the reasons why they are conserved by pressure-cooking.

According to scientific research, the major factors that account for nutritional losses during general cooking may be briefly summarized as follows:

Heat: When prolonged may alter a protein and make it less digestible, destroy some of the amino acids, or cause a breakdown of fats. It may also destroy certain vitamins, such as thiamin, niacin and panthothenic acid.

Oxygen: The oxygen in the air particularly reacts against vitamins A and C, impairing their efficiency by oxidation. Fats are also easily oxidized in the presence of air.

Water: Water by itself does not readily react with nutrients, although when much water is used in cooking it floods or washes out the nutrients. However, combined with heat, water appears to inactivate thiamin—a key member of the B complex vitamin.

Light: This readily destroys riboflavin, another important member of the B complex and hastens the oxidation of fats.

Ideally, cooking should be carried on as rapidly as possible, with a minimum use of water, and in the absence of light and air. With many foods this may be efficiently accomplished by pressure cooking, which eliminates contact with the oxygen of the air, uses minimum liquid, admits no light and speeds up cooking processes by the use of live steam under pressure, which saves from fifty to seventy-five per cent of the usual cooking time and so avoids prolonged heat. This brings me to my next point.

Pressure Cooking Saves Kitchen Hours

Kitchen engineers agree that approximately half of a homemaker's working day is spent in preparing and serving meals, and in cleaning up afterwards. This amount of time is unnecessary, and may be traced to an inefficiently arranged kitchen, to old-fashioned time-consuming cooking methods, and to the use of too many cooking utensils and serving dishes, which makes dish washing a lengthy process. Every thinking woman is making a real attempt to make her kitchen a convenient food workshop. But a very small percentage as yet are using, or learning to use, the New Methods of Cookery. What Mother *did* is still what Daughter *does*. But in this stream-lined age, cookery progresses like any other science. And I have yet to find anyone who can convince me that it is an expression of affection or even good sense to spend unnecessary hours in the preparation of meals—especially when the new methods ensure improved flavor and nutrition. You have to be convinced? Fine, there's nothing I like better than a good argument. So please study the following chart which gives the timings for a few of the old- and new-fashioned cooking methods.

These time-savings you must admit are spectacular—but they are actual facts you can prove for yourself. They range from over 90% down with an average of 75% time-saving. When authorities say that pressure cooking can save from one-fourth to one-third of the usual cooking time, they are being just plain conservative. The majority of time-savings are actually much higher. And these time differentials can be applied to three-fourths of the foods prepared regularly for our tables—not only for dinner, but for breakfast and lunch, special foods for children and

Foods to be Cooked	Old Method	Pressure Method (at 15 pounds)
ASPARAGUS	15 to 20 minutes	1 to 2 minutes
BEETS (whole)	45 minutes	18 minutes
CAULIFLOWER (whole)	25 minutes	5 minutes
POTATOES (medium-sized)	35 minutes	10 minutes
PEAS (fresh)	15 minutes	1½ minutes
DRIED BEANS	2 hours	30 minutes
SOUP-STOCK	4 hours	30 minutes
BEEF STEW	1½ to 2 hours	15 minutes
POT ROAST (4 pounds)	2½ hours	44 minutes
SMOKED TONGUE (3½ pounds)	3 to 4 hours	45 minutes
PORK ROAST (4 pounds)	3½ hours	48 minutes
SPARE-RIBS	2 hours	15 minutes
CHICKEN-ROASTING (4 pounds)	2 hours	28 minutes
CRACKED WHEAT	3 hours	30 minutes
CUP CUSTARDS	30 minutes	6 minutes
STEAMED PUDDINGS	4 hours	50 minutes
DRIED FIGS	1½ hours	10 minutes
BAKED BANANAS	20 minutes	30 seconds

the beforehand cooking of many foods used for party
refreshments.

Lady Come Out of the Kitchen

The right choice of foods and the habitual use of a
pressure-cooker can save the average homemaker at least
an hour a day—365 hours a year—which means around
forty-five eight-hour working days or six and a half working weeks.

Unfortunately, this time cannot be saved in one lump
—to make possible a long house-keeping vacation. But it
can be salvaged at the rate of at least an hour a day. And
who wouldn't welcome 365 *small* vacations? You can save
even more time if you learn to cook ahead, as described in
Chapter XX—MEALS THAT SAVE KITCHEN HOURS. And
this time-saving can all be accomplished, not by speeding
yourself up, wracking your nerves and body in the attempt
to beat the clock, but by the intelligent use of your pressure-
cooker through the application of the principles given in
this book.

You don't hurry—the pressure-cooker hurries for you!
You don't even need to get hot and red-faced, for pressure-
cooking is so fast the kitchen does not become overheated.
As to that tiresome job of washing the pots and pans, it is
cut in half because you will use only half as many.

Yes, I am enthusiastic. I confess I am sold on pressure-
cooking. But it must not be supposed that pressure-cooking
will supplant all other methods of cooking. It can and
should be used for the preparation of all foods calling for
the presence of moist heat; these include cooked cereals,
soups, fresh vegetables, the legumes, meat, poultry and
game (other than when broiled and in some cases oven-
roasted); fish and shellfish in many forms, dried fruits,
certain cooked fresh fruits, and many steamed puddings

and other steamed desserts. The usual methods will still be needed for cooking eggs, most sautéing, rechauffées, deep frying, broiling, some oven-roasting, salads, baking and the making of many desserts, canapés and tidbits, fruit appetizers and cups, etc.

Do Pressure-Cooked Foods Taste Good?

This is a question easily answered. Pressure-cooking conserves full nutritive value, therefore, pressure-cooked foods contain full flavor. Until you have personally eaten these full-flavored foods, you cannot imagine how appetizing they are. In some cases they actually taste a bit exotic, like a de luxe edition of a familiar food. The famous Palmer House in Chicago, where the best in food flavor is appreciated, was the first hotel to feature vegetables pressure-cooked to order, and special vegetable dinners cooked and served in individual pressure sauce-pans. Not only were the vegetables sent to the table superb in flavor, but they were so beautiful and shapely that only a color photograph could show how well the color was retained. And remember, this retention of color pigment means that the actual substance of the vegetable, with all its nutrients and flavor elements, has been conserved; it has not been washed out.

The fine flavors of pressure-cooked meat, poultry and game, fish and shellfish, are due to the same reasons. When brown-heated as necessary, and cooked without too much water, exactly according to the directions given in this book, the flavors are unsurpassed.

Soups are pressured with the exact amount of liquid to make a stated amount; it is not necessary to allow even an ounce extra for evaporation. For this does not take place. The pressure-cooker is sealed during the pressuring period. Consequently every whiff of those delicious meat and vegetable juices and all those flavorful mineral salts are retained in the soup. Because of this conservation of natural elements, less seasoning is needed in pressure-cooking. In fact it is often a better plan to season after cooking.

This is not a book on dietetics. It is a book on pressure cooking. But as a graduate dietitian, privileged to work closely with the medical profession for many years, I must emphasize the health values of pressure-cooked food. Or have I already driven home this point that pressure-cooked foods not only *"taste good* but *are good* for you?" Think a moment: More protein in more digestible form—the amino acids retained to a greater extent; starch grains that are fully cooked and so converted into digestible dextrose; greater conservation of vitamins and minerals; less oxidation; and last of all, better flavored foods with greater appetite-appeal. Doctors recommend pressure-cooked foods for infants; for ulcer and anemia diets. So much for the dietetic and nutritional point of view. The lay person will have full proof when he tastes the fine flavors of the pressured food and discovers that he feels better for the eating.

How About the Thrifty Foods?

Pressure cooking is all very well, you say, for people who can afford to buy frying chickens and fresh peas, tenderized ham, jumbo shrimp and the finest of dried fruits. How about the mortals whose budget indicates cabbage, turnip, dried beans, and the thriftiest cuts of meat? Here is an occasion where they can rejoice—for any thrifty food can be made epicurean in a pressure-cooker. For generations chefs have built great reputations and made fortunes

on tasty dishes based on thrifty foods, which they pains-
takingly slow-cooked for interminable hours. You can cre-
ate dishes of thrifty foods quite as delicious in a fraction
of this time. And while you may not build a fortune with
the money you save, you can salvage a sizable amount
each year, over the cost of more expensive foods. Try keeping track of such savings in a piggy-bank. When you
pressure-cook a pot-roast shoulder of veal instead of a rib-
roast of beef, drop the difference in the cost per pound
in the bank—and don't forget to add enough pennies
to cover the fuel saved by adopting the top-of-the-
stove pressure-method, instead of the oven with its higher
fuel operating costs. I guarantee that you will have a most
agreeable surprise by the end of the year. In fact, the
intelligent use of the pressure-cooker can cut fuel bills at
least a third—an appreciable saving, especially if you are
using bottled gas, or live in a locality where the electric
cooking rate is high. This brings me to a question often
asked.

Can a Pressure-Cooker Be Used on Any Type of Stove?

Yes—pressure cooking can be done successfully with
any kind of stove operated by any kind of fuel, *as long as
the heat is steady* and adjusted to keep the pressure even.
In other words, in pressure cooking the steam pressure
must not fluctuate, or the foods will not be cooked in the
given time. For this reason be sure the range top is level so
the action of the control or indicator will not be impeded.

Gas, bottled gas, electricity, wood, coal, kerosene,
canned alcohol, a good sheltered barbecue grill or outdoor fireplace, or even a large candle-stove will operate a
pressure-cooker. A full-sized range is not necessary. A gas
or electric plate, or even an old-fashioned one-burner kero-

sene stove can be used. You can pressure-cook wherever it is convenient—in a full-sized kitchen, a kitchenette, a trailer, outdoors at barbecues, picnics and when camping; and even in your living-room. For pressure cooking is clean and odorless—and will not harm the furnishings by escaping fat and steam.

The one point I must re-emphasize is to pre-prepare the food according to the directions given in this book. Then close the cooker, bring up the pressure according to the manufacturer's directions, and pressure at 15 pounds with an even steady heat the required length of time. If the pressure gets beyond 15 pounds, reduce the heat, or move the cooker to a less heated part of the range. If using the recipes in this book, cool the cooker at once after pressuring is complete, according to the manufacturer's instructions.

Using a Pressure-Cooker

First to review the basic principles of pressure cooking. A greater pressure than normal is built up inside the cooker by heating water or other liquid to a rapid boil in the covered cooker. This exhausts or drives out the air. The pressure-control is then adjusted so the steam will not escape and the pressure within the cooker can be raised to the required point and maintained with low heat. Cookers are so designed that a pressure higher than fifteen pounds is automatically released through a safety device, so they are safe to use. There is such a safety plug in every cooker top.

This "blows" if the vent becomes clogged or the cooker is overheated or runs dry. The plug can be replaced. They are on sale at the dealers.

Some cookers are adjusted to cooking at three pressures, all others are adjusted to fifteen pounds pressure.

5 pounds pressure equals 228 degrees F. and is used for canning tomatoes and fruits; also for cooking fresh peas, or kernelled corn, and green lima beans if desired.

10 pounds pressure equals 240 degrees F. and is used for canning non-acid vegetables, certain made dishes and soups. Or for cooking certain meats, fish and vegetables.

15 pounds pressure equals 250 degrees F. and is used for all pressuring processes given in this book, as well as for the sterilization of baby bottles or other articles. The advantage of using a single pressuring unit makes it unnecessary to memorize so many timings. It also saves pressuring time and fuel. I personally find foods processed the right length of time at 15 pounds pressure satisfactory in every way.

General Rules for Using a Pressure-Cooker

1. Know your cooker. Carefully study the manufacturer's directions that come with it and follow them. A pressure-cooker is not just another utensil. It is a mechanically designed precision tool and cannot be operated by guess-work. It is accurate in its cooking reactions; it demands accuracy of use. Because of this fact guess-work is eliminated and pressure cooking becomes an easy system to follow.

2. Be sure the vent opening is properly cleaned and clear of all foreign matter after each using.

3. Put in the rack or not as directed. Use the exact amount of water or liquid specified in the recipe.

4. Fill the cooker no more than three-fourths to seven-eighths full of solid food; use three-fourths for a flexible or spring-top cooker, seven-eighths for solid-dome-top types. Under no circumstances should the food touch the top of the cooker while pressuring, as this might clog the vent-pipe or block the safety plug.

5. Fill the cooker no more than half full of soup, liquids, or with cooking cereal.

6. If pressuring frozen meat, poultry or fish, either commercially frozen or from the home locker, it must often be defrosted before pressuring for use in most dishes unless otherwise directed. (See pages 78, 223.)

7. Unless a boiled or stewed effect is desired, use just enough water or liquid to come to the top of the rack, *not over it.*

8. Be sure that a steady flow of cold air with steam is coming out of the vent before pressure is built up. This takes from two to four minutes according to the size of the cooker, and the temperature of the liquid and food when put in.

9. Count pressuring minutes for recipes given in this book, *from the time when the indicator, weight or gauge shows fifteen pound pressure.*

10. Regulate the heat under the cooker so the pressure will keep even. If it tends to go up, even when the heat is lowered, place an asbestos mat under the cooker; use two mats if necessary. Keep a watchful eye on the cooker and the pounds pressure.

11. When pressuring is finished turn off the gas, kerosene or alcohol burner. If using an electric unit or coal range, remove the cooker at once to avoid further cooking from stored heat. Reduce pressure according to the manufacturer's directions. Foods tend to over-cook if allowed to stand in the cooker after pressuring. So in using the recipes in this book reduce the pressure as soon as the processing is finished.

12. When the gauge or indicator shows that all pressure has receded, remove the weight, or indicator if your cooker has one, and open the cooker. If the cover is at all difficult to remove, it is a sign that some steam pressure still exists, so wait a minute or two longer. The cover can be easily removed when all pressure is released. Under no circumstances attempt to force off the cover, even though it seems to stick. You might dent the edge of the cooker, making it impossible thereafter to obtain a perfect seal, or you might get burned if steam pressure still exists.*

How to Cool the Cooker–or Reduce Pressure

Follow the manufacturer's directions. If these say to place the cooker in cold water, do just that. Set it in a pan of cold water, preferably in the kitchen sink. *Do not* allow water from the tap to run over the weight, indicator or gauge. Be careful in using a flexible top cooker not to run water over the top for as soon as the steam recedes and the seal is broken, water can seep into the cooker around the edge. Food in a cooker cooled just to the point where it can be opened, is usually the right temperature for serving. If not, quickly re-heat it.

How to Pressure Cook Two or More Foods at a Time

This subject is discussed in Chapter XX—MEALS THAT SAVE KITCHEN HOURS—and in various other spots in this book. If you are fortunate enough to possess a pressure-cooker equipped with compartment or inset pans, the problem is solved, and you can easily prepare three or

---

*If the cover sticks after waiting a reasonable time, run a piece of wire into the indicator weight, as possibly it has become clogged, and a small amount of pressure, insufficient to operate the safety plug, still exists. Then wait two or three minutes before opening.

even four foods at a time. If you do not own such a cooker, smaller amounts of three or four foods can be cooked at one time in a four-quart cooker by using the divider already described; or by tying vegetables loosely in parchment paper, and placing in the cooker tied-side up. As parchment paper is stiff, it must first be rinsed with cold water and the excess water pressed out, to make it soft enough to handle. It will not tear, and if rinsed and dried can be used over and over again. Waxed paper cannot be substituted.

Only foods requiring the same length of time to pressure-cook can be started and finished together. Otherwise the pressure must be reduced, or the cooker must be cooled, then opened and any additional food put in so the pressure-ing of all will be completed at the same time.

The Care, Cleaning and Storing of the Pressure-Cooker

Handle all indicator weights or controls with care, for dropping may injure them.

If the weight has a handle, hang it on a special hook. Otherwise keep it **inside** the pressure-cooker when not in use so it will not be misplaced.

Do not put an indicator weight in water, as this may cause it to rust. Clean with a pipe cleaner instead of water. Do not use a toothpick or match for it may break off. If the cooker has a gauge it should be checked occasionally by the manufacturer to make sure it is accurate.

Do not pour cold water into a cooker that is dry and overheated as the sudden chill may crack the metal. Let the cooker cool a few minutes, then add boiling water.

Wash the rack with a brush to remove all food particles. Scald and dry it thoroughly.

Wash the cooker with soap and water. Scour inside if necessary with a mild abrasive or metal sponge. Scald and dry thoroughly.*

Sun the cooker occasionally. Careful washing and drying prevents the formation of pits in cast aluminum cookers. These sometimes occur when the water used in them flows through lead, copper or brass pipes. These pits are usually caused by electrolysis started by deposits of other metals on the surface of the aluminum. The two metals in contact in the presence of moisture, form a little electric cell, and after considerable time a speck or pit may form. If there is any tendency toward pitting, scour the cooker with a metal sponge. These pits do not have any deleterious effect on food or health.

If fish, onion or other odors cling to the cooker, fill with warm water containing one tablespoon vinegar to the quart and boil five minutes. Then wash as usual with soap and water.

Polish the outside of the cooker with a suitable cleaner.

Store the cooker with the cover off, or to save space, upside down; this will insure full circulation of air and prevent the possible formation of stale odors.

All pressure-cookers are sold with charts and clearly printed directions for use. Put these under cellophane and tack them up in the kitchen near the range, so that any stranger or member of the family can see at a glance how to operate the cooker.

---

*Spots and discolorations can be easily removed by the use of 2 tablespoons cream of tartar dissolved in 1 quart water. This can be kept in a jar and used when needed.

CHAPTER II

PRESSURE COOKING TERMS, ADAPTING YOUR OWN RECIPES, PRESSURE COOKING FOR TWO, MEASUREMENTS

A NUMBER OF UNFAMILIAR TERMS ARE USED IN THIS book, for pressure cooking is a new science and calls for its own phraseology. Instead of saying "cook" a certain length of time, I have generally used the word "pressure" or "process," as the word "cook" connotes the regulation method, and proves confusing to many pressure-cooker owners.

Correspondingly, I have created a new verb, with the infinitive "to pressure" and the participle "pressuring"; this contrasts with "to cook" or "cooking." So you will find the words "pressured," "pressuring" or "pressure" in constant use as cooking terms. As a synonym to "to pressure," I have used the word "process," long associated with pressure-canning, but little used with pressure cooking. Webster defines the word "process" as follows: "To heat, as fruit, with steam under pressure, so as to cook or sterilize." The length of time and the pounds pressure to which the food is subjected, determine whether it is cooked or sterilized.

In place of the word "sear" which implies scorching almost to burning point, usually in a pre-heated heavy kettle or frying pan, I have used the term *brown-heat* which calls for the slower, more thorough browning required for preparing most meat, poultry and some fish for pressure cooking. (See page 74.)

"Brown-crisp" is the phrase coined to describe the process giving to meat or poultry the appetizing flavor and texture associated with oven-roasting. (See page 75.)

Special names have been given to various pressure-cooking processes, which are adaptations of regulation methods; these include "Pressure-Roasting"; "Pressure-Braising"; "Pressure-Fricasseeing"; "Pressure-Steam-Boiling" and others described in this book. For a complete list of these processes see the Index.

Adapting Home Recipes to Pressure Cooking

Favorite home recipes for the preparation of soups, cereals, meat, poultry, game or fish, usually may be adapted to pressure-cooking.

General Rule: Read the instructions for preparing such foods given in this book. Reduce the amount of liquid in the home recipe to the right quantity to use with the food to be pressured. Correspondingly reduce the amount of seasoning, as there will be less liquid to dilute it. Use a fourth less fat.

For timings required for pressure-roasting, pot-roasting, etc., consult the detailed instructions and recipes given in this book and adapt your own recipes to these patterns.

To select accompanying vegetables that can be pressured at the same time and *in* the same time, consult the Vegetable Time-Table on pages 259 to 267.

GUIDE CHART

For Estimating Pressuring Time for a Few Foods in Favorite Home Recipes

Food	Preparation	Pressuring Time at 15 Pounds
CHOPS	Cut 1 in. thick and brown-heated	8 minutes
MEAT or POULTRY	Cut in ½ in. cubes and brown-heated	8 to 10 minutes according to tenderness
VEAL, BEEF, LAMB or PORK	Thin slices, brown-heated	3 minutes for veal 4 minutes for beef or lamb 6 minutes for pork
BROILING CHICKENS	Sectioned and brown-heated	12 to 15 minutes according to size
DUCKLINGS	Sectioned and brown-heated	12 to 15 minutes according to size
TENDERIZED HAM	Sliced ¼ inch thick	4 to 5 minutes
RAW HAM— Untreated	Sliced ¼ inch thick	10 minutes
FISH FILLETS	Cut ½ to 1 inch thick	5 to 6 minutes

How Much Space to Allow

Fill cooker no more than half full of cooking cereal, soup, or fruit sauce.

Fill no more than comfortably with meat, poultry or vegetables. Be *sure* the food does not touch the cover.

Rice swells about three times its original size, so plan accordingly.

Beans swell from three to four times their original size.

Spaghetti and macaroni double in size; noodles swell only a little.

Dried fruits usually double in size.

Recipes in This Book Serve Four to Six

The exact number of persons to be served food prepared by any recipe cannot be accurately estimated, for this depends on several factors—whether or not they are "big" or "small" eaters; whether they are young children, adolescents or adults. And whether the adults are young or old, or engaged in active or sedentary work. However, as a general rule foods prepared by the recipes given in this book will be sufficient for a family of two adults (a man and woman), one adolescent, and one child up to ten years of age; "seconds" will often be possible, or a little food may be left over toward luncheon, or for a young child's dinner the next day.

In cases where the food is adapted to service a second time, either "as is" or attractively re-serviced in some other form, the recipes are planned to produce sufficient food for serving at two meals. Wherever possible this should be done to save time and fuel. For instance, in pressure-ing potatoes, cook enough for two meals; at the first serve hot flaky potatoes, and the next day serve them cottage-fried or lyonnaise. Cook enough peas, string beans, or mixed vegetables to use hot one day, and in a salad the next; process enough beets or carrots to serve hot, and provide sufficient for quick pickling for service later on.

Pressure Cooking for Two

In cooking for two persons, or two adults and a young child up to five years of age, *halve the ingredients* in the recipes, and write the quantities in the margin next to the printed amounts to save recalculating each time. In dividing recipes it is helpful to know that 16 level tablespoons of anything equal 1 cup or a half pint; and that 3 teaspoonfuls equal 1 tablespoon.

The pressuring time remains the same.

Small quantities can be as successfully pressured as the larger amounts.

Caution: Always use the amount of liquid designated in the recipe. These amounts should not be reduced or augmented.

Measurements and Measuring

A set of standard measuring spoons, and half pint and pint glass measuring cups were used in standardizing the recipes in this book. A nest of four single capacity cups, ¼c., ½c., ⅓c. and 1 c. each, makes the accurate measuring of fractions of a cup much easier.

All measurements are level: Correct measuring is essential.

Flour: Sift all-purpose or cake flour once before measuring; stir all whole grain flours or cereals before measuring. Level off with a kitchen knife.

Liquids: In measuring liquids put the cup on a level surface and fill exactly to the level designated.

Fats: Pack all fats into the measuring unit and level off with a knife.

You Can Expect Fine Results

Adequate knowledge of your pressure-cooker and how to use it; accurate measurements and the careful following of the manufacturer's directions, and the recipes given in this book will produce excellent foods.

There may be a slight variation in pressure-timings due to the finer or poorer quality of the meat used; the garden freshness of vegetables or the fact that they have lost moisture by standing in a city market; or the extra dehydration of dried peas, beans, lentils or some cereals that have been stored a long time. There is also a difference in the amount of moisture foods will absorb. But these instances will not occur frequently. For these recipes have all been standardized with foods bought at super-markets in different parts of the country—the same type bought by homemakers nationwide.

CHAPTER III

SOUPS AND CHOWDERS DOUBLE-QUICK

Don't believe it if someone tells you it is imprac-tical to make soups at home because it takes too much time. For this is a tale handed down by the generations that simmered soup for hours on the back of the range.

Today's soup is something quite different. By pressure cooking, it may be made in a fraction of an hour; and moreover it contains all the fine flavors, vitalizing vitamins and minerals largely lost in the steam evaporating from soup made by old-fashioned methods.

Pressure Cooking Soups

In making pressure-cooked soups, start with the right amount of liquid required to produce the quantity of finished soup desired.

This soup is pressured with no evaporation whatever, and in a small fraction of the time needed by the usual methods. A quart and a half of completed soup can be made in a four quart pressure-cooker, and up to four quarts in a seven quart cooker. This may be soup that is ready to serve, or it may be concentrated soup, made with half the quantity of liquid needed, and diluted before serv-ing with hot water, vegetable juices, milk, meat or fish stock, to bring the quantity of soup to the required amount. For instance, a pint of concentrated soup-stock is diluted before serving with an equal amount of liquid, just as many brands of commercially canned soups are diluted. And by the way, if soup, or soup stock is to be stored in the refrigerator for several days, always make it in concentrated form, as it then occupies less space. In other words, valuable refrigerator room should not be used for storing water. Instead add the liquid when the time comes to ready the soup for serving.

Tantalizing–Appetizing–Thrifty

There is no more tantalizing yet thrifty way to add a luxury touch to a meal, or to provide a satisfying main course dish for lunch or supper than to serve an appetizing soup. And all types of delightful soups from borsch to bouillabaisse can be pressured quickly, as you will see in this chapter. And remember, good use can be made of cracked bones, vegetable tops, outer lettuce leaves, some well-washed vegetables such as onions and carrots, green pea pods, trimmings from celery, string beans, spinach and other greens, by accumulating them from day-to-day for use in making basic soup stock. Needless to say these oddments should be carefully cleaned and refrigerated until used. As the leaves and skins of vegetables contain a major part of the vitamins and minerals better put them in soup to nourish the family instead of putting them in the wastecan.

Do's for Pressure Cooking Soups

Seasoning soups: Underseason, rather than season with a lavish hand. Seasoning can always be added, but it can never be removed.

Crack bones: Always crack open all bones, so the vitamins, minerals, flavor and all nutrients in the marrow can be released into the soup stock.

Remove fat: Before starting to make soup containing meat or poultry, cut off as much fat as possible, as excess fat may clog the pressure-cooker vent.

Amount of liquid: Use sufficient liquid only to *half fill* the pressure-cooker. Vegetables, bones, etc., may come almost to the top, but the liquid should not go beyond the half-way point.

Selecting vegetables for soup: When making a soup containing vegetables, be sure they are kinds that call for the same cooking time, or some of them will be overcooked and mushy. To ascertain these cooking times, see the timetable for cooking vegetables, on pages 259 to 267.

Adding vegetables: When vegetables are to be added to a meat, poultry, vegetable or fish soup stock, first cool the cooker before opening according to the manufacturer's directions. Then strain the stock, return it to the pressure-cooker, add the vegetables, bring again to fifteen pounds pressure, and pressure the length of time the vegetables require.

Cereals As Soup Thickeners

When cereals are used to thicken soups, the cooker should be cooled, opened and the cereal added at the correct time needed for pressure cooking. (See Cereal Time-Table, page 303.) However, if the entire preparation of the soup takes the same time as the entire cooking of the cereal, the cereal may be added when the soup is started to pressure-cook. For example, white rice pressure-cooks in ten minutes. If the entire soup takes only ten minutes' preparation time, the rice may be added in the beginning. Otherwise it must be added at the correct time. Cereals suitable to use in soups include white or brown rice, cracked wheat, white or dark farina, whole cornmeal, Irish oatmeal, buckwheat, and hominy grits.

How to Add Spices–Soup Herbs, etc.

If celery leaves and stalks, soup herbs and whole spices such as bay leaves and peppercorns are tied in a bit of gauze before combining with the soup ingredients, they can easily be removed, and the bother of straining the soup and washing the unnecessary utensils can be avoided.

Soybean Flour for Nutritional Value

If it is advisable to bring up the protein value of a meal in which little or no meat is served, any soup may be thickened by the use of soybean flour. In this case use twice as much soybean as would be used of wheat flour.

How to Thicken Soups

In thickening any soup, whether wheat or soy flour is used, a choice of two methods may be used. In any case, first cool and open the cooker.

Method I: Before adding, stir the flour *smooth* with an equal amount of cold water, cold vegetable juice or cold milk; add to the soup, stir until the soup boils over; then reduce the heat and let it simmer three minutes *without pressure.*

Method II: If the soup is in concentrated form, add the required amount of liquid for serving. Blend the flour with butter or margarine. Add a half cup of the hot soup, stir until *smooth,* pour into the soup in the cooker, and cook and stir until the soup boils, then simmer for three minutes *without pressure.*

To Remove Fat from Hot Soup Stock

Roll up a paper towel tight and use this to blot up the fat from the surface of the broth. When the end is moist, snip it off with the kitchen scissors and continue removing fat with the dry portion.

Adding Garnishes

These should be added after the soup is completely prepared, whether they are garnishes to add to soup before serving, such as minced parsley or chives, sliced lemon or chopped hard-cooked eggs; or whether they are "garnishes" as known to commercial soup canners, such as cooked vegetables, diced meat or fowl; or a cooked cereal, such as rice, barley, or noodles, which are in reality part of the soup itself.

Adapting Your Own Soup Recipes to Pressure Cooking

Read the recipe carefully. If it calls for so much liquid that the pressure-cooker will be more than half full, reduce the quantity proportionately. Also reduce by one-third the usual amount of seasoning as none of the flavor will be lost by evaporation through steam. Go gently on whole spices, such as bay leaf, chili powder, peppercorns and whole cloves. Remember that if raw vegetables are called for, the cooker must be cooled according to the manufacturer's directions and opened when the right moment comes to add them. It is advisable to add thickening at the end of the pressuring time. Allow one-third of the usual time for making cream of vegetable soups, one-fourth of the usual time for pressuring soups of pre-cooked packaged dried peas and beans, and a fourth of the usual time for soups made from non-treated beans or lentils which have not been soaked overnight.

Storing Soup Stock

Whatever kind of soup stock is made, it should be quickly cooled, poured into a glass jar, closely covered and stored in a really cold refrigerator—45 degrees is the temperature required for adequate refrigeration. Remember, pressure-cooked stock contains all the gelatin in the bones, and any gelatinous food needs the protection of cold. Plain soup stock, which does not contain pieces of vegetables or other food, will keep about five days under these conditions. Excellent soup stock can be made with smaller quantities of meat, because there is no evaporation to take off flavor.

Soup stock is useful not only to keep on hand to use in quickly putting together many kinds of soup, but it is also of help in making good gravies, appetizing sauces, and various savory cereal and vegetable dishes. For instance, one of the most delicious vegetables served by the French is potatoes cooked in bouillon.

If considerable cooking is to be done because the family is large, it pays both economically and gastronomically to make soup stock; but if the family is small soup stock is seldom needed. It is often a better plan to use canned bouillon or consommé, or use water with the right amount of one of the yeast extracts that tastes like meat; or use meat extract or bouillon cubes. However, be careful not to add too much as all these products contain considerable salt and so add a salty flavor to any dish. The best proportions to use are one-half teaspoon meat or meat type extract to one cup of boiling water. Or a bouillon cube to each cup and a half of water.

Pressured Soups and Soup Stock

Recipes proportioned to serve four to six.
All measurements are level.
Timings are minutes required for actual pressuring.
Cool cooker as soon as processing is done.

BROWN BEEF SOUP STOCK
1½ quarts
30 minutes

3 pounds shin or shank of beef
6 cups cold water (to half fill cooker)
1 teaspoon peppercorns
3 cloves
½ bay leaf

¼ teaspoon each marjoram and thyme
½ teaspoon celery seed or 1 cup fresh celery leaves
1 scrubbed carrot sliced
1 peeled onion sliced

1⅓ teaspoons salt

1. Cut the meat from the bones; brown it in beef drippings directly in the cooker. Crack the bone and add to the meat. (This adds flavor and calcium from the bone itself and valuable nutrients from the bone marrow.)

2. Add the water and the remaining ingredients.

3. Close the cooker, and bring slowly to 15 pounds pressure. Process 30 minutes.

4. Strain off the liquid and save the meat. The liquid will be highly concentrated. Cool quickly and remove the fat from the surface.

5. Store in a covered glass jar in the refrigerator. Dilute with an equal quantity of hot water before using.

FRENCH ONION SOUP
1 quart
2 minutes

¼ teaspoon sugar
3 tablespoons butter or margarine
3 cups peeled onion sliced thin

2 cups pressure-cooked brown soup stock
2 cups hot water
6 half slices buttered toast
Grated cheese, preferably Parmesan

1. Put the sugar into the pressure-cooker. Let stand over a low heat until it melts. Then add the butter; when melted put in the onions and sauté until yellowed. Do not brown the onions.

2. Add the soup stock and water; close the cooker, bring to 15 pounds pressure for 2 minutes.

3. Meantime cover the toast with the grated Parmesan cheese and place under the broiler until the cheese melts.

4. Serve in soup plates with a piece of the cheese-d toast in each plate.

BROWN MUSHROOM SOUP
1 quart

1. In a heavy saucepan sauté ¾ cup chopped fresh or canned mushrooms in ½ tablespoon butter or margarine.

2. Add ½ cup cooked white or brown rice, and 2 tablespoons minced parsley or sweet green pepper.

3. Put in 2 cups brown soup stock and 2 cups hot water. Add 2 tablespoons Sherry wine if desired.

4. Bring to boiling point and serve with or without a garnish of 1 tablespoon sour cream to each plate.

TOMATO BOUILLON
1 quart

1. In a heavy saucepan combine 1½ cups brown soup stock, 1 cup water, and 1½ cups tomato juice.
2. Bring to boiling point. Season with ½ teaspoon Worcestershire sauce and serve in bouillon cups. Garnish with a thin slice of lemon or lime if desired.

BRAZILIAN SQUASH SOUP
1 quart
3 minutes

1. In a small heavy saucepan melt 1 tablespoon butter or margarine.
2. In this sauté 1½ cups small cubes of summer or winter squash (skin and seeds removed). Add 2 cups brown soup stock, and 2 cups water.
3. Bring to 15 pounds pressure for 3 minutes.

VEGETABLE MEDLEY SOUP
6 cups
3 minutes

1 tablespoon butter or margarine
½ teaspoon sugar
½ cup string beans in inch lengths
1 cup white cabbage shredded fine
½ cup diced celery
½ cup sliced peeled carrot
½ cup sliced peeled turnip
1 peeled onion diced
½ cup shredded peeled parsnip
¼ teaspoon salt
1½ cups canned tomatoes
1½ cups brown soup stock
1½ cups boiling water

1. Melt the butter or margarine in the pressure-cooker, and add the sugar. Cook until beginning to brown. Add all the vegetables and toss lightly in the butter until they begin to turn color. Add the remaining ingredients except the water.

2. Close the cooker. Bring to 15 pounds pressure for 3 minutes.

3. Add the water and serve as is, or with a further seasoning of ½ teaspoon curry powder or Worcestershire sauce; or pour into soup plates in each of which a mold of hot brown rice has been turned out. Almost any mixture of fresh vegetables may be used in making this soup with this exception—do not use beets as they will turn the soup red in color—that is, unless you want a red soup.

CHICKEN SOUP STOCK
1½ quarts
30 minutes

1 (3 to 4 pound) fowl	½ teaspoon pepper
1 teaspoon salt	½ teaspoon celery seed or
1 peeled onion sliced	1 cup celery leaves
⅛ teaspoon nutmeg	1 quart cold water
or mace	

1. Singe, clean, and disjoint the fowl, place in the pressure-cooker with all the remaining ingredients.

2. Close the cooker; bring slowly to 15 pounds pressure and process 30 minutes.

3. Cool soup stock and remove the fat. Store the chicken stock in a covered glass jar in the refrigerator. To use dilute with an equal quantity of hot water. Add ½ teaspoon meat extract to bring up the flavor.

4. Use chicken meat for salad, sandwiches, or chicken à la king.

VEAL SOUP STOCK: Follow the preceding recipe substituting three or four pounds knuckle or neck of veal for the fowl.

CHICKEN AND VEAL SOUP STOCK: Follow the recipe for Chicken Soup Stock, using 1½ pounds chicken necks and backs, and 2½ pounds neck of veal.

CHICKEN SOUP COLBERT
3 minutes

Use Chicken Soup Stock (or Veal). Add a little minced parsley. Poach an egg for each person, place on a slice of toast and put in soup plates. Pour the soup around and serve at once.

CHICKEN NOODLE SOUP
1 quart
15 minutes

1. Prepare 1 quart of chicken soup by combining 2 cups chicken soup stock with 2 cups boiling water, and bring to a rapid boil.

2. Add 1 cup noodles broken in 2-inch lengths; and boil until tender, about five minutes.

3. Serve in soup plates; sprinkle with a garnish of finely chopped hard-cooked egg mixed with a little parsley or chopped water cress; or use minced parsley and small bread croutons fried in butter.

CHICKEN LEMON SOUP GREEK STYLE
1 quart
4 minutes

1. Combine 2 cups chicken soup stock with 2 cups hot water and bring to boiling point.

2. Meantime beat 3 egg yolks light with a few grains of nutmeg and one-half cup sweet or sour cream. Stir into the boiling soup. Add 2 tablespoons lemon juice.

3. Serve at once with a garnish of small croutons fried in butter.

CHICKEN ODDMENT SOUP

Follow the preceding recipe. Before serving add bits of chicken cut from the bone, oddments of cooked mild-flavored vegetables, and a little cooked rice. Or instead of rice, garnish with small cubes of left-over chicken stuffing browned in butter. Dust with minced parsley or chives.

CHICKEN ASPARAGUS SOUP

2 minutes

1. Prepare one quart plain chicken soup by diluting two cups chicken soup stock with 2 cups hot water and bring to a boil.

2. Add inch lengths cooked or canned asparagus.

3. Serve in soup plates; sprinkle with finely minced hard-cooked egg or grated Parmesan cheese.

CHICKEN SOUP CHINESE

1 quart

15 minutes

1. Combine one pint chicken stock with one pint boiling water or liquid drained from cooked vegetables.

2. Bring to boiling point and add 2 or 3 tablespoons finely shredded spinach or chopped water cress.

3. Cook a minute and serve with Won Ton (Chinese dumplings, page 65, which have been cooked separately.

CHICKEN SOUP ITALIAN

1. Combine 2 cups chicken stock with 2 cups boiling water or liquid drained from cooked vegetables.

2. Bring to boiling point and add 1½ cups shredded raw chicory. Heat until tender, about two minutes.

3. Serve in deep soup plates with plenty of grated cheese. Pass bread sticks.

CHICKEN SOUP STOCK FROM THE FRAME
1½ quarts
15 minutes

Bones and trimmings of 1 large or 2 small chickens. All available bits of skin or gristle
1 large onion diced
1 small carrot sliced
1 cup celery leaves

½ bay leaf
1 quart cold water
1 teaspoon meat extract
½ teaspoon salt
⅛ teaspoon pepper
Grated rind ⅛ lemon or lime

1. Break or chop the bones of the chicken after all meat has been removed. Put the bones in the pressure-cooker with the gristle, skin, and trimmings that cannot be used in any other way.

2. Add the vegetables, meat extract, seasonings and water. Close the cooker; bring slowly to 15 pounds pressure and process 15 minutes.

3. Strain; add 2 cups liquid drained from cooked vegetables, or use tomato juice if the flavor is desired.

4. Serve with the desired garnish.

This soup stock is very different from the only-too-frequent wishy-washy soup made from the frame and masquerading as chicken, because pressure cooking extracts all the flavor from the bones and other ingredients.

Turkey Soup Stock from the Frame: Follow the preceding recipe substituting the frame of a turkey.

Duck Soup Stock from the Frame: Follow the recipe for chicken soup stock, using the frame of one or two good-sized ducks.

Soups That Can Be Made from Any Kind of Chicken Stock, or Chicken and Veal Stock, Mixed

Chicken or Turkey Vegetable Soup: Prepare chicken or turkey stock. Dilute if necessary. To serve, add bits of chicken or turkey and oddments of cooked vegetables such as carrots, peas, asparagus, mushrooms or string beans; or use a little left-over rice. Or garnish with cubes of chicken stuffing sautéd in butter.

Chicken, Duck or Turkey Soup Creole: Dilute 1 quart chicken, duck or turkey stock with 1 cup of tomato juice; add ½ diced seeded sweet green pepper, a little onion and ½ cup chopped mushrooms, sautéd until soft in 1 tablespoon butter or margarine. Pour the soup over molds of white or brown rice.

Chicken or Turkey Gumbo: Prepare chicken or turkey Creole soup adding pieces of left-over chicken or turkey and 1 cup canned or pressured okra. (See page 264.) Season with filé powder, a Creole seasoning obtainable at de luxe grocery stores.

SCOTCH BROTH
1½ quarts
15 minutes

2 pounds neck of lamb	1 cup diced peeled carrot
1 quart cold water	1 cup diced peeled turnip
2 tablespoons whole barley	⅔ cup diced peeled onion
1 teaspoon salt	1 tablespoon minced pars-
¼ teaspoon pepper	ley

1. Cut all fat possible from the lamb. Remove the meat from the bones, and cut into half inch pieces.

2. Place in the pressure-cooker with the water, barley, salt and pepper. Close the cooker, bring slowly to 15 pounds pressure and process 11 minutes.

3. Cool the cooker; open, and add the vegetables except the parsley; close, bring the pressure up to 15 pounds again and process 4 minutes longer.

4. Serve with the parsley sprinkled over.

This soup has even a finer flavor if the bones removed from the neck of lamb are put into the cooker while making the broth. In this case, tie the bones in a piece of cheese cloth so they can be easily removed when the soup is finished.

OXTAIL SOUP
1½ quarts
20 minutes

2 oxtails	½ cup sliced peeled carrots
3 tablespoons butter or margarine	¼ cup sliced peeled onion
	½ cup diced celery
1 teaspoon meat extract	3 cups liquid drained from cooked vegetables
1 pint water	
¼ teaspoon ground clove	3 tablespoons flour
½ teaspoon salt	¼ cup dry red wine (optional)
⅛ teaspoon pepper	
¼ teaspoon thyme	

1. Cut the oxtails into pieces at each joint. Rinse and drain.

2. Melt the butter or margarine in the pressure-cooker. Add the oxtails and sauté until lightly browned. Dissolve the meat extract in a tablespoon of water and add. Add the water. Put in the seasonings, close the cooker, slowly bring to 15 pounds pressure and process 16 minutes.

3. Cool and open the cooker. Add the carrots, onions and celery. Bring to 15 pounds pressure again and process 4 minutes.

4. Then cool and open; add the three cups of liquid drained from cooked vegetables and bring to a boil.

5. Thicken with the flour stirred smooth in 3 table-spoons cold water. Add the wine.

6. Serve plain, in soup plates; or pour the soup over molds of cooked barley, cracked wheat or rice, or boiled whole white potatoes.

Oxtail Soup with Tomato: Add one cup thick canned tomato just before serving.

Oxtail Soup with Mushrooms: Add ¾ cup fresh or canned mushroom caps and sliced stems sautéd 3 minutes in 1 tablespoon butter or margarine.

This soup is especially good accompanied by potato pancakes fried in savory fat. Serve as a main course.

RUSSIAN BORSCH
7 cups
17 minutes

½ pound boneless stewing beef

½ pound boneless stewing lamb

1 quart cold water

1 teaspoon salt

⅛ teaspoon pepper

1 teaspoon meat condiment sauce

2 slices salt pork diced very small

1 carrot peeled and diced

1 onion peeled and diced

1½ cups peeled raw beets diced small

1 cup finely shredded white cabbage

2 large peeled white potatoes diced

1 cup canned tomatoes

1 tablespoon butter or margarine

1 tablespoon flour

1 cup finely crumbled rye bread

¾ cup soured cream

2 tablespoons minced parsley

1. Cut the beef and lamb in half-inch dice. Put in the pressure-cooker. Add the cold water, salt, pepper, meat sauce and pork. Close the cooker. Slowly bring to 15 pounds pressure and process 14 minutes.

2. Cool and open the cooker. Put in all the vegetables. Bring again to 15 pounds pressure and process 5 minutes. Cool the cooker, add the tomato and 2 cups boiling water.

3. Thicken with the butter or margarine and flour blended smoothly together. Bring to a boil and add the rye bread.

4. Serve with a tablespoonful of the soured cream in each soup plate. Sprinkle with the parsley.

PHILADELPHIA PEPPER POT
2 quarts
34 minutes

1 pound tripe, fresh or pickled
2 slices lean bacon
3 cups hot water
1½ teaspoons beef extract
1 teaspoon salt
¼ teaspoon pepper
1 peeled onion sliced
1 sweet green pepper seeded and diced
1 cup diced peeled white potatoes
2 tablespoons butter
2 tablespoons flour
1 cup sweet cream or undiluted evaporated milk

1. Cover the tripe, whichever kind is used, with cold water and bring to a rapid boil. Then drain and cut the tripe in thin strips an inch and a half long.

2. Dice the bacon and put directly into the pressure-cooker. Fry until golden brown. Then add the tripe, water and the meat extract dissolved in two tablespoons water. Add the salt and pepper.

3. Close the cooker; bring to 15 pounds pressure and process 30 minutes. Cool and open the cooker and add the vegetables. Close the cooker; bring again to 15 pounds pressure 4 minutes longer.

4. Add two cups water or liquid drained from cooked

vegetables. Then cream together the flour and butter and stir. When boiling stir in the cream or evaporated milk; add salt and pepper to taste.

BEEF AND MUSHROOM SOUP
1½ quarts
10 minutes

2 tablespoons butter or margarine
½ pound chopped raw beef
¼ pound sliced fresh mushrooms
1 peeled onion sliced

5 cups hot water
1 teaspoon beef extract
½ teaspoon salt
Plain, curried or Spanish rice (See pages 305, 312)

1. Melt the butter or margarine in the pressure-cooker. Add the beef, mushrooms and onions; sauté slowly about three minutes or until slightly browned.

2. Add the water, the beef extract dissolved in a little of the water, and the salt.

3. Close the cooker; bring to 15 pounds pressure and process 5 minutes.

4. Serve in soup plates with a mold of rice in each. This is a good way to utilize left-over cooked rice.

Note: If fresh mushrooms are not available, canned mushrooms may be substituted. Or use 2 ounces of dried mushrooms. These should be pre-soaked for 10 minutes in 1 cup of cold water, then drained, chopped and used as directed. The water in which the mushrooms have been soaked should be counted as part of the liquid for the soup.

POT-AU-FEU
29 minutes

3 pounds shank or shin of beef (with bone cracked)
2 tablespoons butter, margarine or meat fat
1½ teaspoons salt
⅛ teaspoon pepper
1 teaspoon sugar
1 large bay leaf
4 cups boiling water

1 pound quartered peeled carrots
1 pound sliced peeled turnip
8 small onions peeled
8 small white potatoes peeled and halved
½ cup diced celery
1 pound cleaned spinach or kale left in small bunches

1. Slowly brown-heat the meat all over in the fat directly in the pressure-cooker. Sprinkle with the salt and pepper. Add sugar, bay leaf and boiling water. Close the cooker; bring to 15 pounds pressure and process 25 minutes.

2. Cool and open the cooker; add the vegetables. Bring again to 15 pounds pressure and process 4 minutes longer.

3. Add 2 cups boiling water to the liquid, spinach and bits of vegetable, and serve in soup plates as the first course. Pass French bread.

4. Slice the meat and arrange in overlapping slices on a platter. Surround with the whole vegetables to act as the main course. Pass sour cream horse-radish sauce. (See page 241.)

FISH STOCK
20 minutes

1 (3 to 4 pound) haddock, cod, or any white fleshed fish	½ cup sliced carrot
	½ cup diced celery **and** celery tops
1 quart cold water	½ bay leaf
1 small onion sliced	½ red pepper
2 sprigs parsley	2 cloves
	¾ teaspoon salt

1. Clean and thoroughly wash the fish. Leave on the head and tail. Cut the fish in four or five pieces; put into the pressure-cooker.

2. Add all the remaining ingredients; bring to 15 pounds pressure and process 20 minutes. Strain through a fine sieve.

3. Dilute before using with 2 cups water or liquid in which vegetables have been cooked.

FISH STOCK FROM TRIMMINGS

An excellent fish stock may be made from the heads, tails, bones and trimmings of fish. Estimate the quantity needed, and follow the preceding recipe.

FISH PURÉE

Follow the preceding recipe for making fish stock. When the fish has cooled sufficiently, remove the skin, bones, etc., and rub the fish through a food mill or purée sieve. Add to the undiluted fish stock; stir in a pint of milk and thicken with 2 tablespoons each flour and butter rubbed together. Bring to boiling point and simmer 10 minutes.

Serve garnished with small croutons, and minced water cress, parsley or a very little minced fresh dill.

SOUPS WITHOUT MEAT STOCK

Soups without meat stock are most of the cream of vegetable soups and those based on legumes, which include lentils and dried beans of all kinds. The usual kettle method of making such soups takes up to three hours according to the type of vegetables used. In contrast, the pressure-cooking method saves many kitchen hours, as these soups can be prepared according to their type, in from five to forty-five minutes, and they include many of the most distinguished soups of many lands.

If to be used as the first course of a meal, they may be sieved or puréed, but if they are to be a principal food, they should be pressure-d so the cooked vegetables, legumes, etc., may be served in them. They will then look and taste substantial and filling and will prove nutritious and satisfying when served at luncheon, supper or as the principal dish at a simple dinner.

CREAM SOUPS

All measurements are level.
Recipes proportioned to serve four to six.
Timings are minutes required for actual pressuring.
Cool cooker as soon as processing is done.

In preparing cream soups to be served with the actual vegetables in them, be sure to watch the time and follow directions, for overcooking quickly reduces vegetable fibers to a pulp. However, this is a real asset if the soup is to be puréed, as the soup may be rubbed quickly through the purée sieve, or may not even need sieving at all.

CREAM SOUPS
General Method
6 cups
3 minutes

1½ cups boiling water
1 teaspoon salt
⅛ teaspoon pepper
½ teaspoon sugar
2 cups of the raw vegetable desired (usually put through the food chopper)

1 quart heated milk
2 tablespoons flour
2 tablespoons butter or margarine
1 egg (optional)

1. Put the water, salt, pepper, sugar and vegetable into the cooker. Close and bring to 15 pounds pressure; process 3 minutes. Then cool and open the cooker.

2. Add the milk and bring to boiling point. Blend the flour and butter, and add a little of the hot soup. Then pour into the soup and cook and stir for two minutes. If the egg is used, beat it light and stir a little of the hot soup into it. Then stir it into the boiling soup and continue to stir for a few seconds over a low heat.

3. Serve at once, if the egg is used. Otherwise the egg will cook in little lumps and cause a curdled appearance.

4. Garnish each serving with minced parsley, minced chives, or very small fried or toasted croutons.

Cream of Onion Soup: Follow the method for making cream soups, using two cups chopped mild onion.

Cream of Leek Soup: Follow the method for making cream soups, using the white part of leeks and about three inches of the green tops.

Cream of Fresh Pea Soup: Follow the general method for making cream soups, using fresh or defrosted green peas that have been put through the food chopper; or use

1½ cups chopped canned drained peas and the liquid. Pass toasted graham crackers.

Cream of Asparagus Soup: Follow the general method for making cream soups, using two cups tender fresh or defrosted asparagus put through the food chopper, or a mixture of asparagus, green peas and carrots.

Cream of Celery Soup: Follow the general directions for making cream soups, using two cups raw celery measured after being put through the food chopper. Add one tablespoon minced onion and season further with a trace of nutmeg.

Cream of Cabbage Soup: Follow the general method for making cream soups, using two cups raw, white cabbage, measured after chopping fine. Season further if desired with ½ teaspoon curry powder dissolved in one tablespoon milk.

Cream of Cauliflower Soup: Follow the general method for making cream soups, using one-half cup tender, outer leaves of cauliflower put through food chopper, and one cup raw caulifleurettes (natural divisions), cut into small sections. Season further with a little nutmeg.

Cream of Spinach Soup: Follow general directions for making cream soups, using two cups finely chopped raw spinach. Add any liquid that may be pressed out while the spinach is being chopped. Season further with a trace of nutmeg or mace.

Cream of Corn Soup: Follow the general method for making cream soups, using two cups fresh or defrosted green corn kernels or kernelled canned corn which has been put through the food chopper. Serve plain, sprinkled with chopped pimiento or garnish with croutons or hot buttered popcorn.

Cream of Corn and Oyster Soup: Prepare cream of corn soup as described. Just before serving drop in two or three small oysters (washed) for each person to be served. Simmer uncovered until the edges of the oysters ruffle. Serve at once with a dusting of paprika.

Cream of Potato and Onion Soup: Follow the general directions for making cream soups, using one-half cup peeled onion and 1½ cups white potatoes, measured after putting through the food chopper. To serve sprinkle with minced parsley.

ROUMANIAN POTATO SOUP
5 cups
3 minutes

1 tablespoon butter or margarine	1 quart soup-stock or 1 quart water and 2 teaspoons beef extract or 3 bouillon cubes
1 medium-sized peeled onion chopped	
1½ cups grated peeled raw white potatoes	1 tablespoon minced parsley

1. Melt the butter or margarine in the pressure-cooker. Add the onion and slightly brown. Add the potatoes and soup-stock.

2. Close the cooker; bring to 15 pounds pressure and process 3 minutes.

3. Serve sprinkled with the parsley and a few croutons.

SOUPS FROM LEGUMES

Be sure to make enough of a legume soup to serve at two meals as they keep well. The portion to be reserved should be quickly cooled and stored in a covered glass jar in the refrigerator. Before reheating, dilute with an equal amount of water or liquid drained from cooked vegetables.

Those who have had experience in making soups of dried beans and lentils know that by ordinary methods it is a long process. Generally the dried vegetables are soaked overnight, and anywhere from an hour and a half to three hours is required actually to cook the soup.

But when pressured, the cooking process is brought

down to about 30 minutes; and modern methods call for only an hour of pre-soaking.

To Pre-Soak Legumes or Dried Vegetables for Pressured Soups

Pick over the dried vegetables. Rinse and cover with boiling water. Put on a lid and let stand one hour. Use as directed.

Soups made from dried vegetables are not only delicious and thrifty, but nutritious. As they supply part of the needed proteins, they can act as a main course at luncheon or supper, or they may be used as the first course of a garden platter meal, or dinner when only a small amount of meat or fish is available for the main course.

CREAM OF LIMA BEAN SOUP
7 to 8 cups
30 minutes

1 cup dried lima beans
1 small bay leaf
1 quart boiling water
1 teaspoon salt
¼ teaspoon pepper
2 tablespoons minced onion
2 tablespoons carrot
2 tablespoons butter or bacon fat

¼ cup flour
1 cup milk
1 cup light cream or evaporated milk
Any desired seasoning
2 tablespoons minced parsley
Croutons

1. Pick over and wash the beans. Add boiling water to cover. Put on lid; let stand one hour, then drain.

2. Place in the pressure-cooker with the bay leaf, boiling water, salt, pepper, onion and carrot. Close cooker; bring to 15 pounds pressure and process 30 minutes. Cool and open the cooker, take out one cup of beans so they will stay whole to garnish the finished soup.

3. Meantime, make a sauce by melting the butter or bacon fat and stirring in the flour, milk, and the cream or evaporated milk. Add to the soup and bring to boiling point. Stir well, as the soup should be in the form of a purée. If not sufficiently smooth, put it through a purée sieve.

4. Add the whole beans, and serve sprinkled with the parsley and croutons. If desired this soup may be seasoned with a little meat condiment sauce, tomato catsup or a half teaspoon curry powder stirred smooth in one table-spoon water.

Cream of Red Kidney Bean Soup: Make according to the preceding recipe using red kidney beans; and adding when the soup is first put on to pressure, one cup diced celery.

YANKEE BEAN SOUP
7 cups
35 minutes

1 cup white pea beans or North Michigan beans	ham or smoked tender-loin
¼ cup salt pork cut in small dice	1 peeled onion sliced
	½ cup carrot diced
1 quart brown soup-stock or water from boiled	2 tablespoons flour

1. Pick over and wash the beans. Cover with boiling water; put on a lid and set aside for an hour. Drain.

2. Place the beans in the pressure-cooker. Add the salt pork, the meat stock, onion and carrot. Close the cooker, bring the pressure to 15 pounds, and process 35 minutes. Cool and open.

3. Add two cups boiling water; then thicken with the flour stirred smooth in ¼ cup water or soup stock. Season to taste with salt and pepper. Sieve if desired.

4. Serve with crisp crackers, or thin sliced or devilled ham mustard sandwiches, plain or toasted.

CONTINENTAL BEAN SOUP
1½ quarts
30 minutes

1 cup red kidney beans
1 quart brown soup stock or 1 quart water and 1½ teaspoons meat extract
½ teaspoon salt
½ teaspoon sugar
1 medium-sized peeled onion chopped
1 (No. 2) can tomatoes
3 tablespoons Madeira or Sherry wine
⅛ teaspoon pepper

1. Pick over and wash the beans. Cover with boiling water; put on a lid and let stand for one hour.

2. Place the beans in the pressure-cooker; add remaining ingredients except wine; bring to 15 pounds pressure and process 35 minutes. Open the cooker and put the soup through a sieve or food-mill.

3. To serve, reheat; add the wine and sprinkle with the croutons.

Other good accompaniments are pulled bread, Melba toast, bread sticks or New England toast.

BAKED BEAN SOUP
5 cups
5 minutes

2 cups baked beans
1½ cups canned tomatoes
1 peeled onion sliced
2 cups soup stock or 2 cups water and 1 teaspoon meat extract
2 tablespoons flour
2 tablespoons butter or margarine
½ teaspoon Worcestershire sauce
Salt and pepper to taste

1. Combine the beans, tomatoes, onion and soup stock in the pressure-cooker. Close the cooker; bring to fifteen pounds pressure and process five minutes. Cool and open the cooker.

2. Stir beans until mashed to bits or put through a sieve. Add 1 cup hot water and thicken with the flour and butter creamed together.

3. Season to taste with salt, pepper and Worcestershire sauce.

4. Serve with croutons or toasted rolls.

DRIED PEA SOUP

As dried peas, when pressured, make a heavy purée likely to clog the vent-pipe of the cooker, no dried pea soup recipes are included in this book.

LENTIL SOUP
5 to 6 cups
30 minutes

2 cups lentils any kind	⅛ teaspoon pepper
4 cups water, or soup stock	1 cup top milk or undiluted
½ cup celery leaves packed down	evaporated milk
⅓ cup chopped onion or leeks	1 tablespoon flour
2 sprigs parsley	1 tablespoon butter or margarine

1. Pick over the lentils; wash, pour over boiling water. Cover, let stand one hour. Then drain.

2. Put into the pressure-cooker with the water or stock and all the vegetables. Close the cooker, bring to 15 pounds pressure and process 30 minutes. Then rub through a purée sieve, or put through a food mill.

3. Add the milk; bring to boiling point and if a medium-thick soup is desired, add an extra cup of water or stock. Thicken with the flour and butter blended, bring to a boil and simmer two minutes. Add pepper and salt if needed.

4. Serve with a garnish of minced parsley, or thin slices of skinless frankfurters.

This soup can also be made with the liquid drained from pressured ham. In this case add as much water as ham liquid, and taste before using to be sure the ham-stock is not too salty.

CHOWDERS

We are all familiar with clam chowder, but many of us have never made the delectable Maine Fish Chowder, a Crab Gumbo, or Bouillabaisse. No matter how good chowders taste when cooked in the usual kettle, they taste much more delicious when pressure-cooked, because all the flavors are retained. And vegetable chowders—which may be termed a relative of the old time fish chowder—gain glamour when pressure-cooked. Serve chowder at luncheon, dinner or supper, as a hearty dish—or serve it right from the pressure-cooker at a picnic or barbecue.

MAINE FISH CHOWDER
1½ quarts
4 minutes

¼ cup salt pork diced
¼ cup sliced onion
1½ pounds cod or haddock
2 cups boiling water
¾ teaspoon salt

¼ teaspoon pepper
1 pint sliced potatoes cut one-fourth inch thick
3 cups milk heated
2 tablespoons flour

Pressured pressed veal buffet style (*Page 135*)

Pressured crab gumbo in a tureen of hospitable size (*Page 55*)

Pressured pork tenderloin dinner with pear and marmalade compote (*Page 152*)

Treat turkey like any other beast—cut it up, then cook. Here's Turkey Marengo in the making, too. (*Page 185*)

1. Put the salt pork in the pressure-cooker and fry slowly until the fat runs freely, and the salt pork is light brown. Remove and reserve the pork. Add the onions and sauté until yellowed but not browned.

2. Meantime remove the skin, bones and fins from the fish. Cut the fish in half-inch cubes and add to the sautéed onion. Pour in the water, add the salt, pepper and potato. Close the cooker, bring to 15 pounds pressure and process 4 minutes.

3. Cool and open the cooker. Add the milk and bring to boiling point; then thicken by stirring in the flour blended smooth with two tablespoons extra milk. Cook and stir until slightly thickened.

4. Serve in bowls or deep soup plates. Sprinkle over the crisp fried salt pork if desired. Traditionally this chowder is always made with salt pork and accompanied by pilot crackers. If desired, 3 tablespoons butter or margarine may be used instead of the salt pork.

Fresh Water Fish Chowder: Follow the preceding recipe using filet of any other kind of fresh water fish.

CLAM CHOWDER MANHATTAN STYLE
2 quarts
15 minutes

¼ cup diced salt pork
1 peeled medium-sized onion chopped
1 quart shelled soft clams
1 section garlic peeled and minced
3 cups water
¼ teaspoon thyme or oregano

1 teaspoon salt
⅛ teaspoon pepper
2 cups canned tomatoes
3 cups peeled raw potatoes cut in inch cubes
1 cup diced raw carrot
1 tablespoon butter
1 tablespoon flour

1. Fry the salt pork and onion together in the pressure-cooker until the salt pork is crisp.

2. Meantime cut off the black necks of the clams, discard them and separate the soft from the hard portions. Chop the hard portions fine and add to the onion and salt pork. Put in the garlic, add the water, seasonings, tomatoes, potato, carrot and the juice from the clams, which should be strained.

3. Close the cooker; bring to 15 pounds pressure and process 10 minutes.

4. Cool and open the cooker; add three more cups boiling water, and the soft parts of the clams. Thicken with the butter and flour which have been blended. Cook and stir until the chowder comes to a boil and boil 2 minutes.

5. Serve in bowls or soup plates with crisp pilot crackers. When clam chowder is to be the main dish it is especially good served with small sandwiches made with thin slices of cold ham or lamb.

Note: This chowder is even more delicious when it stands 24 hours in the refrigerator and is re-heated.

FISH BISQUE
1½ quarts
5 minutes

3 cups fish-stock
2 cups raw white fish, cod, haddock or halibut put through the chopper
1 tablespoon butter or margarine
1 tablespoon flour
1 cup milk

1 cup light cream
½ teaspoon Worcestershire sauce
½ cup fine white cracker crumbs
1 teaspoon lemon juice
1 tablespoon minced parsley

Salt and pepper to taste

1. Pour the fish stock into the pressure-cooker. Add the fish, close the cooker and bring to fifteen pounds pressure and process five minutes.

2. Meantime melt the butter; stir in the flour, milk, cream and Worcestershire sauce, as in making white sauce. Bring to boiling point.

3. Cool and open the cooker. Stir in the milk sauce; add the crumbs and stir a moment to let them soften and thicken the soup. Add the lemon juice. Just before serving sprinkle with the parsley.

4. If desired 2 egg yolks beaten with 2 tablespoons Chablis or dry sherry wine may be stirred into this bisque before serving.

Lobster Bisque: Follow the preceding recipe, using part lobster shells in making the fish stock. Substitute minced boiled or canned lobster meat for the fish. Process only one minute. Finish as directed, adding the egg yolks and sherry.

CRAB GUMBO
7 cups
5 minutes

1 diced seeded sweet green pepper
1 cup diced celery
3 peeled diced tomatoes or 1½ cups canned tomato
1 peeled sliced onion
1 cup sliced okra, stem ends removed
¼ teaspoon powdered bay leaf

⅓ teaspoon thyme
¼ cup water
1 pound flaked fresh cooked or canned crab meat, shell removed
1 quart canned or bottled clam broth
Cayenne pepper to taste
Filé powder
Worcestershire sauce
Pressured rice (optional)

1. In the pressure-cooker combine the green pepper, celery, tomatoes, onion, okra, bay leaf, thyme and water.

2. Close the cooker, bring to 15 pounds pressure and process 5 minutes.

3. Cool and open the cooker. Add the crab meat and clam broth. Bring slowly to boiling point; season to taste with the cayenne, filé powder and Worcestershire sauce and serve with crisp crackers.

4. Or to make the gumbo more substantial, line large soup bowls with a thin layer of the rice; then ladle in the gumbo. Perfect accompaniments are heated French bread and ale.

CORN CHOWDER
2 quarts
4 minutes

2 tablespoons butter or margarine
2 cups fresh or defrosted frozen green corn kernels
4 cups peeled white potatoes sliced one-half inch thick, then halved

2 cups boiling water
4 cups scalded milk
3 tablespoons flour
1 peeled onion chopped
½ teaspoon salt
⅛ teaspoon pepper
Croutons

1. Melt one tablespoon of the butter or margarine in the pressure-cooker; add the onion and sauté until yellowed.

2. Add the corn, potatoes and water. Close the cooker; bring to 15 pounds pressure and process 4 minutes. Then cool and open the cooker.

3. Add the milk; thicken by stirring in the flour blended smooth with the remaining butter or margarine; add the salt and pepper.

4. Sprinkle with croutons or accompany with New England toast or toasted rolls.

Succotash Chowder: Follow the preceding recipe, substituting for one cup of the corn, a cup of fresh or frozen green lima beans.

VEGETABLE CHOWDER
2 quarts
5 minutes

1½ teaspoons granulated
  sugar
4 tablespoons butter or
  savory meat drippings
½ cup diced peeled carrot
½ cup diced peeled onion
2 cups shredded white cabbage
1 cup diced celery
¾ cup diced peeled turnip
1 pint cold water

1 pint tomato juice
2 teaspoons salt
Few grains cayenne pepper
1 tart apple peeled and
  grated
Savory or puffy dumplings
  or pressured white or
  brown rice or cracked
  wheat
Parmesan or sharp Ched-
  dar cheese

1. Put the sugar in the pressure-cooker, and stand over a low heat until the sugar caramelizes and turns dark brown.

2. Add the butter or meat drippings, the carrot, onion, cabbage, celery and turnip. Cook until slightly browned stirring occasionally. Then add the water, tomato juice and seasonings. Close the cooker, bring to 15 pounds pressure and process 5 minutes.

3. Cool and open the cooker; add two cups hot water and the apple. If dumplings are used, cook them in the chowder without pressure.

4. Serve in bowls or soup plates with the dumplings, or pour the chowder over and around cereal molds. Minced chives or parsley may be sprinkled over the top. Pass the grated cheese.

Large kernels of green corn, halved or coarsely shredded string beans, or good sized green lima beans may be added when making this chowder. However, do not put in leafy vegetables such as spinach, or any vegetables that call for quick pressuring such as green peas or cauli-flower, as they will overcook and go to pieces in the pressuring process. Only vegetables needing approximately the same cooking time can be combined to use in this chowder. If desired, small cubes of white potatoes may be added.

Vegetable Chowder with a Meat Flavor: Prepare vegetable chowder as described in the preceding recipe, adding one cup of white potatoes cut in half inch cubes and 2 teaspoons meat extract dissolved in a little of the hot liquid.

Refreshing Cold Soups

A frosty cold soup on a hot summer day is a food not only to be enjoyed, but to be remembered.

If jellied, cold soups should be served in small low soup bowls or bouillon cups. But if in liquid form bouillon cups are a "must."

Assorted canapés, crisp garden relishes, very small thin meat, vegetable or cottage cheese sandwiches, crusty rolls, little hot plain, devilled or cheese biscuits or crisp potato chips, are good accompaniments.

SHCHAV
(Russian Sorrel Soup)
6 cups
1 minute

1 pound shchav (sorrel)	2 raw eggs
1 teaspoon salt	1 hard-cooked egg
4 cups boiling water	½ cup soured cream

1. Pick over the sorrel, wash thoroughly and chop quite fine, both stems and leaves.

2. Place in the pressure-cooker with the salt and boiling water. Bring to 15 pounds pressure and process one minute.

3. Beat the eggs light and pour into them the hot sorrel mixture. Add salt and pepper to taste.

4. Serve ice cold in soup plates with a garnish of soured cream and the hard-cooked egg chopped; grated cucumber, sliced red radishes, or sliced scallions may be added.

A good accompaniment is hot boiled potatoes.

COLD CHICKEN VEGETABLE SOUP
1 quart

This may be served in liquid form or jellied. In the latter case make chicken or veal stock (or use a combination of the two meats) according to the directions on page 33; but do not add the additional water called for after pressuring, as the undiluted stock will form a jelly.

Instead stir into the soup-stock 1½ cups mixed cooked green peas, diced carrot, celery, shredded string beans, and a very little minced raw celery, cucumber or seeded sweet green pepper. Pour into a glass dish, cool, cover and chill a few hours, when the soup will be of the right jellied consistency to serve cold.

TOMATO MADRILENE
3 cups

Combine 1½ cups melted beef stock (page 30) with 1½ cups tomato juice. Season further with a little onion juice and ½ teaspoon meat condiment sauce. Serve very cold in bouillon cups with a wedge of lemon or lime "on the side."

Jellied Tomato Madrilene: If to be served in jellied form, heat together the beef stock and tomato juice, as described above. When boiling stir in 1½ tablespoons plain granulated gelatin previously softened five minutes in two tablespoons cold water. Then add the remaining seasonings.

Transfer to a glass refrigerator dish. Cool, cover and chill until firm in the refrigerator, about four hours. Serve in small, low soup bowls or bouillon cups. Sprinkle with minced parsley, or parsley and chives mixed. Cheese crackers, hot toasted rolls or assorted canapés are nice with this soup.

QUICK COLD BEET SOUP
1 quart

2 cups brown soup-stock (page 30)
½ teaspoon onion juice
½ cup cold water
1 (No. 2) can beets
½ teaspoon salt
1 teaspoon sugar

1 tablespoon lemon or lime juice
½ cup soured cream
⅓ cup grated firm portion peeled cucumber or use minced chives or parsley

1. Combine the soup stock, onion juice and water and heat until soup stock liquefies. Add the juice from the canned beets, the salt, sugar and lemon or lime juice. Chop the beets fine and add. Then chill.

2. Serve in medium-sized bowls or soup plates, topping each with a tablespoonful of soured cream sprinkled with the grated cucumber, chives or parsley. Rye bread, boiled potatoes or hard-cooked eggs are traditional accompaniments.

CHILLED CREAM SOUPS

Any of the cream soups described on pages 45, 46 of this book may be served ice cold in bouillon cups. For a touch of color sprinkle with a little paprika, minced parsley or chives. Hot toast, heated potato chips or almost any hot bread present a pleasant temperature contrast.

Soup Complements and Accompaniments

Crisp crackers are usually served with soup, and they *do* taste good. But if soup is to be the main dish, try serving it with hot toast, plain or New England style; with heated French bread; or cheese-d rolls with thin meat or egg-filled sandwiches, toasted cheese sandwiches or hot plain devilled meat, or cheese frosted biscuits; with dumplings or piroushki (page 66). Butter-fried croutons make for appetite appeal with any soup, and for variety there are buttered popcorn, crisp potato chips and tortilla chips.

NEW ENGLAND TOAST

Spread white bread lightly with butter or margarine, then toast under the broiler, starting with the spread-side up.

CROUTONS

Cut sliced white bread into small dice. Place in a pan thickly rubbed with butter or margarine, and bake in a hot oven until golden brown, stirring occasionally. Or fry slowly in butter or margarine.

HEATED FRENCH BREAD

For each person allow a six-inch strip of French bread cut diagonally from a long loaf. This should be sliced at inch intervals almost through the bottom crust. Spread these slashed sections lightly with butter or margarine;

place the bread in a pan, cover, put in a slow oven and heat about five minutes.

French Bread with Garlic: Prepare as directed above, using butter or margarine seasoned with a little garlic salt, or with a cut peeled section of garlic allowed to stand in the butter a few minutes before spreading.

CHEESE-TOASTED ROLLS

Cut long rolls in halves lengthwise. Spread with grated sharp cheese mixed with butter, a little prepared mustard and some minced chives. Toast slowly until the cheese topping bubbles.

BAKING POWDER BISCUIT
2 dozen small biscuits

2 cups all-purpose flour	½ teaspoon sugar
4 teaspoons baking powder	4 tablespoons shortening
½ teaspoon salt	¾ cup milk

1. Sift the dry ingredients together. Chop in the shortening with a pastry blender or the back and edge of a tablespoon. When flaky add the milk.

2. Turn onto a slightly floured board and pat or roll one inch in thickness. Cut into two-inch squares, or shape into rounds with a biscuit cutter. Transfer to an oiled shallow pan. Brush over with milk.

3. Bake twelve to fifteen minutes in a hot oven 400–425 degrees F.

A commercial biscuit mix may be used. In this case increase the shortening called for on the package by 1 tablespoon to a cup of the mix.

Devilled Meat Biscuits: Prepare baking powder biscuit Roll to one-fourth inch thickness and cut into two-inch squares or rounds. Spread half of these almost to the edge with devilled ham, mixed with a little prepared mustard;

or spread with minced left-over chicken, cooked ham or beef mixed with prepared mustard and a little Worcestershire sauce. Cover with the remaining biscuit, sandwich fashion, and press the edges together lightly. Bake as directed.

Cheese-filled Biscuit: Follow the preceding recipe for baking powder biscuit. Roll the dough to one-fourth inch thickness and cut into two-inch squares or small rounds. On half of the squares or rounds, put a teaspoonful of grated sharp cheese mixed with a little prepared mustard and a few drops of Worcestershire sauce. Top with the remaining biscuit. Press together lightly and bake.

DUMPLINGS IN FIVE LANGUAGES

Every country has its own style of dumpling. As we know them in the United States they are traditionally big and puffy. In England they are Suet Dumplings. In Hungary they become Spaetzel. In Germany they are Kartoffel Klöesse or potato dumplings. In Italy they appear as Ravioli. In China they are called Won Ton. And in Russia the dumplings are baked and called Piroushki. But in any language dumplings are good, so you will enjoy serving them in pressured soups, and with ragouts, fricassees, soupy and platter stews.

AMERICAN PUFFY DUMPLINGS

2 cups all-purpose flour	¾ teaspoon salt
4 teaspoons baking powder	3 tablespoons shortening
¾ cup milk or water	

1. Sift together the flour, baking powder and salt; chop in the shortening with a pastry blender or back of a tablespoon. Add the milk or water.

2. Transfer to a slightly floured board. Pat to one-half inch in thickness; cut into two-inch rounds with a biscuit cutter.

3. Drop into any boiling soup or stew.

4. Cover closely and steam twelve to fifteen minutes, according to size, without pressure.

In pressure cooking soup or any other food to be served with dumplings, stop the pressuring two minutes before the time for it to be completed. Cool and open the cooker. Put in the dumplings and cover but *do not* bring up the pressure again; instead merely slow-boil for twelve minutes.

Puffy dumplings are especially good garnished with coarse bread crumbs fried brown and crisp in butter or margarine.

Savory Puffy Dumplings: Make according to the preceding recipe with this exception. Melt the shortening; add one small seeded and minced green pepper and one peeled and minced small onion. Cook until yellowed. Stir this into the flour mixture. Add ¼ teaspoon thyme, marjoram or poultry seasoning if desired.

KARTOFFEL KLOESSE

6 cold pressured medium-sized white potatoes	½ cup all-purpose flour
1 peeled medium-sized onion grated	3 teaspoons baking powder
	2 tablespoons milk
1 egg	½ teaspoon salt
	Fried bread crumbs
Grated cheese (optional)	

1. Peel and grate the potatoes. Add to the remaining ingredients and mix thoroughly. Form into balls the size of large walnuts.

2. Drop into boiling soup or stew, or into boiling salted water; cover and boil ten minutes. Drain and sprinkle with the fried bread crumbs.

In adding these potato dumplings to any soup or stew prepared in a pressure-cooker, stop the cooking two minutes before the soup or stew is completed. Cool and open the cooker, put in the dumplings and cover; slow-boil for 10 minutes; but *do not* bring up the pressure again.

RAVIOLI

It is possible to make ravioli at home. But it takes considerable time. So it is more sensible to buy canned ravioli either plain or with a sauce. Add directly to the pressure-cooked soup, stew or ragout and reheat.

WON TON

These Chinese dumplings served in a plain meat, chicken or vegetable soup, make a most satisfying and unusual main course. Prepare the pressured soup; and two minutes before it will be done, cool and open the cooker and add the Won Ton; cover and steam for fifteen minutes, but *do not* bring up the pressure again. The following ingredients are needed for Won Ton.

1½ cups all-purpose flour
½ teaspoon salt
1 egg
2 tablespoons cold water
1 cup minced cooked pork, shrimp, beef, veal or poultry

½ tablespoon minced scallion or onion
2 tablespoons minced mushrooms (optional)

Won Ton are really made in two parts.

1. The Won Ton Dough: To make this sift together the flour and salt. Beat and add the egg, and mix in the water. Turn onto a floured board and knead until smooth, as in making a noodle or strudel dough. Let stand 15 minutes.

Then roll as thin as paper and cut in three-inch squares. These are then ready for the filling.

2. The Filling: To make this mix together the cooked pork, shrimp, beef or veal, with salt and pepper to taste, the scallion, and the mushrooms if used. Put a teaspoonful of this mixture in the center of each square of dough. Fold over diagonally to form triangles and press the edges together with a fork. Then cook for 15 minutes in boiling salted water or in thin meat, chicken or vegetable soup.

PIROUSHKI

2 cups all-purpose flour
4 teaspoons baking powder
1 teaspoon sugar
6 tablespoons shortening
1¼ cups chopped cooked meat (any kind)

¾ cup milk
⅓ cup very thick gravy or white sauce
1 egg yolk

1. Sift together the flour, baking powder, sugar and salt.

2. Add the shortening and cut and chop it in with a pastry blender or the edge of a tablespoon until the flour mixture is the consistency of coarse corn meal. Add the milk and mix until blended.

3. Transfer to a slightly floured board; dust the dough with flour, and roll or pat to one-fourth inch in thickness. Then cut in three-inch squares. In the center of each square put a half tablespoon of the meat and gravy or sauce mixed together. This mixture should be dry enough to hold its shape.

4. Fold over to form triangles; press the edges lightly together with a fork, and transfer to an oiled shallow pan. Brush over the tops with the egg yolk slightly beaten with one tablespoon milk. Bake in a moderately hot oven 375–400 degrees F. for 20 minutes, or until puffy and brown.

5. Serve with borsch or with any simple meat or vegetable soup; or use as a main dish for lunch, with gravy, or a cream sauce or tomato sauce.

Soup-Meat Makes Delicious Dishes

Meat or fowl used in making soup should always be utilized—for it can be made most appetizing. First remove the bone, gristle and skin. Then chop and use in making croquettes, loaves, balls to serve with spaghetti; shepherd's pie, piroushki or meat-filled dumplings to serve with soup; or chop and escallop with vegetables and a highly seasoned cream or tomato sauce. Use beef or veal from soup-making, in chili or a curry; and chicken or fish in a curry salad or sandwiches. Add more seasoning than usual because much of the flavor will be cooked out.

But because part of the minerals and nearly *all of the valuable proteins* remain in the meat, it is high in food value and may be used to the last scrap in preparing foods that taste good and are worth eating.

CHAPTER IV

MEAT, POULTRY AND GAME IN THE PRESSURE-COOKER

MEAT FOR DINNER, FULL-FLAVORED, TENDER, JUICY, rich with its vitamins, minerals and proteins; meat in full measure, not shriveled; and no long-time waiting for it to be done ready to eat.

Of course, you can say, "The choicest cuts of steaks fill that description exactly." But we can't always have them. Most of us can't afford them. We have to use the more thrifty cuts of meat, especially when there's a family and the food budget is limited. But when we use these tougher, thrifty cuts we have to plan for long-time cookery, and for most of us this is inconvenient and impractical.

But here's the solution: Use a good pressure-cooker intelligently. Kitchen time will be cut three-fourths. The meat will be fork-tender, and the cost of the cooker will be covered many times over by the money savings effected. You will be able to afford a full quota of the meat your family enjoys and needs, and your own good sense applied to the recipes and suggestions in this book will soon reveal a wide selection of new and appetizing meat dishes that will become family favorites.

What Meats Can It Cook?

The pressure-cooker may be used for preparing any meat, poultry or game dish that requires moist heat; that is, all cuts that are ordinarily boiled or pot-roasted, braised, potted, fricasseed, barbecued, stewed, or served in the form of a ragout. This applies to all cuts of meat, whether they are the choice "tender" or the so-called "tough" or thrifty cuts. Roasts are included.

A four-quart cooker will accommodate a solid, compact piece of meat up to 4 pounds, or a boned small half ham, or a 3½-pound chicken, or a medium-sized rabbit. As to ragouts, stews, casserole-type and barbecued meat, poultry or game, a 4-quart cooker will turn out an ample amount to serve 4 to 6 people, if the quantity of liquid used is concentrated, and diluted if necessary just before serving, with the required liquid. **Use the space in the cooker for cooking the meat and not for boiling water.**

Are Pressured Meats Watery?

If meats taste "watery" it is because a rack is not used, and too much water has been added in preparing them; or it is because the meat is not properly brown-heated before pressure-ing. Unless a "boiled" or braised taste is desired, the amount of liquid put into the pressure-cooker should never come over the top of the cooking rack or "trivet" as it is sometimes called. And the meat should be placed on the rack for cooking. Or if the cooker is equipped with compartments, the meat may be *placed* in a compartment.

However, if a stew, a casserole-type dish, a "boiled" dinner, pot roast or braised dish is being prepared, the meat may be cooked directly in the liquid. But be careful to use just enough—not too much. And this means considerably less than the amount used in ordinary cookery, as there is no evaporation in pressure cooking. *You take out all that you put in.*

Thrifty Cuts of Meat

We are a nation of steak and chop eaters. Many home-makers hesitate to buy the less expensive, thriftier cuts of meat for fear they are not nutritious, or will prove tough and unappetizing. However, the fault lies not with the meat, but with the way it is cooked. When prepared by the usual methods, long, slow cookery almost always produces tender meat that is fully digestible, no matter what cut is used. But if properly pressure-cooked, that period of long, slow preparation is cut to a mere fraction of the usual cooking time, nutrients and vitamins are conserved and fork-tender meat is always the result.

There are nearly a hundred thrifty cuts of beef, pork, lamb and veal available. Yet most homemakers know and use no more than a dozen cuts. This leaves unused a large proportion of the animals which tends to keep prices high. When the demand for the *thrifty* cuts of meat equals the demand for the so-called *choice* cuts, the price of all meat will drop considerably.

Cuts That Cut the Meat Bill

Here is a partial list of thrifty meats that produce deli-cious pressure-cooked dishes in quick time without pre-liminary tenderizing or any other special treatment.

By the way, the word "arm" that is used in several cases, may be unfamiliar as applied to meat. It applies to that portion of meat in the forequarter from the shoulder down. However, any arm cut includes a little shoulder, but shoulder never includes a cut of the arm.

Methods or recipes for preparing most of the following thrifty cuts will be found in this book. Pressure-cooking some of these cuts regularly for three or four meals a week, instead of the more costly cuts, will ensure delectable dishes, save many kitchen hours, and make possible immediate food budget savings; savings that accumulated over a period of months or years will represent an impressive sum of money.

THRIFTY CUTS AND HOW TO USE THEM

Beef

Ground beef—Hamburgers, fricadellen, loaves
Heel of round—Pot roast, braised, pot-au-feu
Hind shank—Stew, soup, casseroles
Flank steak—Broiled, braised, panned
Flank stew meat—Casseroles, ragouts
Beef plate—Pies, casseroles, stews
Short ribs—Roast, pot roast, braised
Brisket of beef—Boiled, braised, jellied loaf
Corned beef brisket—Corned beef dinner, pressed loaf
Knuckle soup bone—Casserole, stew, ragout, soup
Crosscut foreshank—Pot-au-feu, pressed beef
Chuck—Roast, pot roast, fricassee
Round steak—Pot roast, fricassee, barbecued, Swiss
Blade steak—Panned, broiled
Blade pot-roast—Barbecued
Triangle or chuck pot-roast—Braised, boiled
Neck—Stew, casserole
Ox joints—Stew, casserole
Arm pot-roast—Braised, potted, boiled
Beef heart—Braised, casserole

Tripe—Creole, New England style
Beef liver—Panned, braised, with vegetables
Beef kidney—Braised, stewed, pie
Fresh tongue—Braised

Pork

Blade steaks—Panned, broiled
Smoked shoulder butt—Boiled
Boston butt—Boiled
Salt pork—With vegetables, beans, chicken
Spare ribs—Braised, barbecued
Fresh picnic shoulder—Braised, roasted
Smoked picnic shoulder—Boiled, baked
Fresh shoulder hock—Braised, boiled
Arm steak—Panned, broiled
Feet—Braised, boiled with sauerkraut
Knuckles—Braised, boiled, with vegetables
Liver—Panned
Kidney—Stew, pie, with mushrooms
Heart—Potted
Smoked jowl—Boiled, served with greens or cabbage
Neck bones—Stew or ragout, with beans
Back bones—Stew or ragout, with beans
Ham shank—Boiled, with macaroni or green or dried
    beans
End cut pork chops—Panned, cubed

Lamb

Shoulder chops—Panned, jardinière
Square cut shoulder—Roast, pot-roast
Blade chops—Panned, potted, Spanish style
Arm chops—Panned, potted, Spanish style
Neck slices—Stew, casserole
Ground lamb—Balls, lamburgers

Riblets—Panned, barbecued and with mushrooms
Breast of lamb—Roast, braised, stew, ragout
Shanks—Braised, potted, creole
Kidney—Stew
Heart—Braised, panned

Veal

Rump roast—Pot roast, braised
Blade roast—Pot roast, braised
Arm roast—Pot roast, braised
Blade steak—Panned, barbecued
Heel of round—Braised, casserole
Hind shank—Braised, casserole
Round steak (cutlet) leg—Panned, scalloppini
Round roast—Braise, Spanish style
Crosscut shoulder roast—Braised
Breast—Braised, stew, fricassee
Riblets—Braise barbecue
Ground veal—Loaf, Italian meat balls
Foreshank—Braised, potted
Veal kidney—Pie, stew

Pressure cooking effects a great time-saving and is
equally well suited to the preparation of the more tender
cuts, such as pork, lamb or veal chops, meat balls, veal or
ham steaks, or beef steak which is to be cooked in a moist
medium, such as Swiss steak. But for a real grilled or
broiled flavor, obtained through exposure to direct heat,
steaks and chops should be broiled rather than pressure-
cooked.

Pressure-Cooked Roasts

All kinds of meat including beef, pork, veal, lamb, poultry and game can be successfully pressure-roasted no mat-

ter how tough the cut may be, if they are first thoroughly "brown-heated," to insure that delectable roasted taste, and quickly "brown-crisped" afterward. Brown-heating is absolutely essential when a roast-type flavor is desired, as this keeps the juices in the meat to a very large extent. Otherwise juices will be drawn from the meat while pressure-ing. An escape of steam will also cause juices to be drawn from meat. The frying pan and the fat in which this is done should be moderately hot. A searing heat is too high, for brown-heating should not be hurried. It should take from 10 to 20 minutes according to the extent of the surface to be covered. Brush with kitchen bouquet.

Before-hand Brown-heating: Meats may be made ready for pressuring and brown-heated the evening or morning before, and kept in the refrigerator until time to cook.

It is then possible to get dinner with unbelievable rapidity, depending solely on the pressuring time required. Since the recipes in this book give the pressuring time, it will prove an easy matter to choose dinner menus to suit the time-budget.

To Brown-heat Meat, Poultry or Game

Pre-heat the pressure-cooker itself or a heavy frying pan. I prefer a frying pan, as it has lower sides making it easier to turn the meat for even browning, is easier to clean, and prevents possible discoloration of the bottom of the cooker. Melt a little fat in the utensil and slowly brown-heat the food in it all over. Meat will not stick to the utensil if it is sufficiently pre-heated. Onion, garlic or celery may be brown-heated at the same time. If desired the meat may be sprinkled sparingly with flour before brown-heating. Sprinkle on the seasoning after the brown-heating is completed as salt tends to draw out meat or fish juices. If a frying pan has been used, add the water or liquid you expect to put into the cooker, and scrape off any rich brown bits that may stick to the pan before pouring into the cooker. Then proceed with the pressure cooking according to directions.

To Brown-Crisp Meat, Poultry or Game: If a crisp crust is desired after pressure cooking, the roast should be placed under the broiler or in a very hot oven for a few minutes to "brown-crisp." In this case a sizzling metal platter for the meat is not only practical but glamorous. Or glass, or even a plank may be used for the service. Arrange the vegetables around the meat, add a garnish, and the service becomes as distinguished as in the best of hotels. However, if you like oven roasts cooked by long, low heat methods, you will not find it necessary to brown-crisp a pressured roast, as the outer surface will have the same texture.

General Rule for Pressure Cooking All Meats, Poultry and Game

Always put from ½ to ¾ cup of water or other liquid in the pressure-cooker. This is sufficient for 30 to 45 minutes cooking; use ¾ to one cup for 45 minutes to an hour. For roasting or pot-roasting, the water in the cooker should never come over the top of the bottom rack so that it touches the meat, as this would cook out the natural juices. The water is used to prevent drippings from the cooking food from burning on the bottom of the cooker, and to insure the presence of enough liquid to keep the steam pressure at 15 pounds. Meat will never burn in the pressure-cooker as long as there is moisture, and no excess escape of steam. If a boiled effect is desired, use the amount of water designated in the recipes, which is a fraction of the

amount for regulation boiling. If flour or bread crumbs
are used to cover the meat, as with veal cutlets, little more
moisture is required. This is correctly estimated in the recipes in this book.

When Vegetables and Meats Are Cooked Together the Same Length of Time

This can be done without opening the cooker if the
meat and vegetables selected are types that can be pressured an equal length of time. For example, browned
pork chops and peeled large sweet potatoes each take 12
minutes; Swiss steak (cut in strips) and large white potatoes take 12 minutes; panned baby broiling chickens and
small potatoes need 12 minutes; browned chopped beef or
lamb-patties and thickly sliced onions or halved string
beans take 5 minutes.

If the meat or poultry takes longer than the vegetables
to pressure-cook, the cooker should be cooled according
to the manufacturer's directions and the vegetables put
in at the right time; the cooker is then closed again, the
pressure brought back to 15 pounds, and the pressure-ing
completed. However, when cooked *in direct contact,* that
is touching each other, the vegetables take on a little of
the flavor of the meat, and vice versa.

Keeping Vegetables and Meat Flavors Separate

This may be done in one of two ways: Before pressuring, the vegetables may be wrapped in aluminum foil, or

tied in parchment paper first rinsed in cold water, then pressed as dry as possible. Or if you have a large cooker with separate compartments, or a cooker that will permit the use of the divider, recommended by the manufacturer, this will prevent the different foods from coming into direct contact, and the preparation of several foods in the cooker may be done at one time. The pressure of the steam causes a film or quick-sealed coating to form on the outside of the foods, preventing the flavors from merging *as long as the foods do not touch one another.*

Do's in Pressure Cooking All Meats, Poultry and Game

Cut off all excess fat from the meat.

Brown-heat thoroughly all over if a rich flavor is desired.

Season sparingly and always after brown-heating.

Use the amount of liquid designated. Never let it come up over top of the rack unless a "boiled" flavor is desired.

Count cooking time starting when 15 pounds pressure has been attained.

Observe accurately the timings per pound and cooking suggestions given in this book.

Cool the cooker at once according to the manufacturer's directions after the cooking period is completed, unless the recipe states "cool in cooker."

If a crisp-brown crust is desired as with a roast, baked ham or chicken, first brown-heat, then pressure-cook; then place the cooked food in a hot oven or under the broiler a few minutes until the outside becomes brown-crisp.

In pressure cooking stews or so-called "boiled" meats such as boiled beef, never fill the cooker more than half full of water or any other liquid.

If possible cook a piece of cracked soup bone with all stews, ragouts and goulashes to add flavor and mineral value—especially calcium. Remove before serving.

Each time the cooker is used be sure the vent-pipe, all weights or pressure valves are clean and un-clogged.

Pressure Cooking Frozen Meat, Poultry and Game

Frozen meat, poultry and game, whether frozen in the home-locker or commercially frozen may be cooked in the pressure-cooker. If defrosted before pressure-ing it will cook in the time and by the methods allowed for corresponding cuts of fresh meat. For thawing allow from two to four hours at room temperature; or all day in the refrigerator, according to the size of the cut. If meat is cooked while in the **frozen state, allow from 10 to 15 percent additional pressure-ing time.** As it is not possible to brown-heat meat in the frozen state, a longer period of brown-crisping in the oven or under the broiler will be needed at the end of the pressure-ing. Frozen meats and poultry that do not call for the "browned taste" cook satisfactorily solely with the pressuring process.

The bones of pressured frozen meat, poultry and game prove exceptionally soft and porous. The good old-fashioned custom of "gnawing" them is not only permissible, but a step toward better nutrition, as the softness in texture makes the calcium available.

Is the Meat Thermometer Necessary?

It will not be necessary to purchase a meat thermometer if directions given in this book are carefully followed. The only time when it could be needed, is when the starting point of the pressuring was not noted, and consequently it would be uncertain whether the meat was cooked sufficiently in the center. In this case, if you have a meat thermometer, cool and open the cooker when you think the meat should be ready, and test it for "doneness." If the meat is not done, close the cooker, bring up the pressure again to 15 pounds, and pressure as much longer as may seem necessary. When using the meat thermometer, do not let the end of it rest on bone or fat. Bone is a heat conductor, fat acts as an insulator against heat. Only when the bulb of the thermometer is in the center of the lean meat does it accurately register the internal temperature of the roast. Make an incision and insert a meat thermometer so that the bulb reaches the center of the fleshiest part of the meat.

General Methods for Pressure Cooking Meat, Poultry and Game

PRESSURE-ROASTING

Prepare the meat or poultry. Then sprinkle with about 2 tablespoons of flour and slowly sauté (fry) all over until well browned in the pressure-cooker or in a frying pan. In turning be careful not to pierce the meat with a fork, as in this case the juices will escape. Dust with salt and pepper, using half the usual amount. Place the rack in the cooker; pour in ½ cup water if the meat is to cook from 30 to 45 minutes, or about ¾ cup if it is to cook from 45 minutes to an hour. The exact amount depends upon the diameter of the cooker. In any case the water should not come over the top of the rack. Close the cooker; bring the pressure to 15 pounds, and counting the cooking time from that point on, process the meat the required number of minutes per pound designated in the recipes in this book for roasting meats, poultry and game.

Cool the cooker at once. If a crisp, oven-roasted type outer crust is desired, spoon a little fat over the roast and place it in a very hot oven for a few minutes, or under a pre-heated broiler to crisp. In this case lower the broiler-pan and turn the roast several times to brown-crisp it evenly. Use cooking tongs for this purpose. Meantime make gravy from the residue in the pressure-cooker, following the directions on pages 244, 245, 246. If a vegetable or two are to be pressured separately this can be done in the cooker while the meat is brown-crisping.

PRESSURE-PANNING

This method is used for very thin cuts of meat, such as liver, fresh ham or lamb steak, veal, beef or lamb. The great advantage is that thrift cuts may be used.

Method: First thoroughly brown-heat the meat and season. Place on a rack in the cooker, with not more than one-half cup water or vegetable liquid, or enough to barely cover the bottom. Bring up the pressure to 15 pounds, and process the required length of time. For example, 3 minutes for veal scalloppini or sliced liver with onions; 5 minutes for thin shoulder lamb chops. Serve with pan gravy or a special wine, creole or mushroom sauce (see Chapter XIII), or with mixed vegetables.

PRESSURE POT-ROASTING

Pot-roasting is accomplished quickly and easily in the pressure-cooker, and the result is always fork-tender, even when the thrifty cuts of meat are used. We are all familiar with pot roast of beef, but few realize that equally appetizing pot roasts may be made with lamb, mutton, veal, venison or fowl. The main difference between pressure-roasting and pressure-pot-roasting is a slightly longer cooking time per pound, the fact that more water is used, and that a variety of vegetables and seasonings are cooked with the meat for special flavor. A pot roast is not brown-crisped after pressuring.

Method: First brown-heat the meat all over in vegetable or savory fat, or use fat from the meat. Next place the rack in the cooker, and pour in 1 cup of water or liquid from cooked vegetables. This should barely come up *over* the rack and no higher. Dust the meat with salt and pepper and place in the cooker. Cover with diced vegetables for flavor; add additional seasonings, and pressure cook the required time as designated in the recipes in this book for pressure-pot-roasting various meats. When done make gravy from the liquid in the pressure-cooker. (See pages 244, 245, 246.)

PRESSURE-BRAISING

The main difference between pressure-pot-roasting and pressure-braising is in the amount of liquid used—2 cups of water or drained liquid from cooked vegetables being the right amount for braising. During the last 5 minutes of the cookery the cooker may be cooled, opened, and diced vegetables added. The pressure is then brought up to 15 pounds to complete the cookery.

Any cut of meat suitable for pot-roasting may be

braised. First brown-heat, preferably in salt pork fat. To do this, cut enough fat salt pork into dice to make ½ cupful, and sauté until brown-crisp in the pressure-cooker or a frying pan. Reserve the crisp pork scraps, to use in garnishing a vegetable, or a green salad. Brown-heat the meat all over in the fat; add salt, pepper and any other desired seasoning. Put the rack in the cooker; place the meat on it and pour in 1 to 1½ cups boiling water or liquid from cooked vegetables. The liquid should come over the rack and touch the meat. Close the cooker, bring to 15 pounds pressure, and cook the required number of minutes per pound designated in the recipes for braised meats. The selection of diced vegetables to be added depends on the kind of meat that is braised.

Thin cuts instead of large pieces of meat are often braised; Swiss steak (page 100) and lamb chops jardinière (page 122) are familiar examples.

Pressure-potting is the same as pressure-braising.

PRESSURE-BOILING

The ever popular, old-fashioned "boiled" beef, or square cut of mutton or lamb may be cooked to great advantage in the pressure-cooker, because pressuring brings about no loss of flavor or nutrients. In the old-time method, the meat was covered with salted, boiling water and simmered for hours. In the pressuring method the meat is really steam-boiled, and the time is reduced to 12 minutes a pound, thus saving many kitchen hours.

Method: Cut excess fat from the meat and put the meat on the rack in the pressure-cooker. Pour in water to barely half cover, add 1 teaspoon salt to a quart of water, close the cooker, bring up the pressure to 15 pounds, and pressure the required length of time. Various seasonings needed in preparing different kinds of steam-boiled meats are added with the water. To make a complete boiled dinner, the cooker is cooled, opened, and vegetables are put in to cook the last 8 to 12 minutes.

PRESSURED-BARBECUED MEAT, POULTRY OR GAME

All kinds of meat or poultry or game suited to barbecue cookery may be pressure-cooked.

Method: Brown-heat the meat or poultry; season lightly with salt and pepper, then pour over a cup of plain or wine barbecue sauce (page 237). Transfer the meat and sauce to the rack of the pressure cooker, or to a special pan if a compartment cooker is used. Bring to 15 pounds pressure and cook the required length of time. This depends on the size and thickness of the cut; for instance, barbecued bris-ket of beef, which weighs 3 or 4 pounds, takes 50 minutes; spare ribs of pork need 15 minutes; sectioned baby broiler chickens need only 10 to 12 minutes. To gain a glazed crisp outer crust, spread out the cooked meat or poultry on a flat pan or metal or glass sizzling platter, and run this under a pre-heated broiler for a few minutes. Serve with additional barbecue sauce.

PRESSURE-STEWING

Stews of all kinds may be pressure-prepared. In general there are two types which may be called:

1. Soupy-stews: Which are stews consisting of about half thickened soup, and half meat, poultry or game with vegetables. The meat is cut in bite-sized pieces. These stews may be brought to the table in a deep bowl or soup tureen and are served in soup plates, or in shallow bowls if the meat is diced, so that cutting is not necessary. If the meat is in large pieces, choose soup plates.

2. Platter-stews: Which consist of ⅓ thickened gravy and ⅔ meat, poultry or game and vegetables. Deep platters or large shallow bowls may be used for the table service; Mexican pottery is most attractive, with soup or deep plates or shallow bowls. Any thrifty cut of meat or poultry makes an excellent platter stew. These stews are especially good when served on noodles, toasted split rolls, or corn bread squares. Recipes for various stews are in this book.

PRESSURE-FRICASSEEING

Fricassees and platter-stews are closely allied. However, in contrast to platter stews, fricassees are always made with medium-sized portions of poultry or meat, and about one-fourth the amount of gravy; the vegetables are cooked separately, then used as a garnish. A fricassee is usually served on toast, split baking powder biscuit or thin corn bread squares, or in a ring of plain, white, wild or brown rice, or with Spanish, curried, or Persian rice. Looks lovely and tastes grand. There are two types of fricassees:

"White" Fricassee: When the chicken or other poultry or meat is not brown-heated but is cooked "as is."

Brown Fricassee: When the chicken or other meat is first brown-heated before pressuring. All thin or small medium-sized portions or cuts of meat and poultry may be pressure-fricasseed.

Recipes for pressure-fricasseeing several kinds of meat, poultry and game are given in this book.

CASSEROLE-TYPE PRESSURE COOKING

The casserole is most often considered a utensil to use in the oven. But in reality earthen-ware casseroles were first of all top-of-the-stove pots, and they still are in many

ressure cooking in the air, from *Parade,* photographed in the galley of an American Over-Seas Air-Liner, by Ida Bailey Allen and Tad Horton

Pressure cooking in the "Ida Bailey Allen and the Chef" Television Show of the American Broadcasting Company, in New York, Philadelphia and Schenectady. The Herb Tray contributes "ze touch of ze Chef."

Battery of individual pressure cookers used at the Palmer House, Chicago.

countries. Any food that can be casseroled by the oven method may be pressure-cooked. So if you have a pet casserole recipe, you can adapt the procedure to pressure-cooking and serve the finished food in your favorite casserole dish. If you have a large pressure-cooker, or one equipped with compartments, you can often even replace one of the compartments with a tall casserole; but don't do this if it is going to prove a snug fit, as it will then be almost impossible to remove.

Method: In preparing casserole ingredients for pressure-cooking, cut the meat or poultry in ½-inch cubes and brown-heat. Then make the sauce, and add the vegetables cut in larger-than-usual pieces. The pressuring of the whole dish can then be done in the length of time it takes to cook the vegetables, and the rice or spaghetti if used with them. If this pre-preparation is done in the morning, and the food is placed in the refrigerator until time to pressure for dinner, it will be very cold, so allow a few extra minutes to bring the pressure to fifteen pounds. Remember there is no evaporation of liquid from the pressure-cooker, so make a fourth less sauce, or use a fourth less liquid than when a casserole is to be baked in the oven.

When making a casserole-type dish directly in the cooker, the pressure-cooker rack is not used. An extra vegetable may be cooked at the same time if tied in moistened parchment paper and placed on top of the casserole mixture.

STUFFINGS FOR MEAT, POULTRY OR GAME

For pressure cooking choose a dry-moist stuffing, as there will be no oven heat to drive off excess moisture as when cooking is done in the oven.

Any kind of bread may be used, or a combination of accumulated varieties. If the bread is very dry first soak it in hot water. Before making into stuffing, put it in a colander or big strainer and press out all possible liquid; then *omit* any liquid designated in the recipe. If packaged stuffing is used, follow directions, either sautéing or adding less liquid so the stuffing will be half dry when used.

Stuffings may be made by any favorite recipe with this exception: *Do not* add the fat; instead reserve it. After the moistening liquid and seasonings are added, slowly pan-fry the stuffing a few moments in the reserved fat. Then add egg, if used, and spoon the stuffing into the meat or poultry; *but do not pack it in*. Then lace together the edges of the meat or opening. To do this, stick in sharp toothpicks or poultry nails, and lace up the opening with white string, crisscross fashion.

Stuffings

Recipes are proportioned to serve four to six.
All measurements are level.

SAVORY DRY-MOIST STUFFING

2½ cups soft white or entire wheat bread crumbs packed down
1 teaspoon salt
⅛ teaspoon pepper
1 teaspoon onion juice
¾ teaspoon poultry seasoning

1¼ cups hot milk, water or liquid drained from cooked vegetables
2 tablespoons butter, margarine, vegetable fat or savory meat fat

Combine the crumbs, seasonings and liquid. Melt the fat in a frying pan and slowly sauté the stuffing until it is quite dry. If desired a beaten egg may be added after frying.

Onion Stuffing: Add one cup finely chopped onion to the ingredients for dry-moist stuffing before frying.

Vegetabilized Stuffing: Add 1 cup minced celery, grated carrot, onion and parsley mixed to the ingredients for dry-moist stuffing, and decrease the milk to one cupful.

Nut Stuffing: To the ingredients for dry-moist stuffing, add ¾ cup any kind chopped toasted or salted nuts, such as Brazil nuts, pecans, mixed salted nuts, walnuts or filberts.

Mushroom Stuffing: Follow the recipe for savory dry-moist stuffing, with this exception: Fry 1 cup of chopped fresh or canned mushroom caps and stems in the fat before adding the crumb mixture. And add a half teaspoon grated lemon rind if desired. If canned mushrooms are used add the liquid to the stuffing.

GIBLET STUFFING

Giblets from 1 or 2 chickens, duck or a turkey
1 small loaf day-old white bread
½ cup chopped peeled onion

½ cup chopped celery
½ cup chopped parsley
2 tablespoons vegetable fat
1 teaspoon garlic salt
1 teaspoon poultry seasoning

2 eggs

1. Clean giblets, put in pressure-cooker; add ½ cup boiling water, bring to 15 pounds pressure and cook twelve minutes.

2. Cool and chop giblets and add the giblet liquid.

3. Crumb the bread fine. The easiest way to do this is to slice it thick and crumb with a fork; leave on the crust if soft; then add the liquid and giblets.

4. Meantime sauté the onion, celery and parsley lightly in the fat. Add seasonings and the crumb and giblet mixture and sauté a little longer, or until the stuffing is half dried out.

5. Then add the eggs beaten light. Use as desired.

MEXICAN STUFFING

2½ cups white or entire wheat bread crumbs
1 teaspoon salt
⅛ teaspoon pepper
½ teaspoon oregano (Mexican sage)

1¼ cups tomato juice
¼ cup chopped onion
¼ cup chopped seeded sweet green pepper
2 tablespoons butter, margarine or vegetable fat

1. Combine the crumbs, seasonings and tomato juice.
2. Sauté the vegetables in the fat until softened.
3. Add the crumb mixture and continue to sauté until half dried out.

CEREAL STUFFING

2 cups cooked rice, cracked wheat, buckwheat or hominy grits
½ teaspoon salt
⅛ teaspoon pepper
½ teaspoon poultry seasoning or thyme

½ cup chopped or canned tomato, celery, sweet pepper, sautéd mushrooms, halved oysters or minced cooked or raw meat
2 tablespoons butter or margarine

1. Combine all the ingredients except the oysters or meat.
2. Melt the fat; add combined ingredients and slowly sauté until half dry.
3. Then add the oysters or the minced cooked or raw meat.

CORN BREAD STUFFING

⅓ cup butter or margarine
⅓ cup minced onion
¾ cup minced celery
5 cups crumbed unsweet-
    ened corn bread
1½ teaspoons salt

½ teaspoon pepper
1 teaspoon poultry season-
    ing
2 tablespoons minced pars-
    ley
1 egg

1. Melt the butter; add the onion and celery; sauté about 2 minutes.

2. Then add the crumbs and seasoning; mix well. Beat and add the egg. This makes quite a dry stuffing.

If desired more moist, add a little more melted butter or margarine, or bouillon or meat-stock of any kind. This is sufficient to stuff a 10-pound turkey. For a roast chicken or good-sized duck cut the quantities in half.

Meat Garnishes and Platters

It is scarcely possible to talk about meat garnishes without discussing meat platters. Of course the meat itself is the center of interest. Give it plenty of room on the platter. The garnishes and complements should high light the meat and provide contrasting color, but don't overdecorate, and don't fill the platter so full that skillful carving is impossible.

Only edible garnishes are used. We've long since passed the days when "panty ruffles" paraded on lamb chop bones!

Plain Green Garnishes: Use a choice of parsley, water cress, crisp celery tips, crinkly chicory leaves, or feathery finnochio, or carrot tops. Or place the meat on a bed of lettuce, or whole romaine leaves radiating from the center of the platter.

Color Garnishes of Vegetables: Radish tulips are effective. So are scallions cut like lilies. And carrot flowers (p. 374). Red or yellow tomatoes can be used plain, halved or slashed almost to the base to form flowers. There are small pimiento cups, to hold a relish; sliced tomatoes make a nice border, either overlapping or arranged alternately with sliced cucumber.

Color Garnishes of Fruit: These are used with all kinds of meat, poultry or game.

Special Meat Platter
Accompaniments

Pork: You might choose broiled, glacéd or stuffed raisin-d apples, or whole stewed peaches.

Beef: Try halved tomatoes filled with minced Florida Waldorf salad (page 380).

Smoked Meats: Call for pickled peaches, pears, crab apples or prunes. Grilled pineapple is perfect with ham or pork tenderloin.

Lamb: Harmonizes with mint; so use mint sauce or broiled slices of orange first sprinkled with herb vinegar, and after broiling with mint; or serve with fresh currants in any form, or dried currant sauce, or orange-currant-mint sauce (page 240).

Veal: Needs the lift of contrasting flavor. So use sliced oranges, sprinkled with sweet white wine; halves of canned apricots or red cherries or sections of grape fruit in lettuce nests. Or add whole seedless white grapes to the veal gravy, barely heat through, and use fresh grapes as a garnish.

Poultry and Game: Harmonize with sliced oranges or orange sections as a platter border; with clusters of mal-

aga, seedless white or tokay grapes; with overlapping
slices of cored red-skinned apple sprinkled with lime juice
and dipped in chopped nuts; with grilled pineapple,
halved poached apricots or peaches, plain or filled with
tart jam, plum sauce, or red cherries. (Not maraschino,
please!)

Hot Vegetables: Form a pleasant platter decoration.
Choose vegetables with form and contrasting color, as carrots, cut in long, thin strips, or use pressured whole baby
carrots; whole pressured green beans; whole braised tomatoes; stalks of succulent asparagus or dark green broccoli; pickled beets or carrots in lettuce cups. Or border the
platter with grilled tomato slices, fried slices of summer
squash, cucumber, or egg plant. Or use caulifleurettes
sprinkled with paprika; or sautéd mushroom caps or
stuffed mushrooms.

All these are easy to arrange and need cost nothing
extra, because they are part of the meal, adding taste,
color and appeal.

CHAPTER V

BEEF IN APPETIZING WAYS

IF YOU ARE BOTH CAREER AND HOME WOMAN THERE ARE often times when it seems impossible to come home from work and cook a dinner. At that point you decide to "eat out." And eating out certainly makes a big dent in the pay check. Besides, the husband prefers home-cooked food, and for youngsters it is an essential "must."

Careful planning on your part plus the right use of your pressure-cooker will solve this problem. You can even have roast beef, pot roasts or Swiss steak ready to eat in less than an hour after you get home. You need waste no time shopping for expensive steaks and chops, because you can use the abundant thrifty cuts which pressure-cook in a third or less the usual time.

Standards of deliciousness and nutrition will go up in your meals, while the meat bill takes a tailspin. Here are thirty-seven robust ways to pressure cook beef, and here's the best of luck.

Pressure Cooking Beef

Recipes serve from four to six.
All measurements are level.
Timings are minutes required for actual pressure-ing.
Cool cooker as soon as pressure-ing is done.

ROAST SIRLOIN STEAK

7 minutes per pound

2 pounds sirloin steak cut   ½ teaspoon salt
   2 inches thick   ¼ cup hot water

1. Remove excess fat from the steak and slash edges so the meat will lie flat. If too large to fit the cooker, cut in halves so the pieces can be fitted together, but do not pile one on the other in the cooker.

2. Brown-heat slowly on both sides and season.

3. Put rack in cooker; add water and place the steak on the rack. Close the cooker, bring up the pressure to 15 pounds and process 7 minutes per pound for medium-rare.

4. If desired the cooker may be cooled and opened at the end of 3 minutes, and halved white or sweet potatoes, small whole peeled carrots, or mixed vegetables tied in moistened parchment paper, may be processed with the steak the last 4 minutes.

5. To serve, slice thin crosswise. Arrange overlapping on a platter and pour around the pan gravy in the cooker. If vegetables are not cooked with the steak serve with crisp lettuce.

If actually necessary to save room in the cooker, the bone may be removed from the steak, but whenever possible a little bone should be cooked with any pressured meat as it adds both flavor and mineral content.

ROAST BEEF
35 to 50 minutes based on number of pounds

3 to 4 pounds rolled rib or sirloin of beef
2 tablespoons fat
¾ teaspoon salt
⅛ teaspoon pepper
1 peeled section garlic crushed (optional)
½ to ¾ cup hot water

1. Brown-heat the beef thoroughly all over in the fat. Season with salt, pepper and garlic mixed together.

2. Put the rack in the cooker; add the water, put in the meat, close the cooker and bring up the pressure to 15 pounds. For rare roast beef, pressure 9 minutes per pound. For medium roast beef, ten minutes per pound. For well-done roast beef, 12 minutes per pound. Be sure to cool the cooker as soon as the meat has cooked the required length of time. If a crisp crust is desired place in a very hot oven for a few minutes, or put on a heat-proof platter, brown-crisp under the broiler and serve on the platter.

Pass the pan gravy from the cooker (excess fat removed), or make brown gravy. If there is a separate compartment in the cooker, accompany with savory English suet pudding pressured at the same time.

BEEF POT ROAST YANKEE STYLE
11 minutes per pound

2 to 4 pounds pot roast of beef, round, chuck or brisket
1 medium-sized onion sliced
1 teaspoon salt
¼ cup sliced carrot
¼ cup cut celery
2 tablespoons chopped parsley
1 cup hot water or liquid from cooked vegetables

1. Remove excess fat from meat. Brown-heat all over in its own fat with the onion.

2. Place the rack on the cooker and add the liquid.

3. Put in the meat; dust with the salt and strew over the vegetables. Close cooker, bring to 15 pounds pressure and process 11 minutes per pound.

Serve with gravy made from the liquid in the pan. This pot roast is excellent served with slices of fried corn meal or hominy mush; with mashed potatoes, or balls of pressure-cooked whole barley or cracked wheat (page 310). If an inset pan is available the cereal may be pressured with the pot roast as they take approximately the same pressuring time.

SPANISH BEEF POT ROAST
11 minutes per pound

2 to 4 pounds pot roast of beef, round, chuck or brisket

5 sections garlic peeled and quartered

1 teaspoon salt

½ teaspoon marjoram

2 seeded sweet green peppers diced

1 medium-sized onion sliced

¼ cup cut celery

¼ cup sliced carrot

2 tablespoons chopped parsley

1 cup tomato juice

1. Remove excess fat from meat.

2. Gash meat with a sharp knife in 20 places, and press a quartered section of garlic into each. The garlic must be pushed way in so it is covered by the surface of the meat.

3. Brown-heat all over in its own fat and season.

4. Place the rack in the cooker. Add tomato juice (or use 2 tablespoons tomato puree and a scant cup water). Put in the meat and strew over the vegetables. Close cooker, bring to 15 pounds pressure and process 11 minutes to the pound.

Serve with Spanish sauce made from the liquid in the cooker (page 236). Accompany with fried corn meal mush or pressured carbanza beans.

SWEET AND SOUR BEEF POT ROAST
25 minutes

2 to 2½ pounds round, chuck or brisket of beef
1 cup sliced onion
1 peeled section garlic minced
¾ cup hot water or liquid drained from cooked vegetables
1 small bay leaf

2 tablespoons vinegar
1 tablespoon brown sugar or 2 tablespoons brown corn syrup
3 tablespoons tomato catsup
¼ cup raisins
¾ teaspoon salt
⅛ teaspoon pepper

1. Brown-heat the meat in the cooker in its own fat. When browned all over, add the onion and garlic and fry until yellowed.

2. Add the liquid, bay leaf, vinegar, brown sugar, tomato catsup and raisins; season the meat.

3. Close the cooker; bring the pressure to 15 pounds and process 25 minutes.

4. Cool the cooker; thicken the liquid with one tablespoon flour stirred smooth with one-half tablespoon butter.

5. Serve accompanied with boiled or fried noodles, or pressured white, brown or wild rice.

Sweet and Sour Lamb Pot Roast: Substitute a small, rolled boned shoulder of lamb for the beef in the preceding recipe; add ½ tablespoon fresh minced mint, or 1 teaspoon dry mint to the liquid.

BRAISED SHORT RIBS OF BEEF
25 minutes

3 pounds short ribs of beef cracked in three sections	⅛ teaspoon pepper
	¼ teaspoon thyme
¾ teaspoon salt	1¾ cups hot water or liquid from cooked vegetables

1. Remove all fat possible; brown-heat the meat without adding any extra fat; then pour off all fat except two tablespoonfuls.

2. Put rack in pressure-cooker. Pour in liquid. Put meat on rack; season, cover, bring to 15 pounds and process 25 minutes.

3. Make a gravy from the liquid in the cooker (page 244). Arrange the ribs on a platter; pour around the gravy and serve with flaky potatoes or spoon bread (page 201), which may be cooked at the same time if the cooker is equipped with a compartment.

BEEF A LA MODE
14 minutes to the pound

2 cups water	1 carrot sliced
⅓ cup plain or herb vinegar	2 sprigs parsley
1 teaspoon salt	2 lemons sliced with the peel
1 teaspoon poultry seasoning	¼ cup dry wine (optional)
¼ teaspoon mace	4 to 5 pounds round, chuck or brisket of beef
3 whole cloves	

1. Make a marinade by combining the water, vinegar, seasonings, vegetables and lemon. Bring to boiling point and simmer 15 minutes. Add wine if used. Place the meat in a deep bowl. Strain over the vinegar mixture.

2. Cool quickly; cover and stand in the refrigerator 24 hours; turn occasionally.

3. Remove the meat; drain, but save the marinade.

4. Put the meat in the pressure-cooker; brown in beef drippings and at the same time add three additional slices of lemon.

5. Pour in the strained marinade, close the cooker, bring to 15 pounds pressure and process 14 minutes per pound.

6. Make a gravy from the liquid in the cooker. Slice the meat and serve garnished with wedges of lemon. The traditional accompaniment is potato or rice croquettes and small boiled onions.

BRAISED BEEF FLANK MEXICAN
45 minutes

2 pounds trimmed beef flank
1 tablespoon basil or garlic vinegar (optional)
Mexican or Savory Dry-moist stuffing
2 tablespoons fat
¾ teaspoon salt
⅛ teaspoon pepper
1 cup hot water or liquid from cooked vegetables

1. Remove excess fat from meat. Brush all over with the vinegar if used.

2. Spread stuffing to within 1 inch from the edge. Roll up and tie with white string.

3. Brown-heat slowly all over in the fat. Dust with the salt and pepper.

4. Place on rack in cooker. Pour in the liquid. Close the cooker, bring to 15 pounds and process 35 minutes.

5. Place on hot platter. Remove string. Serve surrounded with carrots and flaky potatoes, and pass tomato or brown gravy made from the liquid in the cooker (page 244). Halved potatoes and small whole carrots may be cooked with the meat if desired. To do this cool and open the cooker at the end of 40 minutes. Put in the prepared vegetables, bring up the pressure to 15 pounds and cook 5 minutes longer.

BEEF "BIRDS"
15 minutes

1½ pounds round or flank steak
Savory dry-moist stuffing
1½ tablespoons flour
½ teaspoon salt
⅛ teaspoon pepper
2 tablespoons bacon or any savory fat

¼ lemon rind grated
1½ cups hot water or liquid from cooked vegetables
½ cup evaporated milk, light cream or soured cream

1. Cut the steak in 2-inch squares and pound them until well-flattened with a wooden mallet. Put a teaspoonful of the stuffing on each piece; roll up and skewer into shape with toothpicks.

2. Roll in the flour, salt and pepper mixed, and brown-heat in the fat.

3. Place the rack in the pressure-cooker. Put in the liquid. Place the beef "birds" on the rack, sprinkle over the lemon rind; close the cooker and bring to 15 pounds; process 15 minutes.

4. Cool and open the cooker; remove the "birds," add the milk, light cream or soured cream, and bring the gravy to boiling point.

5. To serve, arrange the "birds" on toast; pour around the gravy and garnish with braised whole tomatoes, pressured whole string beans, diced winter squash, or green peas piled in pressured patty-pan squash.

Veal Birds: Follow the preceding recipe, substituting veal cutlet or steak; or use thin slices of veal from the leg. Mushroom stuffing will prove specially appetizing.

SWISS STEAK
15 minutes

1½ pounds round, chuck or flank steak
1½ tablespoons flour
½ teaspoon salt
⅛ teaspoon pepper
¼ teaspoon thyme
2 tablespoons fat

1 seeded sweet green pepper chopped
1 onion chopped
½ cup hot water or vegetable liquid
2 tablespoons horseradish (optional)

1. Order steak sliced ½ to 1 inch thick; cut in pieces suitable for serving, and rub in the flour, salt, pepper and thyme.
2. Melt the fat in the cooker and quickly brown-heat the meat in it on all sides.
3. Cover with the vegetables; add the liquid. Close cooker, bring to 15 pounds pressure and process 15 minutes. Make a gravy (page 244).
4. Serve with flaky or mashed potatoes, spaghetti al dente, or plain white, brown or Spanish rice.

BARBECUED SHORT RIBS
25 minutes

2 pounds short ribs beef cracked in three sections
1 peeled onion minced
½ cup cut celery
¼ cup mild vinegar
1 tablespoon brown sugar

½ cup hot water
2 tablespoons tomato puree
1 tablespoon Worcestershire sauce
½ tablespoon prepared mustard
1 teaspoon salt

1. If the short ribs are extremely fatty, remove part of it. Then brown-heat in a frying pan without additional fat. Add the onion and celery and continue brown-heating until they are yellowed.

2. Transfer the ribs to the cooker. Do not use the rack. Pour over the remaining ingredients mixed. Rinse out the frying pan with an additional fourth cup of water.

3. Close the cooker, bring to 15 pounds pressure and cook for 25 minutes. Make a gravy from the liquid in the pan. If desired place the short ribs under the broiler to brown-crisp.

4. Serve with mashed potatoes, rice, noodles or spaghetti al dente.

"BOILED BEEF"
12 minutes to the pound

3 to 4 pounds fresh brisket, chuck or rump of beef
2 cups boiling water
1 sliced peeled onion

1 teaspoon salt
½ teaspoon mixed pickle spice or ½ bay leaf (optional)

1. Remove as much fat as possible and place the meat in the cooker. Pour in the water; add the onion and seasonings, close the cooker and bring to 15 pounds. Process 12 minutes per pound.

2. Slice, and serve with horseradish sauce made with part of the liquid in the cooker.

To turn this into a whole course "boiled dinner," cool and open the cooker 10 minutes before the meat will be done. Put in halved medium-sized peeled potatoes, thick wedges of cabbage, peeled young turnips, or carrots peeled and slashed at the thick end. Close the cooker; bring the pressure up to 15 pounds; process 5 minutes and cool at once.

BEEF AND MUSHROOM RAGOUT
12 minutes

1 pound round or flank of beef
2 peeled onions sliced
1 tablespoon fat any kind
1 tablespoon flour
⅛ teaspoon pepper

¼ teaspoon salt
1¼ cups hot water
½ teaspoon beef extract
¾ pound fresh mushrooms or 1 4 oz. can
8 peeled large potatoes

1. Slice the beef paper-thin, then in narrow strips. Add the onions.

2. Sauté in the cooker until lightly browned in the fat. Stir in the flour and seasonings.

3. Dissolve the beef extract in the water and pour it in. Meantime, wash the mushrooms (do not peel), and slice crosswise, tops and stems together.

5. Place the mushrooms on the meat, and over these put the potatoes.

6. Close the cooker; bring to 15 pounds and process 12 minutes.

BEEF STEW "SOUPY STYLE"
15 minutes

2 pounds neck, round, chuck, shank, flank, or shin of beef, freed from bone
2 tablespoons flour
1 tablespoon fat any kind
6 cups hot water, or half water and half vegetable liquid
¼ teaspoon thyme
1 teaspoon salt

⅛ teaspoon pepper
6 peeled small onions halved
4 peeled good-sized potatoes cut in coarse dice
4 carrots peeled and diced coarse
1 tablespoon minced parsley
½ teaspoon beef extract or condiment sauce

1. Cut the meat in inch cubes. Roll in the flour; then brown-heat in the fat, preferably in a frying pan. Put the rack in the cooker.

2. Mix the seasonings with the meat. Transfer to the cooker; add a piece of soup bone if possible. Pour in the water, close the cooker, bring to 15 pounds and process 11 minutes.

3. Cool and open the cooker. Add the vegetables; close; bring up to 15 pounds pressure again; cook 4 minutes longer. Add the beef extract or condiment sauce.

4. Serve in soup plates, bowls or small casseroles; sprinkle with parsley. Pass split toasted rolls or New England toast (page 61).

BEEF STEW PLATTER STYLE

Follow the preceding recipe, using only 2½ cups of liquid. If dumplings (page 63) are served, make them small; arrange around the edge of the platter, and sprinkle with minced parsley, or dust with paprika.

CHILE CON CARNE
15 minutes

1 tablespoon fat	⅛ teaspoon pepper
5 peeled onions chopped	1 tablespoon chili powder
1 peeled section garlic chopped	1½ cups canned tomatoes
	1 cup hot water
1 pound beef (any cut) chopped coarse	1 No. 2 can kidney beans or 2 cups cooked kidney beans
1 teaspoon salt	

1. Melt the fat in the cooker; fry the onions and garlic in it until yellowed. Add the beef and slowly brown-heat.

2. Add the seasonings, tomato, water and ½ cup of

the beans thoroughly mashed to give thickness to the gravy.

3. Close the cooker; bring up the pressure to 15 pounds and process 15 minutes.

4. Cool and open the cooker; add the remaining beans, bring to boiling point, and serve on white or brown rice; with mashed potatoes, New England toast, corn bread, or the traditional crackers.

BEEF WITH CUCUMBER CHINESE STYLE
6 minutes

2 tablespoons butter or vegetable fat
1 pound flank, chuck or round steak cut in shoe-string strips
2 teaspoons corn starch
1 teaspoon soy sauce
½ teaspoon salt
⅛ teaspoon pepper
1 cup beef bouillon, or 1 cup hot water and one bouillon cube
2 large cucumbers
4 tablespoons chopped scallions and their green tops

1. Melt the fat in the pressure-cooker. Meantime stir the corn starch, seasonings and soy sauce with the meat. Then brown-heat in the fat. Add the bouillon, or water with the bouillon cube dissolved in it. Bring to 15 pounds pressure and process 5 minutes.

2. Meantime, wash and half peel the cucumbers. Quarter lengthwise, discard seeds, and cut the cucumber in inch-long pieces.

3. Cool and open the cooker; add the cucumber, bring to 15 pounds pressure and process 1½ minutes longer.

4. Serve topped with the chopped scallions; accompany with rice.

Veal with Cucumber: Instead of beef, use veal from the shin or shank cut in shoe-string strips.

STEAK RUSSIAN STYLE
16 minutes

1½ pounds round, flank or chuck steak cut in three-inch pieces
2 tablespoons flour
2 tablespoons fat

2 cups peeled sliced onions
½ teaspoon salt
⅛ teaspoon pepper
1 cup hot water
1 cup soured cream

1. Pound the pieces of steak until flattened, at the same time pounding or rubbing in the flour.

2. Melt the fat in a frying pan and fry the onions in it until yellowed. Then remove and reserve.

3. Brown-heat the steak in the fat on both sides. Pour the water into cooker. Season the meat and transfer to the cooker. Bring the pressure to 15 pounds and process 15 minutes.

4. Cool and open the cooker. Add the onions mixed with the soured cream; bring the pressure up to 15 pounds and process 1 minute longer.

5. Serve with flaky or fried white potatoes.

CHINESE PEPPERED BEEF
3 minutes

1 tablespoon fat
1 pound round, chuck or flank steak, cut in narrow inch-long strips
½ teaspoon salt
Few grains pepper
1 peeled crushed section garlic
4 tablespoons shredded scallions or onions

4 large sweet peppers seeded and shredded
¾ cup celery cut in inch lengths
1 bouillon cube
1 cup hot water
2 tablespoons corn starch
2 teaspoons soy sauce
⅓ cup cold water

1. Melt the fat in the pressure-cooker. Put in the meat and thoroughly brown-heat stirring occasionally. Add the salt and pepper.

2. Add the garlic, scallions, peppers and celery, and the bouillon cube dissolved in the water.

3. Close the cooker; bring to 15 pounds pressure and process 3 minutes.

4. Cool and open the cooker; thicken with the corn starch smoothly blended with the soy sauce and cold water. Stir until the mixture boils. Cook 2 minutes.

5. Serve with rice or boiled or fried noodles.

CURRIED BEEF
15 minutes

1½ pounds round, neck or chuck of beef

3 tablespoons flour

1½ teaspoons curry powder

3 tablespoons beef drippings

¼ cup sliced onion

1½ cups beef-stock, or water and 2 bouillon cubes

¾ tablespoon lemon juice

¼ cup dry Sauterne (optional)

1. Cut the meat in inch cubes; roll in the flour and curry until thoroughly mixed.

2. Melt the beef drippings in the pressure-cooker; put in the meat and brown-heat, turning occasionally. Add the onion and cook until it begins to turn yellow.

3. Put into the cooker the stock, or the bouillon cubes dissolved in 1½ cups water. Close the pressure-cooker, bring the pressure to 15 pounds and process 15 minutes.

4. Cool and open the cooker. Add the lemon juice and Sauterne; reheat and serve with boiled rice. Traditionally, the curried beef would be served strewn with grated fresh coconut. Defrosted fresh coconut may be used instead. Pass chutney sauce.

BOEUF STROGONOFF
5 minutes

2 tablespoons butter or margarine

1 pound tenderloin or chuck steak cut in shoe-string strips

1 tablespoon chopped onion

½ teaspoon salt

⅛ teaspoon pepper

2½ tablespoons flour

½ teaspoon beef extract

1½ cups hot water

½ pound fresh mushrooms sliced top through stem

3 tablespoons soured cream

1. Melt butter or margarine in the pressure-cooker. Brown-heat the steak and onion in this. Stir in seasonings and flour.

2. Dissolve the beef extract in the water and add to the steak mixture. Stir in the mushrooms. Close, bring to 15 pounds pressure and process 5 minutes.

3. Cool at once, and stir in the soured cream.

4. Serve with flaky or fried white potatoes.

SPANISH BEEF CASSEROLE STYLE
15 minutes

2 tablespoons fat

1½ pounds round or chuck steak cut in inch cubes

2½ tablespoons flour

1 peeled section garlic minced

2 onions sliced

2 seeded sweet green peppers shredded

1¼ cups canned tomato or 1 pound diced peeled fresh tomatoes

1 teaspoon salt

¼ teaspoon pepper

½ tablespoon brown sugar or corn syrup

¼ cup dry red wine (optional)

½ cup sliced stuffed olives

1. Melt the fat in the cooker. Roll the meat in the flour and lightly brown-heat. Then add garlic, onions and pepper and sauté until slightly soft.

2. Add the tomato and seasonings.

3. Close the cooker, bring to 15 pounds pressure and process 15 minutes.

4. Cool at once; stir in the wine, add the olives, bring to boiling point, and serve in a border of mashed potatoes, or white, brown or wild rice or barley, any one of which may be pressure-prepared in a compartment while the meat is pressuring.

BEEF CHOP SUEY
5 minutes

See recipe on page 178 for Chicken Chop Suey. Instead of chicken use round, chuck or flank steak cut into small thin pieces. Sauté the steak for 2 minutes in the oil; then complete as directed for Chicken Chop Suey.

HUNGARIAN GOULASH
15 minutes

2 pounds chuck or neck of beef cubed
2 tablespoons butter or margarine
2 peeled onions sliced
1 peeled section garlic minced

Plenty of paprika
½ teaspoon marjoram
1 teaspoon salt
1 cup water or tomato juice
A piece of cracked bone

1. Cut meat into 1-inch cubes. Melt the butter or margarine in the cooker. Add the onion, garlic and meat and brown-heat lightly.

2. Add enough paprika to effect a noticeable red color,

about 1½ teaspoonfuls. Add the remaining seasonings, the water or tomato juice, or use 2 tablespoons tomato purée in one cup water. Add the bone.

3. Close the cooker; bring to 15 pounds pressure and process 20 minutes.

4. Serve with flaky white potatoes. These may be cooked with the goulash if desired. To do this, cool and open the cooker at the end of 5 minutes; put in medium-sized potatoes, bring the pressure to 15 pounds again and cook 10 minutes longer.

5. Remove the bone before serving. It is used to give additional flavor to the goulash.

BEEF AND VEGETABLE BALLS
5 minutes

1 pound chopped beef	1 egg
2 medium-sized potatoes peeled	¼ teaspoon thyme or marjoram
2 small carrots peeled	½ teaspoon salt
1 cup cut celery	⅛ teaspoon pepper
1 medium-sized onion peeled	½ cup hot water
2 sprigs parsley	½ teaspoon beef extract

1. Put the beef, potatoes, carrots, celery, onion and parsley through the food chopper twice to make very smooth. Beat in the egg and add the seasonings.

2. Form into flattened balls containing one tablespoon each, shaping with the hands first dipped in flour.

3. Slowly brown-heat in two tablespoons fat in a frying pan.

4. Dissolve the beef extract in the water and put in the cooker. Put in the rack, and place meat balls on it.

5. Close the cooker, bring to 15 pounds and process 5 minutes.

6. Serve on toast or thin squares of unsweetened corn bread; accompany with a green salad tossed with herb flavored French dressing.

5-WAY HAMBURGERS
5 minutes

Plain Hamburgers

1 pound chopped raw beef   ⅛ teaspoon pepper
½ teaspoon salt

1. Put the meat through the chopper twice with the salt and pepper. Form into flat round cakes one-half inch thick.

2. Brown-heat in butter or margarine if possible. Put ½ cup water in the cooker. Put in the rack, place the hamburgers on it and bring the pressure to 15 pounds; process 5 minutes. If there is more than one layer of hamburgers, put a piece of moistened parchment paper between the layers.

3. Serve on toasted split buns, buttered before toasting. Use only ½ to a hamburger. Top each with a thin slice of raw onion, a bit of green pepper and ½ stuffed olive; or vary in any of the following ways:

Curried Hamburgers: Mix ½ teaspoon curry powder with the chopped beef before shaping into patties. After brown-heating, cook directly in the cooker without a rack. When done, remove the hamburgers, stir 1 cup soured cream into the drippings in the cooker. Thicken with 1 tablespoon flour stirred smooth in 1 tablespoon water. Add salt and pepper to taste. Serve with rice.

Tomatoed Hamburgers: Prepare plain hamburgers. Before shaping add 1 teaspoon scraped onion, or ½ teaspoon onion or garlic salt to the chopped beef. Cook as described. Serve on toast or halved toasted unsweetened buns as follows: Place a fresh or broiled slice of tomato on each. Top with the hamburger, and decorate each with a slice of hard-cooked egg and minced chives or scallions relish style (page 374).

Garlicked Hamburgers Extraordinary: Prepare plain hamburgers. Place in a dish, pour over 3 tablespoons garlic wine vinegar mixed with ½ cup cold water. Let stand at room temperature for 2 hours. Drain, and pat dry with paper towels. Cook as directed for plain hamburgers.

DANISH MEAT BALL PLATTER
5 minutes

½ pound lean raw beef	1 large egg
½ pound lean raw pork	½ cup boiling water
1 small onion peeled	3 tablespoons savory fat
½ cup flour, wheat or soy	2 sliced onions for gravy
1¼ teaspoons salt	Whole barley
¼ teaspoon pepper	Poached eggs
¼ teaspoon nutmeg	

1. Put the beef, pork and onion through the food chopper 3 times to blend and make very smooth.

2. Stir in the flour and seasonings. Beat the egg light and add. Stir in the boiling water and beat briskly until the mixture looks light.

3. Form into 8 flattened balls with the hands first dipped in a little flour. Brown-heat slowly in the fat.

4. Put the rack in the cooker; add the water; put in meat balls.

5. Close; bring the pressure to 15 pounds and process 5 minutes. Meantime, make a brown gravy in the frying pan (page 244); add 2 cups steam-fried onions.

Serve on a large sizzling platter.

To carry out the Danish idea, alternate the meat balls around the edge of the platter with balls of whole barley, shaped with an ice-cream scoop or a demi-tasse cup. Place a poached egg on each of the meat balls arranged down the center of the platter. Dust the poached eggs with paprika. Top each barley ball with half a stuffed olive or a bit of parsley or green pepper. Carefully spoon the onion gravy around the meat and barley balls.

HAMBURGER STEW
7 minutes

½ pound chopped raw beef
½ teaspoon sugar
2 onions sliced
1 tablespoon fat any kind
2 tablespoons flour
3 cups boiling water or liquid from cooked vegetables
1 teaspoon salt
⅛ teaspoon pepper
1 teaspoon beef extract
4 peeled white potatoes sliced thick
½ pound string beans cut in half lengthwise
2 peeled carrots cut thick crosswise
1 tablespoon chopped fresh herbs or ½ teaspoon thyme

1. Brown-heat the beef, sugar and onions in the fat, using the pressure-cooker without the rack. Stir in the flour; when well mixed, add the water, seasonings and all remaining ingredients.

2. Close the cooker, bring the pressure to 15 pounds and process 7 minutes.

3. Serve in deep soup plates, with hot rolls, New England toast, or butter-heated French bread (page 61).

Hamburger Stew Creole: Follow the preceding recipe, using 1 cup solid-pack canned tomatoes in place of one cup of water, and adding to the vegetables 2 medium-sized seeded sweet green peppers, shredded coarse. When done, add 2 tablespoons dry Sherry wine. Do not use red wine as this will discolor the vegetables.

THREE MEATS LOAF
25 minutes

¾ cup soft bread crumbs
½ cup hot milk
½ pound ground beef
½ pound ground veal
½ pound ground fresh pork
2 sprigs parsley
1 egg beaten

1 teaspoon salt
⅛ teaspoon pepper
½ teaspoon mace
¾ teaspoon poultry seasoning
1 teaspoon onion juice

1. Simmer the crumbs and milk together for 3 minutes or until soft and pasty. Stir often.

2. Put the beef, veal, pork and parsley through the food chopper. In other words, the meats should be chopped twice. Combine with the crumb mixture and add all the remaining ingredients.

3. Shape into a short thick loaf with the hands, which should be first dipped in flour. Brown-heat the loaf all over in the fat. Then roll in a piece of moistened parchment paper.

4. Put ½ cup water in the cooker. Put in the rack, place the loaf on it, close the cooker, bring to 15 pounds pressure and process 25 minutes.

5. If desired the cooker may be cooled and opened 5 minutes before the loaf is done, and mixed vegetables, or corn and soybean succotash may be added; or quartered sweet potatoes, yams or white potatoes may be put around the loaf to cook. In this case, bring the pressure again to 15 pounds and process the remaining 5 minutes.

6. To serve, remove the wrapping from the loaf. Place

the meat on a platter and surround with any vegetable that may be cooked with it. A plain brown gravy may be made from the fat in which the loaf was brown-heated. Or a tomato or mushroom sauce is in order. Or serve the loaf cold with potato salad, or Florida Waldorf salad. If served with plain sliced tomato and cucumber, accompany with Vinegarette Sauce and quartered hard-cooked eggs.

SPICED JELLIED BEEF LOAF
15 minutes to the pound

4 pounds shin or shank of beef, thick portion

2 teaspoons salt

¼ teaspoon pepper

½ teaspoon thyme or marjoram

½ teaspoon mace

1 cup hot water

1. If the meat will be too large to go into the pressure-cooker easily, ask the butcher to cut it in half.

2. Place directly in the cooker with no rack. Mix the seasonings with the water and pour in.

3. Close the cooker; bring to 15 pounds pressure and process 15 minutes to the pound. Cool the cooker.

4. Slightly cool the meat. Cut in pieces, place in a chopping bowl and chop fine with a chopping knife. Do not use a food chopper for this purpose. Add salt and pepper to taste; stir in the liquid from the cooker.

5. Rinse a bread pan or oblong glass refrigerator dish with cold water and pack in the meat and liquid. Weight this down by placing a second pan of the same size over the top with some heavy article in it. Chill overnight in the refrigerator to stiffen. This is possible because of the natural gelatin contained in the bone and sinews of the meat.

6. Cut in thin slices and serve with potato salad, asparagus vinegarette, stuffed tomato salad, or with macaroni and olive salad; garnish with tomato or cucumber slices.

Jellied Beef Loaf Buffet: Cook the ingredients for Jellied Beef Loaf as described in the preceding recipe but prepare it for chilling and stiffening as follows: In the bottom of the bread pan or glass dish make a design of sliced hard-cooked eggs, sliced scallions and bits of parsley. Carefully spoon enough of the beef mixture onto this to make a layer 1-inch deep. Into this press a layer of minced sautéd mushrooms and scallions mixed. Spoon on another inch-thick layer of the beef. Cover with sliced hard-cooked eggs, minced mushrooms and scallions. Then spoon on the remaining meat. Chill overnight.

To serve, unmold on a large platter; surround with individual servings of potato or egg salad, or halved tomatoes stuffed with macaroni salad, or with a ring of alternating slices of tomato and cucumber. Garnish with lettuce, chicory or water cress, and wedges of lemon or lime.

A NEW ENGLAND CORNED BEEF DINNER
36 to 50 minutes according to cut

3 to 5 pounds corned beef, brisket or plate
1 tablespoon garlic wine vinegar (optional)
3 cups boiling water
6 small peeled whole potatoes

6 medium-sized peeled young turnips
6 large carrots peeled and slashed at the end
1 medium-sized cabbage cut in six wedges

1. Put the corned beef into the cooker. Cover with cold water. Bring to boiling point; simmer 5 minutes then drain off the water. If very salt simmer 10 minutes to remove excess salt.

2. Put the rack in the cooker; put the corned beef on

it, add the garlic vinegar if used, and the three cups boiling water. Close the cooker; bring to 15 pounds and process 20 minutes per pound for a thick piece of corned beef, or 12 minutes per pound for a thin piece.

3. Open the cooker 8 minutes before the meat will be done and put in the vegetables. Close the cooker, bring the pressure to 15 pounds again and process 8 minutes longer.

4. Serve on a very large platter. Arrange the meat in overlapping slices down the center, and surround with the vegetables. Garnish with parsley. Serve with mustard or horseradish or catsup sauce (pages 241, 243).

If beets are to be included they may be pressure-cooked with the other vegetables by tying them in moistened parchment paper; place in the cooker tied-side up. For if they come directly in contact with other foods the red color of the beets will discolor them. If desired the beets may be cooked separately in some of the liquid in which the corned beef was pre-cooked. Traditionally a New England corned beef dinner is accompanied with some form of corn bread, usually steamed.

How to stuff and truss a shoulder of lamb (*Page 120*)

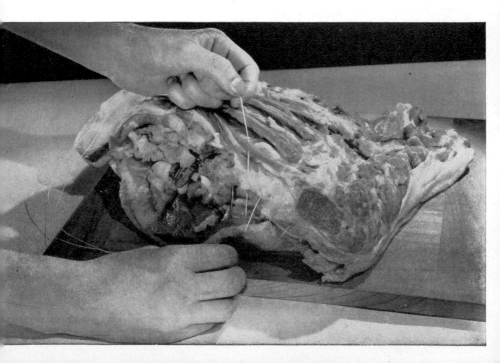

Pressured stuffed roast of lamb with mushrooms (*Page 120*)

Five-minute pressured lamb chop platter (*Page 121*)

CHAPTER VI

LAMB AND MUTTON SPECIALS

LAMB AND MUTTON ARE APPETIZING WELL-FLAVORED meats that deserve much wider usage in the United States. In many countries of Europe and the Orient they are favorites. The famous sword-broiled Kebabs of Arabia are made from lamb; the most popular dishes of Turkey and Armenia are based on it. "Down under," in New Zealand, it is scarcely Sunday without the traditional roast mutton dinner. In Scotland lamb and mutton are the principal meats; and Irish mutton is so famous that when the overseas air liners stop at Shannon they often take on choice legs of mutton which are promptly pressure-roasted while the plane flies on to its next destination.

Why is it that we do not serve lamb and mutton more often in the United States? There are two possible reasons. We may be prejudiced against them or we may not understand their cookery. I am inclined to think the difficulty is a combination of the two. Prejudice is present because we do not know how to cook these meats to bring out the best flavor. If we learn how to cook them well, prejudice will disappear.

The best procedure to follow in preparing lamb or mutton is pressure cooking. And all methods of preparing them, except broiling, may be followed when carried out according to the directions given in this book. But always be sure to observe the following rule unless otherwise indicated.

General Rule for Pressure Cooking Lamb or Mutton

Remove all excess fat from lamb or mutton before cooking. Brown-heat the meat thoroughly when brown-heating is indicated. Season sparingly with salt, but well with other seasonings. Be sure all excess fat is removed from the liquid in the cooker before making gravy.

Pressure Cooking Lamb and Mutton

Recipes are proportioned to serve four to six.
All measurements are level.
Timings are minutes required for actual pressuring.
Cool cooker as soon as pressuring is done.

ROAST LAMB
12 to 14 minutes to the pound

3 to 4 pounds square cut of lamb
1 tablespoon fat
¾ teaspoon salt

⅛ teaspoon pepper
2 sections peeled garlic crushed (optional)
¼ cup hot water

1. Brown-heat the lamb or mutton thoroughly all over in the fat. Season with salt, pepper and garlic mixed together.

2. Put the rack in the cooker. Add the water, put in the meat; close the cooker and bring the pressure up to 15 pounds. Cook thoroughly allowing 12 to 14 minutes to the pound.

3. Cool the cooker as soon as the lamb or mutton has cooked the required length of time. If a crisp crust is desired, place in a very hot oven for a few minutes, or put on a heat-proof platter, brown-crisp under the broiler and serve sizzling on the same platter.

4. Pass brown gravy made from the liquid in the cooker—but be sure to remove any excess fat; or accompany with a caper gravy, chopped dill pickle sauce, or with the traditional mint sauce (page 237).

LAMB POT ROAST
12 minutes to the pound

3 to 5 pounds short leg or boned rolled shoulder of lamb
2 tablespoons fat
1 teaspoon salt
⅛ teaspoon pepper
Worcestershire sauce
½ teaspoon marjoram or thyme
2 sliced peeled carrots
2 sliced peeled onions
1 cup cut celery stalks
1 cup hot water

1. Remove all excess fat from the lamb. Then brown-heat slowly in the fat. Season with salt, pepper and the marjoram or thyme.

2. Place on rack in the cooker; add the vegetables, pour in the water, close the cooker, bring to 15 pounds pressure and process 12 minutes to the pound.

3. Serve with brown gravy made from the liquid in the cooker. Season with Worcestershire sauce.

If desired, whole good-sized peeled potatoes may be cooked with the lamb the last 12 minutes. In this case, cool and open the cooker at the right time, put in the potatoes, bring the pressure back to 15 pounds and finish cooking.

PRESSURED STUFFED ROAST LAMB
WITH MUSHROOMS
12 to 14 minutes to the pound

Square cut lamb shoulder   Dry-moist stuffing (page
Salt and pepper   86)
                  2 (4 oz.) cans mushrooms

1. Order the lamb boned. Season with salt and pepper
and sew up the two sides with white string.

2. Fill loosely with the stuffing; and lace the edges together.

3. Brown-heat slowly all over in a frying pan.

4. Put the rack in the cooker. Pour in ½ cup water,
and put in the roast. Close the cooker.

5. Bring to 15 pounds pressure, and process 12 to 14
minutes to the pound.

6. Serve surrounded with mushrooms lightly sautéd in
a little butter. Garnish with chicory and romaine or parsley. Brown or tomato gravy may be made and passed if
desired.

LAMB SHANKS CALIFORNIA
20 to 25 minutes

4 lamb shanks   2 tablespoons fat
1 teaspoon salt   ½ cup hot water
⅛ teaspoon pepper   1 small bay leaf
1 teaspoon paprika   ½ cup lemon juice
1 section garlic crushed   2 tablespoons grated lemon
2 tablespoons flour   rind

1. Remove all excess fat from the shanks. Rub with the
salt, pepper, paprika, garlic and flour mixed.

2. Brown-heat slowly in the fat. Put the rack in the

cooker; add the water and bay leaf. Pour the lemon juice over the meat and sprinkle with the lemon rind. Close the cooker, bring to 15 pounds pressure and process 20 minutes for small shanks, 25 minutes for large shanks.

3. Serve with a gravy made from the liquid in the cooker; be sure to remove any excess fat before making it.

Accompany with mashed potatoes, curried rice, yams or sweet potatoes.

LAMB CHOP PLATTER
5 minutes

4 rib lamb chops	4 sections canned grape-
½ pound mushrooms	fruit
2 tomatoes	Scallions

1. Remove outside edge of fat from chops. Brown-heat chops on both sides. Add salt and pepper.

2. Pour one-half cup hot water into the pressure-cooker. Put in rack. Place chops on rack.

3. Add mushrooms, washed but not peeled. Put in tomatoes halved crosswise. Dot with butter; dust with salt, pepper and a little powdered mint if desired.

4. Close the cooker. Bring to 15 pounds pressure, and process 5 minutes.

5. To serve, garnish each chop with a section of canned grapefruit and arrange the entire course on a platter. If desired quartered peeled white or sweet potatoes may be pressured at the same time.

KIDNEY LAMB CHOPS
8 minutes

4 thick kidney lamb chops   Salt and pepper
½ lemon

1. Remove as much fat as possible from the chops. Roll up each chop and fasten with a skewer. (The butcher will do this on request.)

2. Rub the surface of the chops with the cut side of the lemon; dust with salt and pepper. Quickly brown-heat.

3. Pour 4 tablespoons water in the cooker, or enough to barely cover the bottom. Put in the rack, place the chops on it; close the cooker, bring to 15 pounds and process 8 minutes. Before serving brown-crisp a minute under the broiler.

4. Serve garnished with lemon wedges and water cress or parsley.

LAMB CHOPS OR STEAKS JARDINIÈRE
5 to 7 minutes

4 shoulder lamb chops or   Salt and pepper
    lamb steak   ¼ cup hot water
1 peeled section garlic   Vegetables jardinière (page
    (optional)   279)

1. Remove excess fat from meat. Rub the lamb with the cut surface of the garlic and dust with salt and pepper. Brown-heat in the cooker without additional fat. Place on the rack in the cooker; add the water.

2. Close the cooker; bring to 15 pounds and process 5 to 7 minutes according to thickness.

3. Serve surrounded with vegetables jardinière, that is, mixed vegetables.

BOILED LAMB ENGLISH STYLE
10 minutes to the pound

3 to 5 pounds short leg of   ¼ teaspoon pepper
    lamb   1 section garlic crushed
1 teaspoon salt   2 cups water

1. Remove all excess fat from the lamb. Rub meat with the salt, pepper and garlic mixed.

2. Place on the rack in the cooker. Add the water. Close the cooker, bring to 15 pounds pressure and process 10 minutes per pound.

3. Serve with caper sauce or dill pickle sauce made from the liquid in the cooker (page 235).

LAMB OR MUTTON CURRY
15 minutes

1½ pounds lamb or mutton stew meat
1 peeled onion chopped
1 teaspoon curry powder
2 tablespoons butter or vegetable fat

1½ cups water
½ teaspoon salt
⅛ teaspoon pepper
2 tablespoons flour
Pressured white or brown rice

1. Remove all fat from the meat; then brown-heat with the onion and curry powder in the butter right in the cooker.

2. Add the water, salt and pepper; close the cooker, bring to 15 pounds pressure and process 15 minutes.

3. Cool and open the cooker. Thicken with the flour mixed smooth with ¼ cup cold water.

4. Serve surrounded by the rice.

LAMB À LA MODE PLATTER STEW
15 minutes

1½ pounds lean stewing lamb cut in inch cubes
¼ cup wine vinegar
½ cup cider
2 tablespoons flour

3 peeled medium-sized onions sliced
½ teaspoon pickle spice
1 teaspoon salt
⅛ teaspoon pepper

1. At least 6 hours in advance combine the lamb with the vinegar, cider, onions and pickle spice. Cover closely and stand in refrigerator till ready to cook, up to 24 hours.

2. To cook, drain the lamb, but strain and reserve the spiced liquid. Dust the meat with the salt and pepper; place it in the pressure-cooker (no rack), add the spiced liquid, close the cooker, bring to 15 pounds pressure and process 15 minutes.

3. Remove excess fat from the liquid in the pan; add an extra cup of bouillon, or water containing ½ teaspoon beef extract; bring to a boil and thicken with the flour smooth-blended with two tablespoons cold water. Cook and stir 2 minutes.

4. Serve on toast, split baking powder biscuit or bordered with barley or rice balls (page 310).

IRISH LAMB STEW
17 minutes

2 pounds lamb
3 cups boiling water
1½ teaspoons salt
⅛ teaspoon pepper
1¼ cups scraped carrots cut
   in inch lengths

4 peeled medium-sized on-
   ions quartered
4 peeled white potatoes
   sliced thick
3 tablespoons flour
Condiment sauce (op-
   tional)

1. Remove as much fat from the lamb as possible, and cut in inch cubes.

2. Put in the pressure-cooker with the water and seasonings. Close the cooker, bring to 15 pounds and process 12 minutes. Cool and open cooker.

3. Add vegetables. Bring to 15 pounds pressure again and process 5 minutes longer.

4. Stir in the flour blended with 3 tablespoons cold water, and simmer 2 minutes.

If dumplings are to be cooked with the stew, make them small. Place on top of the stew, put on the cover, and steam 10 minutes without pressure. (See page 63.)

FRICASSEED LAMB CREOLE
16 minutes

3 pounds shoulder of lamb cut in serving portions	1 cup solid-pack canned tomatoes
1 tablespoon fat	1 teaspoon salt
2 peeled onions sliced	⅛ teaspoon pepper
1 peeled section garlic minced	¼ teaspoon marjoram or thyme
2 seeded sweet green peppers shredded	1½ cups water
	3 tablespoons flour

1. Brown-heat the lamb in the fat directly in the pressure-cooker. Add the onions, garlic, pepper, tomatoes, seasonings and water.

2. Close the cooker, bring to 15 pounds pressure and process 16 minutes.

3. Thicken the sauce with the flour stirred smooth in ¼ cup cold water or vegetable liquid.

4. Serve with rice or hominy grits.

LAMB RAGOUT SPRING STYLE
16 minutes

2 pounds shoulder of lamb cut in serving portions	1½ cups hot water
1 tablespoon fat	2 tablespoons flour
1 peeled onion sliced	½ teaspoon Worcestershire sauce
1 teaspoon salt	Flaky white potatoes
⅛ teaspoon pepper	Whole minted carrots
Green peas	

1. Brown-heat the lamb all over in the fat directly in the cooker. Add the seasonings and water or liquid from cooked vegetables.

2. Close the cooker; bring to 15 pounds pressure and process 16 minutes. Thicken the liquid with the flour stirred smooth in 2 tablespoons water. Add Worcestershire sauce, arrange on a platter and surround with the vegetables.

LAMB WITH GREEN BEANS GREEK STYLE
16 minutes

2 pounds lean stewing lamb
½ teaspoon salt
½ teaspoon raw onion chopped
1 cup hot water

1 cup solid-pack canned tomatoes
1 teaspoon powdered mint (optional)
¼ teaspoon pepper
1 pound fresh string beans
3 tablespoons flour

1. Remove all possible fat from the lamb. Then cut the meat in 1-inch cubes and brown-heat in its own fat directly in the pressure-cooker. Add the salt, onion, water, tomatoes, mint and pepper.

2. Close the cooker; bring to 15 pounds and process 11 minutes. Then cool and open the cooker.

3. Add the string beans cut in lengthwise strips; again bring to 15 pounds pressure and process the remaining 5 minutes.

4. Cool and open the cooker, and stir in the flour blended with 2 tablespoons cold water. Simmer 2 minutes.

5. Serve with rice, barley, noodles or flaky or baked white or sweet potatoes.

LAMBURGERS
5 minutes

1 pound lean raw lamb put
   through the chopper
   twice
1 teaspoon salt

1 tablespoon margarine
⅛ teaspoon pepper
1 teaspoon scraped onion
   (optional)

¼ cup hot water

1. Combine the ingredients; form into flat cakes containing 1 tablespoon each and brown-heat in the cooker.

2. Place the rack in the pressure-cooker; add the water. Place the lamburgers on the rack; dot with the margarine, close the cooker, bring to 15 pounds pressure and process 5 minutes.

3. Serve on halved buns, buttered before toasting; or with fried onions, or a tomato gravy made from the liquid in the cooker.

Lamburger Variations: Follow the suggestions for 5-Way Hamburgers (page 110).

LAMB WITH LIMA BEANS
30 minutes

½ pound dried lima beans
1 pound lean shoulder of
   lamb
2 tablespoons bacon or sausage drippings
1 small peeled onion
   chopped

1 peeled section garlic
   chopped
1½ teaspoons salt
⅛ teaspoon pepper
Boiling water and tomato
   juice, equal parts

1. Cover the lima beans with boiling water and let stand one hour. Then drain.

2. Cut the lamb in inch cubes and brown-heat in the bacon or sausage drippings with the onion and garlic. Add salt and pepper.

3. Combine with the lima beans in the pressure-cooker. Add liquid barely to cover. Bring to 15 pounds pressure and process 30 minutes. If desired place in a hot oven or under the broiler to brown-crisp the top. Serve accompanied with a tossed green salad.

ENGLISH HOT POT
15 minutes

1½ pounds half-inch cubes of lamb or mutton any cut
½ tablespoon flour
1 cup meat broth or liquid drained from cooked vegetables
1½ teaspoons salt
⅛ teaspoon pepper
4 good-sized peeled onions sliced thick
6 large white potatoes peeled and sliced one-inch thick
1 tablespoon minced parsley (optional)

1. Brown-heat the meat in its own fat in the pressure-cooker. Add the flour and broth or vegetable liquid. Stir in the seasonings and vegetables.

2. Close the cooker; bring the pressure to fifteen pounds and process ten minutes.

CHAPTER VII

SCINTILLATING WAYS WITH VEAL

As veal is an immature meat, it lacks both flavor and fat. So in cooking we must add fat, and season the meat quite highly, or else serve it with a tasty sauce. But remember that in pressure-cooking, high seasoning does not mean adding a large quantity of salt; but rather the discreet use of spices, herbs, lemon or lime, mushrooms, tomatoes or vegetables with their juices.

The finest fats to use in preparing veal, are butter, margarine and soured cream because they blend best with the delicate flavor of the meat. If a heavier more "hearty" taste is desired, use bacon or sausage fat.

All cuts of veal are suited to pressure cooking and some of the most thrifty make the most epicurean dishes. A good example is Veal Scalloppini (page 135). This can be pressure-cooked even from thin slices of veal shank which costs little. But if you purchase this dish in a good Italian restaurant you will pay a high price. No matter how veal is pressure-cooked, it is never dry, but always tasty and succulent.

Pressure Cooking Veal

Recipes proportioned to serve four to six.
All measurements are level.
Timings are minutes required for actual pressuring.
Cool cooker as soon as processing is done.

PANNED VEAL CHOPS OR STEAKS
10 minutes

4 large veal chops or 1¼ pounds veal steak cut one-inch thick

Onion, celery or garlic salt or marjoram

2 tablespoons flour

1½ tablespoons bacon, ham or sausage drippings

¼ cup hot water or vegetable liquid

1. Rub veal all over with a choice of onion, celery or garlic salt, or a little marjoram.

2. Dust with the flour and brown-heat in the fat.

3. Put the rack in the cooker; add the liquid. Close the cooker; bring to 15 pounds pressure and process 10 minutes.

4. Serve with brown gravy and a choice of rice or hominy grits; or with medium-sized sweet potatoes or yams peeled and cooked the same length of time in the cooker.

Veal Chops Jardinière: Prepare veal chops according to the preceding directions and serve with mixed vegetables.

Veal Chops or Steaks Creole: Follow directions for panning veal chops or steaks. Serve with creole sauce (page 236).

Veal Chops with Mushrooms and Soured Cream: Follow directions for panning veal chops, adding ¼ pound mushrooms sliced down through caps and stems. When done make a gravy from the liquid in the cooker, and stir in ¾ cup soured cream.

ROAST VEAL
10 minutes to the pound

3 pounds loin, boned leg or rolled shoulder of veal
4 peeled sections garlic quartered, or use minced parsley
1½ teaspoons salt
⅛ teaspoon pepper
2 tablespoons flour
¼ cup bacon, sausage or ham fat
½ cup hot water or liquid drained from vegetables

1. Cut 16 gashes one-half inch deep, about 2 inches apart in the meat. Insert a piece of garlic in each, or omit the garlic and tuck in some minced parsley. Rub in the salt, pepper and flour mixed.
2. Brown-heat slowly in the fat.
3. Put the rack in the cooker; add the water; place the meat on the rack, close the cooker; bring to 15 pounds pressure and process 10 minutes to the pound.
4. Serve with white or sweet potatoes cooked with the meat the right length of time, or with Spanish rice or whole barley (page 236).

VEAL MEXICAN STYLE
5 minutes

1½ pounds veal cutlet or shank sliced one-fourth inch thick
2 tablespoons flour
½ teaspoon salt
⅛ teaspoon pepper
2 tablespoons savory fat
¾ cup minced cooked ham
1 cup tomato juice
¼ cup chopped chives
1 tablespoon minced parsley

1. Pound the veal until well flattened.

2. Mix together the flour, salt and pepper and rub into the veal.

3. Melt the fat in the cooker and brown-heat the veal in it. Add the ham and tomato juice; close the cooker, bring to 15 pounds pressure and process 5 minutes.

4. Serve sprinkled with chives and parsley. Accompany with flaky or mashed white potatoes, or fried cornmeal mush.

POT ROAST OF VEAL
10 minutes to the pound

3 pounds boned rolled shoulder of veal, stuffed if desired
2 tablespoons savory fat
2 peeled sections garlic

1 teaspoon mixed minced herbs
1 teaspoon salt
1 peeled onion sliced
½ cup water or meat bouillon

1. Brown-heat the veal slowly in the fat together with the garlic and onion. Then dust on the herbs and salt.

2. Place the rack in the cooker; add the liquid, put the veal on the rack, close the cooker, bring to 15 pounds pressure, and process 10 minutes per pound.

3. Serve with brown gravy or mushroom gravy (page 245), made from the cooker-liquid. Accompany with balls of barley, plain or Spanish rice or mashed potatoes dusted with minced parsley, chives or scallions.

BARBECUED VEALBURGERS
5 minutes

Prepare Italian Veal Balls as described, but shape into flat round patties. Then brown-heat directly in the cooker. Add ½ cup barbecue sauce (page 237); bring pressure to 15 pounds and process 5 minutes.

VEAL STEW
15 minutes

3 pounds knuckle of veal
4 cups (one quart) cold water
½ teaspoon peppercorns
2 cloves
Bit of bay leaf
2 peeled onions diced

1½ teaspoons salt
2 cups solid-pack canned tomatoes
1 cup diced celery
½ teaspoon sugar
½ cup brown rice

1. Cut the meat in 1-inch squares. Put with the bones and water in the cooker. Add the spices tied in a bit of gauze, the onions and salt. Close the cooker; bring to 15 pounds pressure and process 7 minutes.

2. Cool and open the cooker. Add the tomatoes, celery, sugar and rice; bring the pressure back to 15 pounds and cook 8 minutes longer. Cool. Open cooker. Drop in dumplings if you wish (page 63). Cover and cook without pressure as directed in dumpling recipe.

3. Serve in deep soup plates or bowls. In case dumplings are not used, crisp croutons are a pleasant garnish.

RAGOUT OF VEAL PARISIENNE
17 minutes

3 pounds knuckle of veal
1 teaspoon sugar
1 peeled onion sliced
2 cups boiling water or liquid from cooked vegetables
1 teaspoon salt

¼ teaspoon pepper
¼ lemon rind grated
3 tablespoons flour
3 tablespoons butter or margarine
½ cup sweet or soured cream

1. Cut the veal in pieces suitable for serving, but reserve the bone to cook with the meat.

2. Melt the sugar in the bottom of the pressure-cooker. When golden brown add the onion and stir until coated. Add the meat, bone, liquid and seasonings.

3. Close the cooker; bring to 15 pounds pressure and process 17 minutes.

4. Remove the bone. Thicken the ragout with the flour and butter rubbed together.

5. Serve surrounded with boiled white or brown rice, either plain or curried.

ITALIAN VEAL BALLS
6 minutes

½ cup soft white bread
   crumbs
¼ cup milk
1 pound chopped chuck of
   veal
1 egg
¾ teaspoon salt

⅛ teaspoon nutmeg
¼ cup chopped parsley
3 tablespoons flour
2 tablespoons margarine
½ cup hot water or vege-
   table juice
Spaghetti Italienne

1. Combine the crumbs with the milk; simmer and stir three minutes. Add the veal, the egg beaten, the seasonings and parsley.

2. Form into balls containing a tablespoonful each, shaping with the hands first dipped in the flour.

3. Brown-heat in the fat. Place the balls on the rack in the cooker; add the liquid. Close the cooker, bring to 15 pounds pressure and process 6 minutes.

4. Serve with Spaghetti Italienne (page 316), or with tomato or green pepper sauce.

PRESSED VEAL BUFFET STYLE
30 minutes

4 pounds knuckle of veal
   sawed in two pieces
1½ cups boiling water

1¼ teaspoons salt
½ teaspoon pickle spice
1 tablespoon lemon or lime
   juice

1. Put the veal in the pressure-cooker. Add the water, salt, and the spices tied in a bit of gauze. Close the cooker; bring the pressure to 15 pounds and process 30 minutes.

2. Drain and cool meat immediately. Chop it fine; add the lemon or lime juice and additional salt and pepper if needed. Mix in the liquid from the cooker. Pack into a bread pan or oblong glass dish first rinsed with cold water. Put a second pan or dish on top of this and weight it down to press the loaf into shape. Refrigerate at least 12 hours.

3. Unmold on a large platter; garnish with sliced hard-cooked eggs, and lettuce nests containing a tomato relish salad or cucumber sour cream salad.

VEAL SCALLOPPINI
As served on American overseas air liners.
3 minutes

1 pound very thin slices leg
   of veal
½ teaspoon salt
⅛ teaspoon pepper
4 tablespoons flour

⅓ cup butter
¼ cup hot water
⅓ teaspoon meat extract
3 tablespoons dry Sherry

1. Pound the pieces of veal with a wooden mallet till very flat. Mix the salt, pepper and flour and rub into the meat.

2. Brown-heat in the butter directly in the cooker. Dissolve the meat extract in the liquid, and add with the wine. Close the cooker; bring to 15 pounds pressure and process 3 minutes.

3. Serve with spaghetti al dente, flaky rice or fried potatoes, and a garnish of parsley or water cress.

CHAPTER VIII

TASTE-TEASING SPECIALS WITH FRESH PORK, SMOKED AND CURED MEATS

PORK IS A MEAT THAT MUST BE THOROUGHLY COOKED. Pressure cooking is especially adapted to preparing it, for this makes possible thorough cooking in a short time. Pork is one of the best sources of the Vitamin B Complex, and as there is little loss of these vitamins during the cooking process, this is a second good reason for pressure cooking pork. Besides, it tastes extra delicious. There is just one rule to follow.

General Rule for Preparing Pork for Pressuring

Before cooking, cut off all excess fat; pressure the right length of time. And before making gravy, be sure to remove any extra fat from the liquid in the cooker.

Pressure Cooking Fresh Pork

Recipes proportioned to serve four to six.
All measurements are level.
Timings are minutes required for actual pressuring.
Cool cooker as soon as processing is done.

BONED ROAST SHOULDER OF PORK
10 minutes to the pound

4 to 5 pounds boned shoulder of pork
Dry-moist savory, celery or onion stuffing
1 peeled section garlic crushed

½ teaspoon marjoram
1 teaspoon salt
⅛ teaspoon pepper
2 tablespoons flour
¾ tablespoon fat
½ cup hot water

1. Fill the shoulder with the stuffing and truss (see stuffed lamb, page 120).

2. Mix together the garlic, seasonings and flour; rub into the meat. Brown-heat slowly in the fat.

3. Put the rack in the pressure-cooker; add the water or use liquid drained from cooked vegetables; close the cooker, bring to 15 pounds pressure and process 10 minutes to the pound. Make gravy from the liquid in the cooker (page 244), but be sure first to remove all excess fat.

4. Serve with whole stuffed apples baked style (page 341), white or sweet potatoes and a green vegetable.

Roast Pork Spanish Style: Follow the preceding recipe using a dry-moist stuffing containing 2 seeded chopped sweet green peppers, 2 chopped peeled onions and 2 peeled sections garlic; and moisten with tomato juice instead of water. When done, serve with tomato gravy, with Spanish sauce (page 236), or with canned tomato sauce heated with minced green pepper and sliced stuffed olives.

ROAST LOIN OF PORK
10 to 12 minutes to the pound

3 to 4 pounds loin of pork, bones cracked
1 teaspoon salt
⅛ teaspoon pepper

1 teaspoon powdered sage
2 tablespoons flour
½ tablespoon fat
½ cup hot water

1. Rub the pork all over with the salt, pepper, sage and flour mixed.

2. Brown-heat slowly all over in not more than one-half tablespoon fat.

3. Put the rack in the pressure-cooker; add water, close the cooker, bring to 15 pounds pressure and process 10 to 12 minutes per pound. Make brown or tomato gravy from the liquid in the pan.

4. Serve with medium-sized white potatoes, and sauerkraut seasoned with onion and caraway seed and pressured together for 10 minutes. Or with sweet potatoes and green beans, which may be pressured together after the pork has been processed. In this case shred the beans fine, peel and quarter the potatoes, and pressure 4 minutes.

BRAISED PORK CHOPS WITH POTATOES
12 minutes

4 large pork chops cut one-half inch thick
1 tablespoon flour
½ teaspoon salt
⅛ teaspoon pepper
½ cup hot water or liquid from cooked vegetables

½ teaspoon powdered sage or cumin seed
½ tablespoon fat
Good-sized peeled white or sweet potatoes

1. Cut off all excess fat from the pork. Mix together the flour and seasonings and rub into the meat.

2. Brown-heat in the fat. Put the rack in the cooker, add the water and place chops on the rack. Surround with the potatoes.

3. Close the cooker, bring to 15 pounds pressure and process 12 minutes.

4. Serve plain, or with a gravy made from the liquid in the cooker (page 244). Pork chops prepared this way are especially good served with kale, spinach or string beans.

Stuffed Pork Chops: Order thick loin pork chops. Remove excess fat and cut a slit in each to make a pocket. Fill with any dry-moist stuffing or with 2 prunes, the stones removed. Finish according to the preceding directions.

Pork Chops with Onions: Prepare pork chops for pressure-cooking as directed for braised pork chops. Brown-heat; at the end of the brown-heating add as many small peeled onions as desired. Turn them over in the fat so they will be slightly browned. Put the chops in the cooker, bring to 15 pounds pressure and process 8 minutes. Then cool and open the cooker, put in the onions, bring the pressure to 15 pounds again and process 4 minutes longer.

PORK STEAKS
12 minutes

1½ pounds pork steak cut one-half inch thick	⅛ teaspoon pepper
1 tablespoon prepared mustard	2 tablespoons flour
	1 tablespoon fat
½ teaspoon salt	¼ cup hot water
	¼ cup dry white wine (optional)

1. Cut the steak in portions for serving. Spread with the mustard, and rub in the seasonings and flour mixed.

2. Brown-heat on both sides in the pressure-cooker, using as little fat as possible. Add the water and wine, or use instead one-half cup water or liquid drained from cooked vegetables.

3. Close the cooker, bring to 15 pounds pressure and process 12 minutes.

4. Serve with gravy made from the liquid in the cooker. Pork steak cooked this way is especially good with yams or sweet potatoes glazed with a little sugar and lime juice.

PIGS KNUCKLES WITH VEGETABLES
40 minutes

4 pigs knuckles
½ teaspoon salt
⅛ teaspoon pepper
¼ teaspoon allspice
6 halved peeled large white
    potatoes

8 peeled good-sized onions
4 large carrots peeled and
    slashed
4 peeled medium-sized
    white turnips
1 cup liquid from cooked
    vegetables

1. Scrub the pigs knuckles thoroughly. Drain and dry on paper towels. Dust with salt and pepper.

2. Put the rack in the cooker and add the liquid and allspice. Put in the pigs knuckles. Close the cooker, bring to 15 pounds pressure and process 33 minutes.

3. Cool and open the cooker. Pile the prepared vegetables around and over the meat. Dust with a little salt; close the cooker, bring to 15 pounds pressure and process 7 minutes longer.

4. Make a gravy from the liquid in the cooker (page 244). Thicken with 1 tablespoon each margarine and flour stirred to a smooth blend. Season with meat condiment sauce.

5. Serve the pigs knuckles surrounded with the vegetables. Garnish with crisp parsley or Scallions Relish Style (page 374). Pass corn muffins.

FRESH PORK TENDERLOIN
15 minutes

1½ pounds fresh pork ten-
    derloin sliced one-inch
    thick
3 tablespoons flour
1 teaspoon salt
⅛ teaspoon pepper
1 teaspoon meat condiment
    sauce

2 tablespoons butter or mar-
    garine
1½ cups solid-pack canned
    tomatoes
½ teaspoon sugar
1 peeled onion sliced
½ seeded sweet green pep-
    per diced

1. Rub the meat with the flour and seasonings mixed. Then brown-heat in the butter or margarine directly in the cooker. Add the tomatoes, sugar, onion and green pepper.

2. Close the cooker, bring to 15 pounds pressure and process 15 minutes.

3. Serve with flaky rice, or whole or mashed white or sweet potatoes, or with noodles or spaghetti al dente.

PORK TENDERLOIN WITH MUSHROOMS
16 minutes

1½ pounds fresh pork ten-
    derloin sliced ½-inch
    thick
⅛ teaspoon pepper
2 tablespoons flour
½ tablespoon butter or mar-
    garine

1½ cups thin white sauce
    (no salt)
Good-sized peeled white po-
    tatoes
½ pound mushrooms sautéd

1. Rub the pork all over with the pepper and flour and brown-heat directly in the cooker with the butter or margarine. Add the white sauce.

2. Cover the cooker; bring to 15 pounds pressure and process 4 minutes.

3. Cool and open the cooker. Put in the potatoes, bring the pressure to 15 pounds and process 12 minutes.

4. Before serving, season the sauce with a little salt. Place the sliced pork overlapping in the center of the platter; surround with the sauce, cover with the mushrooms, put the potatoes around the edge and garnish with plenty of water cress or parsley.

SAVORY SPARERIBS
15 minutes

2 tablespoons flour
1 teaspoon salt
¼ teaspoon pepper
½ teaspoon marjoram

2 sections spareribs separated
½ cup liquid drained from cooked vegetables

1. Combine the flour and seasonings and rub the spareribs all over with it. Brown-heat in their own fat. If it is necessary add a little margarine to start the brown-heating.

2. Put the rack in the cooker; add the spareribs and liquid, bring to 15 pounds pressure and process 15 minutes. If a brown-crisp crust is desired slip the spareribs under a pre-heated broiler about 2 minutes.

3. Serve with brown gravy made from the liquid in the cooker (page 244). Accompany with white or sweet potatoes in any form.

Barbecued Spareribs: Follow the recipe for savory spareribs substituting barbecue sauce for the liquid (page 237). Pour an extra ¼ cupful of barbecue sauce over the spare ribs before putting to brown-crisp under the broiler.

PIGS KNUCKLES WITH SAUERKRAUT
40 minutes

4 pigs knuckles	1 pint sauerkraut
½ cup hot water	½ teaspoon caraway or cumin seed (optional)

1. Scrub the pigs knuckles. Drain and dry on paper towels. Season with salt and pepper.

2. Put in the pressure-cooker and add the water. Close the cooker. Bring to 15 pounds and process 30 minutes.

3. Cool and open the cooker. Add the sauerkraut and caraway or cumin seed. Bring to 15 pounds pressure again and process 10 minutes.

4. Serve the pigs knuckles on the sauerkraut. Garnish with crisp croutons if convenient. Flaky white or mashed potatoes are good with this.

Smoked and Cured Meats

All smoked or cured meats may be pressure-cooked with mouth-watering conservation of flavor and nutrients. But —know your meat! For in pressure cooking there is not enough water to draw out excess salt as in regulation "boiling." To produce a dish that will not be salty, the problem is to learn whether or not the meat contains excess salt, and if so, how to get it out before pressuring. In some cases the meat-man can enlighten you, especially regarding corned beef or pickled tongue prepared in his own establishment.

As to smoked ham, the wrapper often indicates the type, whether it is one of the new tender hams, or whether it is the regulation old-time heavily smoked and salted type. Your meat-man will know.

DO'S FOR PRESSURE COOKING SMOKED OR CURED MEATS

Tender Raw Hams need no pre-preparation before pressure-ing. Keep refrigerated until cooked.

Old-Fashioned Regulation Type Hams, whether boned or not, and all cottage or picnic hams, should be covered with cold water, and soaked for at least two hours; then bring slowly to boiling point. Discard the water and pressure as directed.

Center Cuts or Smoked Ham Slices: If from a tender raw ham, cook "as is." But if from an old-fashioned smoked ham, cover with boiling water and let stand from 5 to 15 minutes according to saltiness. Then drain and pressure-cook according to directions.

Smoked Pigs Jowl: Follow directions for old-fashioned hams.

Smoked Pork Tenderloin: Cover with cold water, bring to boiling-point, discard the water and pressure as directed.

Smoked Beef Tongue: Cover with cold water, soak at least 2 hours, bring to boiling-point, discard the water and pressure as directed.

Corned Beef or Corned Lamb: Cover with cold water. Bring slowly to boiling point, and simmer 5 minutes. Then discard liquid. If the meat has been in the brine more than 3 days, simmer for 10 minutes before pressure-ing.

Salt Pork or Bacon Squares: Cover with boiling water; let stand 5 minutes, drain off water and pressure as directed.

Pressure Cooking Smoked or Cured Meats

Recipes proportioned to serve four to six.
All measurements are level.
Timings are minutes required for actual pressuring.
Cool cooker as soon as pressuring is done.

GLAZES FOR BAKING HAM

Orange Mustard Glaze: Combine grated rind of one orange, 2 tablespoons orange juice and 1 tablespoon prepared mustard with ½ cup dark corn syrup; spread over the ham; press in whole cloves if desired, and bake in a hot oven until well glazed, about 15 minutes.

Cranberry Glaze: Cover the ham with equal parts of thick cranberry sauce and fine dry bread crumbs seasoned with a little prepared mustard. Spread over the ham and bake in a hot oven until well glazed.

Spiced Honey Glaze: Combine 3 tablespoons honey and 1 tablespoon prepared mustard. Spread over the ham; dust with fine dry bread crumbs, press in whole cloves at inch intervals, and bake in a hot oven until browned.

Southern Molasses Glaze: Spread the ham sparingly with dark molasses mixed with a very little vinegar from sweet pickles. Cover with fine bread crumbs; press in cloves if desired and bake in a hot oven.

Pineapple Glaze: Combine ¾ cup canned grated pineapple with 1 teaspoon powdered ginger and 1 tablespoon sweet pickle or basil vinegar. Add ½ cup fine dry bread crumbs. Spread over the ham. Press in whole cloves at half-inch intervals. Bake in a hot oven until browned.

STEAM-BOILED TENDERIZED HAM
6 minutes to the pound

4 to 5 pounds tenderized   ½ cup hot water
   ham

1. Place rack in cooker and pour in water.

2. Place ham on rack, close the cooker, bring to 15 pounds pressure and process 30 minutes.

Baked Tenderized Ham: Follow preceding directions. Remove ham from the cooker and cover with any desired glaze (page 146).

Place in a hot oven and bake until the glaze is a rich golden brown.

HAM BURGUNDY STYLE
Tenderized—10 minutes to the pound
Regulation—20 minutes to the pound

1½ pounds center slice ten-   1 teaspoon honey or brown
   derized or regulation   sugar
   style ham cut two-   12 whole cloves
   inches thick   ½ cup Burgundy wine (or
1 teaspoon prepared mus-   use grape juice)
   tard

1. Remove all excess fat from the ham; brown the ham in this fat on both sides. Brush with the mustard and honey. Then press in the cloves.

2. Put the rack in the cooker. Place the ham on the rack and pour over the wine or grape juice.

3. Close cooker, bring to 15 pounds pressure and process the required minutes to the pound.

4. Serve with a sauce made from the liquid in the cooker. Garnish with glazed sweet potatoes, and asparagus or broccoli.

PICNIC HAM, STEAM-BOILED OR BAKED
12 minutes to the pound

Half or whole picnic ham, 2 cups hot water or cider
   regular type

1. Cover ham with cold water. Soak at least 2 hours.
Bring slowly to boiling point and discard water.
2. Place the rack in the cooker; pour in the hot water
or cider and put in the ham.
3. Close the cooker; bring to 15 pounds pressure and
process 12 minutes to the pound.
4. When the ham is done, pare off the rind and excess
fat; bake if desired. To do this spread with any interesting
glaze and brown in a hot oven.

HAM BAKED IN WINE
Tenderized—5 minutes to the pound
Regulation—10 minutes to the pound

1¼ pounds tenderized or ½ cup dry red or white
   regulation style ham   wine
   cut very thin

1. Remove excess fat from the ham and lightly brown-
heat the slices in it.
2. Place directly in the cooker; pour in the wine, bring
to 15 pounds pressure and process the required length of
time.
3. If a crisp crust is desired, put the ham slices under a
pre-heated broiler for one minute.
4. Serve with a gravy or sauce made from the liquid
in the cooker.
Ham Slices Hawaiian: Follow the preceding recipe. Put
the ham slices on the broiler. Top with very thin slices of

Pressured green peas with onion spice seasoning, raw vegetable relishes and a decorative vegetable arrangement for the table (*Page 274*)

An hors d'oeuvre
supper platter
(*Page 381*)

Pressured shrimp-stuffed cucumbers with potato chips and radishes (*Page 289*)

A trio of grapefruit salads (*Page 382*)

Little pressured Christmas puddings Brazil style (*Page 332*)

canned pineapple, put prunes in the "holes" and broil 1 minute.

HAM SLICE WITH APPLES
Tenderized ham—8 minutes
Regulation ham—15 minutes

1½ pounds center slice ham cut one-inch thick

1 teaspoon prepared mustard

1 teaspoon honey or brown sugar

½ cup water

Raisin-d apples (page 341)

1. Remove excess fat from edge of ham and slash the edge so the meat will lie flat. Brown-heat ham on both sides.

2. Rub sparingly with the mustard and honey or sugar.

3. Place the rack in the cooker; pour in the water; put the ham on the rack and process the required time according to the type of ham used.

4. Serve garnished with raisin-d apples.

ENGLISH HAM DINNER
Tenderized—6 minutes to the pound
Regulation—10 minutes to the pound

1 pound raw ham sliced very thin, tenderized or regular style

6 large white potatoes peeled and sliced ½ inch thick

6 peeled onions sliced ½ inch thick

4 tablespoons flour

¼ teaspoon salt

½ teaspoon prepared mustard

⅛ teaspoon pepper

½ teaspoon meat condiment sauce

½ cup grated sharp Cheddar cheese

1 pint heated milk

1. The ham should be cut in 2-inch pieces. The potatoes, onions, flour and seasonings should be mixed together.

To arrange these ingredients for pressuring proceed as follows:

2. Put a thin layer of the ham in the bottom of the cooker. Cover with a layer of the potatoes, onions, flour and seasoning thoroughly mixed. Sprinkle on a little cheese. Put on a second layer of the ham, then one of potatoes, onions and seasonings. Sprinkle over the remaining cheese. Pour in the milk.

3. Close the cooker, bring to 15 pounds pressure and process the required time.

4. Serve as is; or transfer to a shallow casserole, dot with a little butter or margarine, and place under the broiler 2 or 3 minutes to brown on top.

HAM SHANK WITH BEANS
(Regulation Type)
30 minutes

1 ham shank about 3 pounds
Cold water
2 cups navy or pea beans

1 peeled onion sliced
¼ cup molasses
2 teaspoons dry mustard

1. Put the ham shank in the pressure-cooker. Cover with cold water, let stand 2 hours, then bring to boiling point. Drain the water from the shank and take out of cooker. In the meantime pick over the beans, cover them with boiling water and let stand for an hour. Then drain off the liquid.

2. Place the ham shank in the cooker. Add 5 cups boiling water, the beans, the onion, molasses and mustard.

3. Close the cooker, bring to 15 pounds pressure and process 30 minutes.

Ham Shank with Black-Eyed Peas: Follow the preceding recipe using black-eyed peas. Before putting the ham and peas together, add ⅓ cup chili sauce or tomato catsup.

HAM AND EGG TIMBALES AUSTRALIAN
6 minutes

1½ cups minced cooked ham
6 eggs
Salt and pepper

6 large slices grilled or fried tomato
Rounds buttered toast
Cheese or Rarebit sauce

1. Line custard cups or individual molds with the ham, making it about ⅛ of an inch thick.

2. Break an egg in each mold; dust with a little salt and pepper. Put the rack in the cooker, pour in ½ cup water, put in the molds, close the cooker, bring to 15 pounds pressure and process 6 minutes.

3. To serve, unmold on the tomato placed on rounds of buttered toast; surround with the sauce. Top each mold with a bit of parsley.

SMOKED PORK TENDERLOIN
35 minutes

1½ pounds smoked pork tenderloin
½ cup hot water

2 tablespoons sweet pickle or herb vinegar

1. Soak the tenderloin 2 hours in cold water. Then drain. Place on rack in the cooker; add the hot water and vinegar.

2. Close the cooker; bring to 15 pounds pressure and process 35 minutes.

3. Serve sliced, with a sauce made from the liquid in the pan, or with a mustard or horse-radish sauce (pages 232, 241). Accompany with mashed or flaky potatoes and a green vegetable or cabbage.

Grill-Topped Smoked Pork Tenderloin: Brush the cooked pork tenderloin with a mixture made of 1 tablespoon each sweet pickle vinegar, honey, brown sugar or molasses. Place in a pre-heated broiler until brown and glazed. Serve with yams or sweet potatoes glazed at the same time, and with cabbage or cauliflower, or a green vegetable.

Glazed Smoked Pork Tenderloin with Peppers: Prepare grill-topped pork tenderloin. Serve with a sauce made from the residue in the cooker, in which 2 or 3 chopped sweet green peppers have been simmered 2 or 3 minutes. Serve with barley or rice balls (page 310), and broccoli or carrots.

Pork Tenderloin with Pressured Pear Compote: Follow directions for preparing smoked pork tenderloin, using 1 cup grapefruit juice in place of the water and sweet pickle vinegar. At the end of 28 minutes, cool and open the cooker. Add peeled carrots, and very small peeled white potatoes (or use halved peeled potatoes). Bring back to 15 pounds pressure, and process 8 minutes longer. Serve with pressured pear-relish compote.

Pressured Pear-Relish Compote: Cover pressured pears with orange marmalade mixed with any kind of chutney available.

BACONIZED POTATOES
12 minutes

½ pound bacon squares or   Good-sized peeled white
　　Irish bacon   potatoes
½ cup hot water

1. Scald the bacon squares with boiling water and let stand 5 minutes. Drain. Put in the pressure-cooker together with the desired number of peeled potatoes. Add the water.

2. Close the cooker; bring the pressure to 15 pounds and process 12 minutes.

3. Then score the top of the bacon. That is, cut through the rind to make ½-inch squares. Place under a pre-heated broiler to crisp and brown.

4. Serve with the potatoes sprinkled with parsley, and a choice of sauerkraut, green beans, a tossed green salad, or plain or Creole cole slaw.

CANADIAN BACON WITH POTATOES AND CABBAGE
8 minutes

Thick slices white cabbage
½ pound Canadian bacon sliced ¼-inch thick
Peeled white potatoes halved

½ teaspoon prepared mustard
1 tablespoon vinegar drained from sweet pickles
½ cup hot water

1. Put a layer of the cabbage and bacon in the bottom of the pressure-cooker. Cover with a layer of potatoes and top with cabbage. Add the vinegar and water.

2. Close the cooker; bring to 15 pounds pressure and process 8 minutes.

3. Arrange for service on a platter. Sprinkle with freshly ground black pepper if possible. Dust with minced parsley, or a little fresh dill. Serve with plenty of hot toast or corn bread.

SMOKED BEEF TONGUE
14 minutes to the pound

3 to 4 pounds smoked beef tongue
2 cloves
6 peppercorns

1 small bay leaf
1 tablespoon vinegar
1 cup hot water

1. Let the tongue stand in cold water to cover for 2 hours. Bring to a boil, simmer 5 minutes and discard the water.

2. Place in pressure-cooker with vinegar, spices and water. Close the cooker; bring to 15 pounds pressure and process 14 minutes to the pound.

3. When sufficiently cool, pull off the skin and remove the bones and root ends.

4. Slice the tongue and serve with horse-radish sauce made from the liquid in the cooker. Accompany with parslied or whipped potato, and a green vegetable.

Glazed Smoked Tongue: After removing the skin and root ends from tongue prepared according to the preceding directions, spread it lightly with a mixture made of 1 tablespoon prepared mustard, 1 tablespoon honey and ⅓ teaspoon ground clove. Dust with fine dry bread crumbs; fit into a small deep pan, pour in just enough of the tongue liquid to cover the bottom of the pan, and bake slowly for 30 minutes or until the tongue is lightly glazed. The tongue may be pressured a day or two in advance of use, and glazed and heated just before using. Serve with oven browned potatoes, minted carrots and cole slaw.

CHAPTER IX

THE ORGAN MEATS AS HONOR FOODS

IT TOOK A WAR, BACKED UP BY SCIENTIFIC EXPERIMENTS and findings, to prove to us that hearts, kidneys, brains, sweetbreads, liver, tripe, lungs, all the "innards" of the animals we had often passed up, really taste good. And they are "good for us" we know, because they contribute class A proteins, with small amounts of fat, no bone, little waste, and high vitamin and mineral content. In most countries, other than the United States, the organ meats are honor foods. Witness the famous Minestra de trippa (tripe soup) of Italy; the Kidneys "en brochette" of Paris; the beef and kidney stew of England; the famous mixed grill of Argentina which includes liver, brains, kidney, lamb's fry and sliced heart.

As many of these organ meats call for slow cooking when prepared by the usual methods, many kitchen hours can be saved when they are pressure-cooked.

Regarding Hearts

Here we have quite a selection—beef and pork, lamb and calves' hearts. Beef and pork hearts weigh the most, and call for longer cooking because they come from mature animals and so are inclined to be a little tough. Pressure-cooking cuts the time two-thirds. Lamb and calves' hearts are small and tender, a good-sized one will serve two persons. All hearts are high in vitamin B complex, provide extra quantities of G and a little C, and contain appreciable amounts of phosphorus and iron.

Recipes serve four to six.
All measurements are level.
Timings are minutes required for actual pressuring.
Cool cooker as soon as pressuring is done.

STUFFED BEEF HEARTS
16 minutes to the pound

3 pounds beef heart
Salt and pepper
3 slices bacon
Dry-moist stuffing any kind

3 tablespoons flour
¾ cup water or liquid drained from cooked vegetables

1. Wash the heart thoroughly. Remove any tubes. Split down half way from the top to make a pocket.

2. Season the inside cavity with salt and pepper. Meantime dice the bacon, fry it in the pressure-cooker until crisp, add to the stuffing and press into the heart. Truss loosely into shape with toothpicks and lace together with white string.

3. Dust with salt and pepper; roll in the flour and slowly brown-heat in the bacon fat in the pressure-cooker.

4. Put the rack in the cooker; add the water, place the heart on the rack, close the cooker, bring to 15 pounds pressure and process 16 minutes to the pound.

5. Serve sliced, accompanied with brown gravy made from the liquid in the pan. Add a dash of sherry if desired. Use horse-radish, Creole or red wine sauce.

Stuffed Pork, Lamb or Veal Hearts: Use 2 pork, lamb or veal hearts, onion stuffing, 3 slices bacon or 3 tablespoons savory fat, tomato, creole, horse-radish or Madeira sauce.

(pages 231–247). Follow directions given in the preceding recipe for stuffed beef heart.

FRICASSEED LAMB HEARTS
10 minutes to the pound

3 lamb hearts	1 cup peeled carrots sliced
¾ teaspoon salt	thick
⅛ teaspoon pepper	1 cup solid-pack canned
3 tablespoons flour	tomatoes
3 tablespoons savory fat	½ cup hot water or liquid
2 peeled onions sliced	from cooked vegetables

1. Wash and clean the hearts. Slice across the grain ½-inch thick and cut into ¾-inch pieces. Roll in the salt, pepper and flour mixed. Brown in the fat directly in the pressure-cooker.

2. Add the vegetables, tomatoes and hot water.

3. Close the cooker, bring to 15 pounds pressure and process 10 minutes to the pound.

4. Serve with flaky or mashed potatoes, barley or rice in any form. Sprinkle with a little minced mint if desired.

Fricasseed Veal Hearts: Follow the preceding recipe adding ¼ teaspoon marjoram when the hearts are put in the cooker.

Fricasseed Pork Hearts: Follow the recipe for Fricasseed Lamb Hearts substituting pork hearts. Add ½ teaspoon powdered sage.

Kidneys

Some people do not like kidneys because of their pronounced flavor. But when properly prepared this marked taste disappears. Beside their high protein content, beef, lamb and veal kidneys all contain good amounts of vitamin B and G, and are rich in iron. But in order to supply these in appreciable amounts kidneys should not be cooked over-long. That is why pressure cooking is especially adapted to them. The basic preparation is as follows:

To Pre-Cook Kidneys: Remove all fat and render it for cooking. Wash the kidneys, remove the tubes, gristle and all white centers (called "eyes"); then soak the kidneys 15 to 30 minutes in cold water containing 1 teaspoon salt and 1 tablespoon vinegar to a quart. This improves the flavor and texture, but does not cause loss of food value as when vegetables are soaked in water, because the action of the salt and vinegar combined tends to firm the meat and keep in the juices. Rinse the kidneys under running water. They are then ready to cook as desired.

BRAISED VEAL KIDNEYS
8 minutes

3 veal kidneys	¼ teaspoon marjoram
½ teaspoon salt	2 teaspoons chopped onion
⅛ teaspoon pepper	½ cup chopped celery (op-
3 tablespoons flou:	tional)
2 tablespoons butter or	1 cup solid-pack canned to-
margarine	matoes

1. Prepare kidneys as previously directed in this section. Then cut in halves lengthwise. Roll in the salt, pepper, marjoram and flour mixed.

2. Melt the butter or margarine in the pressure-cooker and put in the kidneys. Cook until light brown; add the onion and celery, and cook until they begin to turn yellow. Add the tomatoes.

3. Close the cooker, bring to 15 pounds pressure and process 8 minutes.

4. Serve on toast.

Braised Pork Kidneys: Follow the preceding recipe, using pork kidneys.

Braised Lamb Kidneys: Use 8 lamb kidneys in place of the veal kidneys.

BEEF KIDNEYS BRITTANY STYLE
8 minutes

3 beef kidneys
Bit of bay leaf
¼ cup water
1 cup dry red wine
2 tablespoons flour

2½ tablespoons butter or margarine
½ teaspoon salt
⅛ teaspoon pepper
Cooked noodles
Minced chives

1. Prepare the kidneys as previously described in this section. Be sure to remove all the "eyes." Slice the kidneys thin.

2. Place in the cooker with the bay leaf, water and wine. Bring to a boil and stir in the flour blended smooth with the butter, salt and pepper. Cook and stir until the sauce is boiling. Add the sliced kidneys.

3. Close the cooker, bring to 15 pounds pressure and process 15 minutes.

4. Serve with the noodles and sprinkle with the chives.

BEEF AND KIDNEY STEW
15 minutes

2 beef kidneys or 6 lamb
  kidneys
1 pound round or chuck
  steak
½ cup sliced onion
1½ cups boiling water
2 teaspoons prepared mustard

1 teaspoon salt
Few grains pepper
2 tablespoons flour
1 tablespoon margarine or
  savory fat
⅓ cup dry red wine
Buttered toast

1. Prepare the kidneys as previously directed in this section. Drain thoroughly and dry on paper towels. Cut into 1-inch cubes. Place the kidneys and beef in the pressure-cooker. Add the onion and water.

2. Close the cooker, bring to 15 pounds pressure and process 15 minutes.

3. Meanwhile cream together the mustard, salt, pepper, flour and margarine. Stir into the cooked meat and cook and stir until it reaches a rapid boil. Add the wine; simmer a minute longer and serve on hot toast. Or accompany with small savory dumplings, noodles, plain Spanish or curried or yellow rice (pages 311, 312).

Sweetbreads
5 minutes

No matter in what form they are used sweetbreads must always be pre-cooked. They are then ready to be broiled, to be used in Sweetbreads à la King, en casserole, with mushrooms or in sweetbread salad.

To Pre-Cook Sweetbreads: Wash and place in the pressure-cooker. Add 1 cup boiling water, ½ tablespoon vinegar or lemon juice and ½ teaspoon salt. Close the cooker, bring to 15 pounds pressure and process 5 minutes. Cool cooker. Then plunge the sweetbreads into cold water to firm. Remove the tubes and membrane. The sweetbreads are then ready to use as desired.

BROILED SWEETBREADS

1 pair sweetbreads	⅓ cup dry bread crumbs
¼ cup tart mayonnaise	Sauce tartare

1. Split the prepared sweetbreads in half lengthwise. Roll each piece in the mayonnaise, then in the bread crumbs, and place in a shallow pan.

2. Broil slowly 6 to 8 minutes in a pre-heated broiler, keeping the sweetbreads at least 3 inches from the flame. Turn as soon as they are light brown.

3. Serve with sauce tartare.

SWEETBREADS A LA KING

1 pair sweetbreads   Patty or pastry shells or but-
À la king sauce (page 233)   tered toast

1. Prepare the sweetbreads as described in this section. Cut in dice and add to the à la king sauce. Heat in a double-boiler until very hot.

2. Serve in the patty or pastry shells or on toast with a garnish of parsley, or sautéd mushroom caps, or broiled halved stuffed tomatoes.

Brains to Cook Brains

It needs "brains" to prepare any foods to the best advantage. For no matter how intrinsically good food may be in itself, it can be spoiled by unintelligent cooking. When correctly cooked, brains have a smooth, rather firm texture similar to that of sweetbreads. Because of this the two meats may be used interchangeably in many dishes. As brains are rich in the vitamin B complex they should be gently but quickly cooked. However they are to be served, the basic preparation is the same. When this method is followed, brains will not have the too soft consistency that has often caused them to be disliked.

To Pre-Cook Brains: First soak the brains in cold water at least an hour, changing the water twice during this time. Then drain.

Place in the pressure-cooker; cover with boiling water,

add ½ teaspoon salt and ½ tablespoon vinegar or lemon juice.

Close the cooker, bring to 15 pounds pressure and process 5 minutes. Then cool and open the cooker. Plunge the brains into cold water to make them firm.

Brains prepared in this way may be diced and scrambled with eggs and tomatoes; creamed with mushrooms and sprinkled with chives. Or serve with Spanish sauce as an entree, or with sliced tomatoes as an hors d'oeuvre salad.

ENTREE OF BRAINS VITAMIN STYLE

Mince ¼ cup each celery, radishes and carrot, and moisten with French dressing made with lemon juice. Slice chilled cooked brains; arrange individually on crisp salad greens, and garnish with the vegetable mixture and lemon wedges. Pass pumpernickel or any dark bread.

Braised Beef, Lamb or Pork Liver

5 minutes

1¼ pounds beef or pork liver sliced one-inch thick
½ teaspoon salt
⅛ teaspoon pepper
¼ teaspoon marjoram (optional)
1 peeled section garlic crushed (optional)
¼ cup butter or savory fat
½ cup hot water or tomato juice

1. Scald the liver and remove the tough outer skin and veins. Dry the liver on paper towels. Dust with salt and pepper, marjoram and garlic mixed. Brown-heat in the fat.

2. Place the rack in the cooker. Pour in the liquid. Place the liver on the rack and process 5 minutes.

3. Serve with brown gravy, onion gravy, tomato or Spanish sauce (pages 235, 236, 245).

BRAISED CALVES' LIVER WITH ONIONS
3 minutes

Prepare the liver as above. Process 3 minutes. Serve surrounded with steam-fried onions.

CHAPTER X

CHICKEN, DUCK, TURKEY, GUINEA HEN, AND GAME

THE FINAL CHOICE OF A BIRD TO PRESSURE-COOK DEPENDS on the size of the cooker; for instance, a big capon or small turkey is too large to fit into the average-sized pressure-cooker, but if you have a seven-quart cooker, a fairly large bird can be used. In any case, there's a treat in store; because pressure cooking properly done retains all the fine flavors of poultry, and produces a velvety smooth tender texture; never stringy even when the bird is a bit mature!

However, bear in mind that large chickens or ducks are as delicious when sectioned, browned and pressure-panned, as when cooked whole; that turkey makes a superb fricassee; and that guinea-hen is delightful pressure-panned, or smothered in cabbage Holland style.

Do's for Pressure Cooking Poultry

Clean, scrub and thoroughly wash the poultry.

Dry on paper towels or with a cloth.

To achieve a roasted or panned effect, brown-heat before pressuring, and brown-crisp afterward.

Use only enough water or liquid to bring up steam and maintain 15 pounds pressure during the cooking period.

Use larger amounts of water or other liquid only when

steam-boiling, braising, fricasseeing or stewing, and then only according to the directions given.

To Prepare Poultry for Pressure Cooking

Singe the long hairs from the bird by holding over a low flame, or by applying a lighted wax taper or candle. Remove pinfeathers with kitchen tweezers. Clean the bird, removing the entrails and kidneys, cut out the oil sac from the tip of the tail. Save the giblets, feet, neck and tips of wings for soup-stock or gravy. Scrub the skin of the bird all over with a brush dipped in mild soap suds. Rinse all over several times in tepid water. When this is done, excess oil (and dirt) are thoroughly removed from the skin. The improvement in flavor is amazing. Drain thoroughly and pat dry with paper towels or a clean cloth.

Rub inside and out with the required seasoning. Stuff if indicated, and truss. Weigh, to determine the number of pounds after stuffing, so you can estimate the pressuring time. Finish according to directions.

To Truss Poultry: Fold the skin of the neck over on the back, and fasten in place with sharp toothpicks or poultry nails. Close the vent with toothpicks or poultry nails, and lace together with white string. Lightly bind the legs and wings close to the bird with white string. Remove strings and toothpicks or poultry nails before serving.

To Buy a Whole Chicken or Chicken Parts

That is the question. From the cost angle there is little difference pound for pound, and cut for cut. But from the standpoint of time-saving and convenience there is no comparison, the chicken parts are so much easier to use. And there's no discussion of who will get the white or the dark meat.

If you are giving a dinner party and wish to serve chicken Virginia style, it is certainly more sensible to buy chicken breasts and serve a half to each person. Your money buys just what you wish to serve. If it is to be a fricassee, equal weights of chicken breasts and drum sticks or a mixture are just the thing. If you are on a small budget and serving a chicken curry, your guests will appreciate chicken wings and giblets in curry sauce with rice. And if it's an old fowl you must tender up, try Chicken Irish Style.

As to chicken soup, why buy a whole bird and cook the life out of it, when chicken backs, necks and wings can be purchased at a third the cost and make better soup.

Pressure Cooking Frozen Poultry

If poultry is to be steam-boiled or plain pressured whole, without brown-heating, it may be pressured in the frozen state, by increasing the pressuring time from 10 to 15 per cent. This assumes that the poultry was eviscerated, scrubbed and singed before freezing. If this was *not* done, or if the poultry is to be brown-heated, or sectioned before pressuring it must be completely defrosted. This takes at least 3 hours for a small bird, longer for a large one; allow 2 hours for cut-up sections, all at room temperature. Be sure to remove the giblets from a whole bird—they are inside wrapped in parchment paper.

Singe, remove pinfeathers, wash, rinse, drain, dry and season as for fresh poultry; and follow the same timings.

Pressure Cooking Poultry

Recipes are proportioned to serve four to six.
All measurements are level.
Timings are the minutes required for actual pressuring.
Cool cooker as soon as processing is done.

FRIED CHICKEN
15 minutes

2 young frying chickens
1 tablespoon lemon juice
½ teaspoon salt
⅛ teaspoon pepper
3 tablespoons flour

¼ cup butter or margarine
1 small peeled onion sliced
  (optional)
½ cup hot water

1. Singe, clean, wash, dry and cut up the chicken into sections. Rub with lemon juice. Then dip in the salt, pepper and flour mixed.

2. Melt the butter or margarine in a heavy frying pan; slowly brown-heat the chicken in it. Add the onion the last few minutes of frying.

3. Put the rack in the cooker; pour in the hot water. Place the brown-heated chicken on the rack, close the cooker, bring to 15 pounds pressure and process 15 minutes.

4. Make gravy from the liquid in the cooker by adding 1 tablespoon each butter and flour creamed together; stir until smooth and add ¼ cup water and ½ cup sweet or soured cream. Season to taste with salt and pepper.

5. Serve plain, on buttered toast, cornbread squares, or in a border of plain, yellow or Spanish rice or mashed potatoes.

SOUTHERN FRIED QUARTERED CHICKEN
15 minutes

1 (2½ pound) frying chicken quartered
½ lemon
½ teaspoon salt
⅛ teaspoon pepper
3 tablespoons flour
¼ cup butter or vegetable fat

1 small peeled onion sliced (optional)
¼ cup boiling water
1 hard-cooked egg chopped
1 tablespoon minced parsley

1. Follow the directions given in the preceding recipe. Process the chicken at 15 pounds pressure for 20 minutes.

2. Make gravy from the liquid in the cooker. Serve sprinkled with the chopped hard-cooked egg and minced parsley.

PANNED BABY BROILERS WITH SHERRIED MUSHROOMS
10 to 12 minutes

2 baby broiling chickens
½ teaspoon salt
⅛ teaspoon pepper
4 tablespoons butter

½ pound cleaned, fresh mushrooms
¼ cup water
3 tablespoons dry Sherry wine

1. Singe, clean, wash and dry the chickens; cut in quarters. Slowly pan-fry in the butter until brown, about 5 minutes. Add the salt, pepper and mushrooms last, the stems sliced crosswise, the caps whole. Fry 1 minute more.

2. Place the rack in the cooker; add the water; put the chickens on the rack; surround with the mushrooms. Pour over the Sherry. Close the cooker, bring to 15 pounds pressure and process 8 minutes.

3. If desired brown-crisp, arrange the pressured broilers and mushrooms on a sizzling platter, dot with 2 table-spoons butter or margarine, and heat under the broiler for 2 minutes.

4. Serve plain or with wild rice, Jerusalem artichokes or sweet potatoes and asparagus.

BARBECUED CHICKEN
15 to 17 minutes

Prepare chicken for frying, and brown-heat as described in recipe for fried chicken. Place chicken direct in the cooker. Pour over plain or wine barbecue sauce (page 237). Close the cooker, bring to 15 pounds pressure, and process 15 minutes. If roasting chicken is used, process 16 minutes.

ROAST CHICKEN (Not Stuffed)
7 minutes to the pound

1 (3 to 4 pound) roasting chicken	⅛ teaspoon pepper
½ lemon or 1 teaspoon dry ginger	2 tablespoons flour
	¼ cup butter, margarine or vegetable fat
½ teaspoon salt	½ cup hot water

1. Singe, clean, wash and dry the chicken. Rub inside and out with the ginger, or the cut surface of the lemon. Dust outside with the salt, pepper and flour mixed.

2. Slowly brown-heat all over in the fat, using a frying pan.

3. Put the water (or liquid drained from cooked vege-tables), in the pressure-cooker; put in the rack; place the chicken on the rack, together with the giblets. Close the cooker, bring to 15 pounds pressure and process 7 minutes to the pound.

4. To brown-crisp the skin, place the chicken in a hot oven or under the broiler for a few minutes. Make a gravy from the liquid in the cooker (page 244).

5. Carve, and serve garnished with parsley; surround with Franconia style white potatoes, or sweet potato glacé and asparagus or broccoli.

Roast Chicken with Fresh Herbs: Prepare the chicken as described, but fill the cavity with little sprigs of fresh parsley, mixed with 1 teaspoon of minced fresh thyme, marjoram, tarragon or basil. Finish as directed.

Roast Chicken, Stuffed: (7 minutes to the pound.) Follow the preceding recipe with this exception. Fill the cavity at the neck and body of the chicken with cornbread stuffing, or with plain, dry-moist stuffing, or any of its variations (page 86). Then truss. Weigh the chicken, as the amount of stuffing added must be counted in the cooking time. Finish as directed. Serve with giblet gravy.

Chicken Roasted with Wine: Follow the recipe for roast chicken, plain, with herbs or stuffed. Before pressuring pour over 1 cup dry white wine. Omit water. Serve with a sauce made from the liquid in the cooker.

STEAM-BOILED CHICKEN
30 minutes

1 (3 to 4 pound) chicken   1½ cups water
1 teaspoon salt   4 slices onion (optional)
⅓ cup celery tips

1. Singe, clean, wash and dry the chicken. Sprinkle with salt.

2. Put rack in pressure-cooker. Add water. Place chicken on rack. Add remaining ingredients. Close cooker. Bring to 15 pounds pressure and process 30 minutes. Cool at once according to directions.

3. Remove and save skin. Remove the chicken from the bones in good-sized pieces. Heat in chicken gravy or in mushroom, tomato or creole sauce (pages 233, 235, 236).

4. Serve in a border of rice or mashed potatoes, or on unsweetened cornbread squares, or hot split baking powder biscuits.

5. Cut the chicken skin in inch squares, fry crisp in chicken fat or butter, and sprinkle over the chicken.

Note: Use the neck, tips of wings, feet and giblets for chicken giblet soup.

Steam-boiled Fowl: For a 4 to 5 pound fowl, follow the preceding directions allowing 35 minutes cooking under pressure.

CHICKEN SHORTCAKE

Prepare plain steam-boiled chicken. Remove the skin and flake the chicken meat. Mix it with giblet or chicken cream gravy, and serve between and on top of New England toast, split buttered large thin baking powder biscuits, or squares of unsweetened corn bread. A little fresh or dried marjoram or thyme may be added to the gravy.

CHICKEN PAPRIKASH
20 minutes

1 (3 pound) tender chicken
1 teaspoon salt
1½ teaspoons paprika

1 peeled onion sliced
3 tablespoons butter or margarine
1 cup tomato juice

1. Singe, clean, wash, dry and section the chicken. Dust all over with the salt and paprika. Then brown-heat with the onion and butter.

2. Place the tomato juice in the cooker and adjust the rack. Put the chicken on the rack, close the cooker, bring to 15 pounds pressure and process 25 minutes. Make a thin gravy from the liquid in the cooker (page 244).

3. Serve with flaky white potatoes.

WHITE CHICKEN FRICASSEE

5 minutes to the pound for roasting chicken
7 minutes to the pound for fowl

1 (3 to 4 pound) roasting chicken	⅛ teaspoon pepper
½ lemon (optional)	1 cup hot water
1 teaspoon salt	1 cup diced celery
	1 peeled small onion sliced

1. Singe, clean, wash, dry and section the chicken. Season with salt and pepper; put the rack in the cooker; pour in the water or use liquid from cooked vegetables. Place the chicken on the rack; add the vegetables and the giblets.

2. Close cooker; bring to 15 pounds pressure and process 5 minutes to the pound for roasting chicken, 7 minutes to the pound for fowl.

3. To serve, make a gravy from the liquid in the cooker, by adding an equal amount of water, liquid drained from cooked vegetables, or light cream. Bring to boiling point and thicken with 3 tablespoons flour creamed smooth with 2 tablespoons butter or margarine. Mix this gravy with the chicken.

4. Serve on toast, split baking powder biscuits, over noodles, or in a ring of plain, yellow or Spanish rice (see pages 311, 312). The giblets may be chopped and added to the gravy, or they may be stirred into the rice. To add color, sprinkle the chicken with mixed minced parsley and hard-cooked egg.

BROWN CHICKEN FRICASSEE
5 minutes to the pound for roasting chicken
7 minutes to the pound for fowl

Follow the preceding recipe with this exception. Roll the sectioned chicken in 3 tablespoons flour, seasoned with ½ teaspoon salt and ¼ teaspoon pepper. Then brown-heat slowly in ¼ cup margarine or vegetable shortening. Place on the rack in the pressure-cooker and pressure as directed.

Chicken Smothered with Mushrooms: Prepare white or brown chicken fricassee. Add one cup sautéd sliced mushrooms to the gravy, and garnish the platter with sautéd fresh or stuffed mushroom caps, or with sautéd canned whole mushrooms.

CHICKEN STEW JACK DEMPSEY
25 minutes

1 (3 to 4 pound) chicken or fowl
4 tablespoons butter or vegetable fat
½ teaspoon salt
⅛ teaspoon pepper
1 small onion peeled
1½ teaspoons meat extract
3½ cups water or liquid from cooked vegetables
8 small slashed peeled carrots
8 small peeled white potatoes
Minced parsley

1. Singe, clean, wash, dry and section the chicken.

2. Brown-heat lightly in the butter or fat directly in the pressure-cooker. Add the seasonings, onion, liquid and meat extract. Close the cooker.

3. Bring to 15 pounds pressure and process 17 minutes.

4. Cool and open the cooker; put in the vegetables. Then close again, bring to 15 pounds pressure and process 8 minutes longer.

5. Serve the chicken, vegetables and broth in deep soup plates. Sprinkle with the parsley.

CHICKEN CREAM SAUCE

3 tablespoons butter
3 tablespoons flour
⅓ teaspoon salt
⅛ teaspoon paprika
1 cup chicken-stock

½ cup light cream
1 egg yolk, beaten
1 tablespoon dry sherry wine (optional)

1. Melt the butter. Stir in the flour and seasonings. When smooth gradually stir in the chicken-stock and cream, bring to boiling point and simmer 2 minutes.

2. Combine the egg yolk with the sherry or 1 tablespoon cold water. Stir into the sauce, cook and stir half a minute and serve.

CHICKEN VIRGINIA STYLE
10 to 12 minutes

6 small chicken breasts
½ teaspoon salt
Few grains pepper
½ cup heavy cream
⅓ cup flour
Butter or margarine for frying
½ cup chicken-stock or hot water

2 tablespoons butter (extra)
6 individual slices broiled tenderized ham
Chicken cream sauce
Asparagus tips
Sautéd mushroom caps

1. Season the chicken breasts with the salt and pepper. Brush all over with cream, then dust thickly with the flour.

2. Brown-heat in the butter in the pressure-cooker. Remove, put in the rack with ½ cup chicken-stock or hot water.

3. Put chicken on rack, dot with remaining butter; close cooker, bring to 15 pounds pressure and process 10 minutes for small breasts, 12 minutes for large ones.

4. Meantime broil the ham, and make the sauce.

5. To serve, arrange the ham on a large platter. Top each piece with a chicken breast. Pour around the sauce; arrange the asparagus tips around the edge of the platter, and garnish the chicken with the mushroom caps.

CHICKEN IRISH STYLE
25 to 30 minutes according to tenderness

1 (3 pound) roasting chicken or fowl
½ pound lean bacon, Irish preferred
½ teaspoon salt
1 cup hot water
1½ tablespoons butter or margarine

3 tablespoons flour
1 cup light cream
½ cup capers
Flaky white potatoes
Cooked sliced cabbage
Minced parsley

1. Singe, clean, wash and dry the chicken. Put rack in cooker; put chicken on the rack with the whole piece of bacon. Dust the chicken with the salt. Pour in the water.

2. Close the cooker; bring to 15 pounds pressure and process 30 minutes. Remove the bacon; score the top, (that is cut through the rind in squares); dust with a trace of sugar and place under a pre-heated broiler to brown the top.

3. Remove excess fat from the liquid in the cooker, and make a caper gravy by melting the butter or margarine, stirring in the flour, then the liquid from the cooker. Bring to a rapid boil; add the cream. Stir in the capers.

4. To serve, put the chicken (whole or sectioned) on a platter; pour over the caper gravy. Surround with flaky white potatoes and sections of cabbage; dust with minced parsley. Slice the browned bacon and serve separately. Small, peeled white potatoes and thick slices of cabbage may be pressured together for this dish. Allow 8 minutes at 15 pounds pressure.

CHICKEN CURRY HAWAIIAN
30 minutes

1 (3 pound) chicken
½ package frozen coconut or 1 fresh coconut grated
1 pint milk scalded
1½ tablespoons butter or margarine
1 peeled large onion chopped
1 peeled section garlic minced

1 root fresh ginger chopped or ½ teaspoon powdered ginger
1 tablespoon curry powder
½ teaspoon brown sugar
2 tablespoons flour
Pressure-cooked white or brown rice

1. Singe, clean, wash, dry and season the chicken. Steam-boil in the pressure-cooker (page 170). This will take 30 minutes.

2. Meantime make the curry sauce as follows: Add the coconut to the scalded milk and let stand 10 minutes. Then put through a fine sieve and press the coconut until it is dry; reserve the coconut to use later.

3. Melt the butter; add the onion, garlic and ginger and sauté slowly until browned. Add the curry powder and sugar mixed and stir in the flour. Then gradually stir in the milk squeezed from the coconut meat and cook and stir until the sauce boils all over.

4. When the chicken is cooked, remove the skin and the bones; flake the meat and add to the sauce; then season to taste with a little salt. Do not cook after the salt is added or the sauce will curdle.

5. To serve, heap the rice on a deep platter, and surround with the curried chicken; sprinkle with the coconut and decorate with parsley, water cress or scallions relish style. Pass chutney sauce.

Curried Chicken Wings Hawaiian (15 minutes): Follow the preceding recipe substituting chicken wings for the whole chicken. Process the chicken wings 15 minutes at 15 pounds pressure. Whichever of the preceding recipes is used, a delicious Hawaiian style chicken curry will be ready to eat within 30 minutes—quite different from the 2 or 3 hours time usually allowed for the preparation of this dish.

COLD CHICKEN CURRY
30 minutes

1 (3 pound) roasting chicken	1 tablespoon tomato purée
¼ cup butter	One recipe cream or white sauce
⅓ teaspoon salt	2 egg yolks
⅛ teaspoon pepper	3 tablespoons dry sherry wine
½ teaspoon paprika	½ cup sweet cream
2 teaspoons curry powder	

1. Singe, clean, wash and section the chicken. Then steam-boil allowing 30 minutes at 15 pounds pressure. Cool and remove skin.

2. Meantime make the sauce as follows: Melt the butter, add the salt, pepper, paprika, curry powder and tomato purée, and simmer together about three minutes. Add the cream sauce and the chicken. Bring slowly to boiling point. Then stir in the egg yolks slightly beaten with the sherry wine. Cook and stir for a minute then add the sweet cream.

3. Cool quickly uncovered. Serve very cold in small deep plates or individual casseroles; sprinkle with minced parsley.

CHICKEN CACCIATORE
15 minutes

1 (3 pound) chicken
½ cup olive or vegetable oil
1 peeled onion diced
1 (No. 2) can tomatoes or 6 fresh tomatoes
½ teaspoon salt
⅛ teaspoon pepper
Spaghetti al dente (page 306)

1. Singe, clean, wash, dry and section the chicken.

2. Heat the oil in the pressure-cooker; fry the chicken in it gently until golden brown. Then add the onion. When yellowed, add the tomato, salt and pepper.

3. Close the cooker, bring to 15 pounds pressure and process 15 minutes.

4. Meantime prepare spaghetti al dente. Arrange on a platter. Pour over the chicken and sauce, and serve with or without grated Parmesan cheese.

CHICKEN CHOP SUEY
3 minutes

1 tablespoon salad oil
¾ cup finely shredded Chinese cabbage
⅔ cup celery cut in strips
¼ cup canned bean sprouts or bamboo shoots
⅓ cup sliced canned mushrooms
¼ cup shredded peeled onion
¾ teaspoon salt
½ teaspoon sugar
1 cup soup stock
⅛ teaspoon black pepper
½ cup diced cooked or canned chicken

2 teaspoons cornstarch

1. Heat the oil; add the vegetables, seasonings and soup stock. Close the cooker, bring to 15 pounds pressure and process 3 minutes. Cool and open the cooker. Add the chicken.

2. Thicken with the cornstarch blended smooth with 1 tablespoon cold water or extra soup stock. Bring to a rapid boil and simmer 2 minutes.

3. Serve poured over pressured rice; garnish with extra shredded chicken; with shredded egg; with sautéd extra mushroom caps; or with the chopped tender green tops of scallions.

Chinese Shredded Egg: Beat an egg till well-blended. Fry very slowly until firm in a little oil in an individual omelet pan. Cool, and cut in paper thin shreds with a very sharp knife.

CHOP SUEY VARIATIONS
3 minutes

Add 1 large seeded, diced green pepper when the vegetables are sautéd. Or after the chop suey has been pressured and just before the thickening is added, stir in one large peeled tomato cut in 8 or 10 pieces; or use 2 slices drained canned pineapple which have been cut into 10 pieces each.

Duck and Less Used Poultry

Many a taste treat is in store when duck, guinea hen, pigeon or squab reach the table. And they are so easy to pressure-cook as well as delicious to eat that they deserve a fair trial.

ROAST DUCKLINGS
6 minutes to the pound

Follow the directions for preparing roast duck, using ducklings. If desired they may be filled with a sausage stuffing. Process 6 minutes to the pound. Serve with gravy or orange sauce, a green vegetable and a tossed celery and grape salad. Raisin-d apples or stuffed oranges (pages 341, 342) are an accompaniment de luxe.

ROAST DUCK
7 minutes to the pound

1 (4 to 5 pound) duck
½ lemon
Dry-moist stuffing or fruit
    stuffing

Salt and pepper
3 tablespoons butter, mar-
    garine or vegetable fat
½ cup hot water

1. Singe, clean, wash and dry the duck. Rub with a cut lemon. Fill with the desired stuffing and truss (page 165). Dust with salt and pepper.

2. Brown-heat all over in the fat, using a frying pan. Place the rack in the cooker; pour in hot water, put in the duck, close the cooker, bring to 15 pounds pressure and process 7 minutes to the pound.

3. Serve with a gravy made from the liquid in the cooker, excess fat removed (page 244). If fruit stuffing is used accompany with brown or wild rice.

Fruit Stuffing for Duck: Remove the pits from ¼ pound prunes, leaving the prunes whole. Add sections from 2 oranges, and 1 peeled cored apple cut in eighths. No further ingredients are necessary.

FRICASSEE OF DUCK
20 minutes

1 (4 to 5 pound) duck
¼ cup flour
½ teaspoon salt
¼ teaspoon pepper

1 teaspoon garlic or onion
    salt
¼ cup vegetable shortening
1 cup hot water

1. Singe, clean, wash, dry and section the duck. Mix the flour and seasonings. Roll the duck in this. Brown-heat slowly in the fat using a heavy frying pan.

2. Put the water (or use liquid drained from cooked vegetables) in the pressure-cooker. Drain the duck from the fat. Put in the rack and place the duck on it.

3. Close the cooker, bring the pressure to 15 pounds and process 20 minutes. When done cool and open the cooker. Remove the duck and keep it warm. Remove any excess fat from the liquid in the pan. Make a gravy (page 244).

4. Serve the duck on split baking powder biscuits or crisp waffles; with hominy, brown or wild rice; or in a mashed potato border. If desired a little dry sherry or white wine may be added to the gravy when it is being made.

SWEET AND PUNGENT DUCK

Pressure-cook duck as described in the preceding recipe. Instead of making gravy, serve with a sweet and pungent sauce made as follows:

SWEET AND PUNGENT SAUCE

2 large sweet green peppers, seeded and diced

2 tablespoons vegetable oil or butter

4 slices canned pineapple, drained and diced

½ cup mild vinegar

⅓ cup sugar

⅔ cup chicken or veal-stock

2 tablespoons cornstarch

2 tablespoons cold water

2 teaspoons soy sauce

1. Simmer the peppers 5 minutes in water to cover, then drain.

2. Heat the oil or butter in a saucepan; add the pine-apple and the duck liquid from the pressure-cooker, the excess fat removed. Stir in the vinegar, sugar, veal or chicken stock, or use canned chicken bouillon.

3. Last thicken with the cornstarch stirred smooth with the cold water and soy sauce. Cook and stir until the sauce boils rapidly all over. Then simmer for two minutes.

4. Pour over and around the duck and serve with molds of rice.

Sweet and Pungent Chicken: This can be prepared by the same recipe; just substitute chicken for duck.

PANNED GUINEA CHICKEN
15 minutes

4 slices bacon
1 (2 to 3 pound) guinea chicken
⅓ teaspoon salt
⅛ teaspoon pepper

¼ teaspoon thyme
¼ cup hot water
Small croutons
1 tablespoon butter or margarine

1. Fry the bacon until almost crisp in a frying pan, then remove.

2. Singe, clean, wash and dry the guinea chicken. Cut it into quarters if small, and into sections if large.

3. Brown-heat in the bacon fat. Put the rack in the pressure-cooker, add the water and place the guinea chicken on the rack. Dust with the salt, pepper and thyme. Close the cooker, bring to 15 pounds pressure and process 15 minutes.

4. Place the pieces of guinea chicken in a pan; cover with the nearly cooked bacon and put under a pre-heated broiler to finish cooking the bacon and brown-crisp the guinea chicken.

5. Serve with a thickened gravy made from the liquid in the pan. Accompany with yellow or brown rice, or small white or sweet potato croquettes. Sautéed mushrooms and water cress make an attractive garnish.

GUINEA HEN HOLLAND DUTCH STYLE
18 minutes

1 (3 pound) guinea hen
3 tablespoons butter or margarine
½ cup hot water
½ cup dry white wine
½ teaspoon salt

⅛ teaspoon pepper
1 small green cabbage cut into 6 slices
Freshly ground black pepper

1. Singe, clean, wash, dry and section the guinea hen. Brown-heat in the butter, using a frying pan. Place the water and wine in the pressure-cooker. Put in the rack. Place the guinea hen on it. Dust with the salt and pepper. Close the cooker, bring to 15 pounds pressure and process 12 minutes.

2. Cool the cooker; open it and put in the sliced cabbage. Close and bring to 15 pounds pressure again; process 6 minutes. Season with the black pepper.

3. Serve the cabbage and guinea hen together. The liquid in the pressure-cooker should be slightly thickened and used as a gravy. If desired, ½ teaspoon caraway seed may be added.

POTTED PIGEONS
15 minutes

4 to 6 pigeons
Yellow, wild or savory brown rice (page 309)
3 tablespoons butter or margarine
1 cup meat-stock or 1 cup hot water and 1 bouillon cube

3 tablespoons dry white wine
½ teaspoon salt
⅛ teaspoon pepper
1½ tablespoons flour
½ tablespoon tart jelly
Toast

1. Allow 1 pigeon to each person. Singe, clean, wash and dry the birds on paper towels. Stuff with the rice, then truss (page 165). Brown-heat slowly in the butter using a frying pan.

2. Put in the rack. Pour the stock, or water with the cube dissolved in it, into the pressure-cooker; add the wine. Place the pigeons on the rack; dust with the salt and pepper.

3. Close the cooker, bring to 15 pounds pressure and process 15 minutes.

4. Remove the pigeons. Make a gravy from the liquid in the cooker. To do this, thicken it with the flour well mixed with the jelly; cook and stir until boiling and simmer two minutes. Place each pigeon on a slice of toast and pour around the sauce. If desired the pigeons may be brown-crisped before serving by dotting with butter and placing in a hot oven or under a pre-heated broiler.

Potted Squab: Follow the preceding recipe, using squab. Add a few finely chopped mushrooms to the stuffing. Process 10 minutes at 15 pounds pressure.

As to Turkey

Why enjoy turkey only once or twice a year? It's too big you say—we can't eat it up, and it takes so long to cook. Besides the small birds are so expensive and a big bird, although it costs less per pound, takes dollars from the budget. I know. But all this is not necessarily so; not if you look on turkey as on any other large "critter"; cut it up and cook it in various ways at leisure. Part can be steaked, or pressure-pot-roasted; some fricasseed or stewed, and while waiting to be cooked, sections of the cut-up bird can be frozen in the ice-making compartment of the refrigerator. Or you can buy a turkey half or quarter. At any rate a turkey can play peek-a-boo for two weeks with the menu. The illustration shows how a whole bird should be cut up.

1. Cut off the drum sticks, thighs and wings, ready to fricassee or stew.

2. Cut the breast away from the back and away from the neck, too. This makes what might be called a nice big "saddle" of meat. But this breast meat is dry. So it should be marinated for 2 or 3 days to season and "take on" fat. This takes care of part of the turkey for a few days, when it can be pressure-pot-roasted. Or the turkey breasts can be sliced and cooked in the form of steaks.

3. The bony back and the stringy neck and the wings, can be frozen, or cooked the next day and kept up to 48 hours in the refrigerator. This meat and broth will make a fine basis for turkey stew, little turkey pies, turkey à la king, or turkey soubise.

TURKEY MARENGO
15 to 20 minutes

Giblets
1 oz. dried mushrooms
Turkey legs and wings
4 tablespoons fortified margarine
Salt and pepper
⅓ cup flour
2 tablespoons minced onion

1 peeled section garlic minced
½ teaspoon celery salt
1 can tomato purée
¼ teaspoon dried basil
¼ teaspoon dried thyme
1 grated carrot
Giblet stock
¼ teaspoon paprika
½ cup dry sauterne

1. Clean turkey giblets; place in pressure-cooker with the mushrooms and 2 cups hot water; close the cooker, bring to 15 pounds pressure and process 15 minutes. Then cool and mince the giblets. Save liquid.

2. Meantime section the turkey legs and wings; add salt and pepper, and rub in the flour.

3. Brown-heat in the margarine, using a frying pan. Add the onion and garlic.

4. Then put directly into the cooker (no rack). Add the remaining ingredients, close the cooker, bring to 15 pounds pressure and process 15 minutes for young turkey, 20 minutes if old and inclined to be tough.

5. Serve in a border of pressured white, brown or wild rice.

TURKEY FRICASSEE
5 to 7 minutes to the pound

Follow the recipe for white or brown chicken fricassee using the drum sticks, thighs and wings of the turkey. Pressure 5 minutes to the pound for young turkey, 7 minutes to the pound for an old bird; if the pieces are too large for individual portions, cut meat from the bone and add to the gravy. Serve in a border of rice. Decorate the fricassee with sautéed mushrooms and pressured peas.

SADDLE OF TURKEY POT-ROASTED
15 minutes

½ cup dry white wine
1 teaspoon mixed pickle spice tied in a bit of gauze
½ teaspoon garlic salt
1 tablespoon salad oil
½ cup hot water
Saddle of turkey breast
2 tablespoons butter or margarine
½ teaspoon salt
⅛ teaspoon pepper
1 egg yolk
½ cup fine dry bread crumbs
1 tablespoon melted butter or margarine additional

1. Combine the wine, pickle spice, garlic salt and oil, and heat. Pour over the turkey breast meat. Cover and place in the refrigerator for two or three days to season. Turn occasionally. Pierce the meat with a fork to take up more seasoning.

2. When ready to pressure-cook, brown-heat the top surface of the turkey meat in a skillet, using the butter or margarine. Season with the salt and pepper.

3. Put the rack in the pressure-cooker. Add the water; put in the turkey and pour over the marinating sauce. Close the cooker, bring to 15 pounds pressure and process 15 minutes.

4. Place in a baking pan, brush over with the egg yolk, beaten, and dust with the crumbs mixed with the additional butter or margarine. Bake a few minutes or until the crumbs brown.

5. Serve with a gravy made from the liquid in the cooker.

TURKEY STEW NO. 1

Follow recipe for chicken stew Jack Dempsey (page 173) in this book. Be sure the sections of turkey are not too large. If so, remove the meat from the bones and cut in large dice. If the bird is a bit mature, better remove the skin and bones before serving. A few raw oysters may be added when the stew is done, and simmered 3 minutes until the edges curl.

TURKEY STEW NO. 2

Follow recipe for Irish stew (page 124) substituting raw diced turkey meat. Season with 1 teaspoon meat extract or 2 bouillon cubes. Add 1 cup cooked or canned peas if desired.

Serve with plain or savory puffy dumplings (page 63).

USING TURKEY WINGS, BACK AND NECK
15 minutes

Steam-boil back, wings and neck of the turkey. Follow the recipe for steam-boiled chicken on page 170, and process 30 minutes at 15 pounds pressure.

When cold, dice the meat and use in any of the following ways:

1. Turkey à La King: Add diced turkey meat to sauce à la king (page 233). Heat and serve on mounds of rice or between and on top of thin slices of toast, sandwich style.

2. Turkey Soubise: Make a sauce as follows: Peel and slice 16 young button onions, or use scallions with ½ inch of the green tops. Add ½ cup water or turkey-stock and ¼ teaspoon salt. Close the cooker, bring to 15 pounds pressure and process 3 minutes. Thicken with 1½ tablespoon each flour and butter blended together, and add ½ cup sweet or soured cream. Add 1½ cups diced turkey meat and heat. Serve on toast or split buttered thin baking powder biscuits.

3. Turkey Salad: Dice or flake cooked turkey meat. Add half as much diced celery, ¼ the quantity of seeded halved white grapes, ¼ cup French dressing and 1 tablespoon chutney or Chinese plum sauce. Chill. Add a few roasted walnut meats, or toasted butternut meats. Blend with a little mayonnaise and serve in nests of lettuce; or heap onto split slices of canned pineapple. Garnish with grapes and lettuce or chicory.

A Covey of Game Recipes

Recipes proportioned to serve four to six.
All measurements are level.
Timings are minutes required for actual pressuring.
Cool cooker as soon as processing is done.

All kinds of game may be prepared in the pressure-cooker. As some types are likely to be a little tough as usually cooked, the use of the pressure-cooker is a great asset. Remember, however, that the natural "gamey" taste will be entirely retained. So if game of strong flavor is to be prepared, it should first be scalded or even par-boiled for 5 minutes to draw out a little of the excess flavor.

In arranging game for service, use an attractive green garnish such as water cress, fresh dandelions, radishes or cucumbers; provide a tart fresh or prepared relish, as chutney. Or use cooked fruit such as raisin-d apples or stuffed oranges (page 342); or accompany with Chinese plum sauce (page 243), or tart jelly made from wild fruit, such as the beach plum. In other words, try to serve game with foods that suggest the out-of-doors.

Rabbit should be thoroughly cleaned and the little kernels under the paws removed. It is then ready to pressure-roast or fricassee, just as chicken is prepared (page 173), or to be prepared according to the following recipes.

RABBIT PIE

Prepare fricassee of rabbit (see recipe for chicken fricassee page 173). Combine the rabbit with potatoes cut in inch cubes, peeled button onions and a few sliced mushrooms first pressured together 4 minutes. Place the boiling hot mixture in a deep pottery dish and top with rich pie-pastry cut to fit; bake 20 minutes in a hot oven 375 to 400 degrees F. Or top the bubbling hot rabbit fricassee with small rounds of baked pie-pastry.

SAVORY RABBIT RAGOUT
15 minutes

1 (3 pound) frying rabbit	1 tablespoon Worcestershire
1 peeled small onion	sauce
1 teaspoon salt	¼ cup flour
1 teaspoon poultry season-	3 tablespoons butter or mar-
ing	garine
⅛ teaspoon pepper	½ cup dry red wine
2 tablespoons vinegar, herb	½ cup hot water
preferred	

1. Clean, wash and dry the rabbit on paper towels; cut in sections as for frying.

2. Combine the onion, salt, poultry seasoning, pepper, vinegar and Worcestershire sauce, and rub over the rabbit. Cover and let stand in the refrigerator 4 or 5 hours, or overnight if more convenient.

3. Drain the rabbit; roll it in the flour, and brown in the fat directly in the cooker. Add the wine and vinegar mixture.

4. Close the cooker, bring to 15 pounds pressure and process 15 minutes.

5. Make a gravy from the residue in the pressure-cooker.

6. For serving, arrange the rabbit in a ring of wild rice or on squares of toast. Pour around the gravy.

FRIED RABBIT

Clean the rabbit thoroughly. Remove the kernels from under the front paws, and cut the rabbit into sections. Then proceed as for pressure-cooked fried chicken (page 167).

Serve with gravy made from the liquid in the pressure-cooker, diluted with soured cream.

Fried rabbit is especially good served with red and white coleslaw containing sprigs of water cress and put together with tomato French dressing.

BARBECUED RABBIT

Wash, clean, dry and disjoint the rabbit. Cook according to the recipe for barbecued chicken on page 169, using plain or wine barbecue sauce (page 237).

Serve with whipped white or sweet potatoes or with yellow, brown or wild rice.

SQUIRREL

Squirrel may be pressure cooked in a variety of ways—barbecued, fricasseed or in the form of a stew. Any of the recipes for pressure cooking chicken in this book can also be used for cooking squirrel.

Young squirrels can be fried. (See recipe for pressure-frying chicken on page 167.)

Properly prepared squirrel meat is delicious. The flesh is light red or pink, and there is very little "gamey" taste.

SQUIRREL STEW
25 minutes for young squirrel
30 minutes for older squirrel

2 squirrels cleaned and dis-
    jointed
5 cups hot water
1 teaspoon salt
⅛ teaspoon pepper
2 peeled onions diced
1 cup diced celery

1 cup diced carrot
1 seeded sweet green pep-
    per shredded
2 tablespoons butter or mar-
    garine
½ cup white or brown rice
3 tablespoons flour

1. Put the squirrels in the pressure-cooker with the water, salt and pepper. Close the cooker, bring the pressure to 15 pounds and process 25 minutes for young squirrels, 30 minutes if older.

2. Meantime fry the vegetables in the butter or margarine till soft and yellowed.

3. Drain the broth from the squirrel. Return it to the pressure-cooker, add the vegetables and rice and pressure 7 minutes. Dice the squirrel meat, roll it in the flour and add to the stew. Bring to boiling point and serve with old-fashioned cornbread.

Squirrel Pie: Prepare squirrel stew using ½ the amount of salt and water. Add 1 cup sliced fresh mushrooms. Transfer to a deep baking dish; cover with little baking powder biscuits or rich piecrust, and bake 25 to 30 minutes in a hot oven 400 degrees F.

VENISON

The cuts of venison are almost the same as those of mutton—the leg, the haunch and the saddle. The flank is the thin portion of the lower part of each side of the saddle.

This is usually removed before roasting and can be made into a ragout or stew by following the recipes for beef, lamb or veal ragout or stew in this book.

However venison is served, a tossed green salad and tart jelly is the usual accompaniment.

POT ROAST OF VENISON

Follow the recipe given in this book for pot roast of beef (page 94).

Venison à La Mode: Follow recipe given in this book for beef à la mode (page 95).

Barbecued Venison: Follow recipe for barbecued short ribs of beef (page 100).

VENIBURGERS
5 minutes

Put sufficient venison or reindeer meat through the food chopper twice to make 2½ cups
½ cup fine soft bread crumbs

¼ cup milk
1 tablespoon minced parsley
1 teaspoon salt
⅛ teaspoon pepper
¼ teaspoon thyme
¼ cup red wine
3 tablespoons water

1. Combine the ingredients except the wine and water. Shape into large, round flat cakes, and brown on both sides in butter or margarine in the pressure-cooker.

2. Put in ¼ cup red wine and 2 tablespoons water; add the veniburgers, bring to 15 pounds pressure and process 5 minutes.

3. Serve with wine gravy made from the residue in the cooker.

Garlicked Veniburgers: Follow recipe for garlicked hamburgers on page 111.

BRAISED BEAR STEAK
15 minutes

1½ pounds bear steak cut   2 tablespoons fat
   1½ inches thick   1 teaspoon salt
2 tablespoons flour   ⅛ teaspoon pepper
1 teaspoon ginger   ½ cup water or liquid
¼ teaspoon clove   drained from vege-
                                    tables

1. Trim the steak removing excess fat. Cut meat in portions for serving.

2. Mix together the flour, ginger and clove, and pound and rub into the steak.

3. Melt the fat in the cooker and brown-heat the steak in it on both sides.

4. Add salt and pepper, and the liquid.

5. Close the cooker. Bring to 15 pounds pressure and process 15 minutes.

6. Make a gravy with the liquid in the pan.

7. Serve with wild rice or barley balls, and a highly flavored green vegetable, as Brussels sprouts or Savoy cabbage.

GENERAL DIRECTIONS FOR COOKING PHEASANT

No matter how pheasant is to be cooked it must first be dry-picked. It should not be skinned as both fat and flavor lie under the skin. Carefully remove any shot, then clean the birds. Scrub them inside and out with mild soapy water. Rinse well, then drain and dry on paper towels. Rub all over with cut lemon and plenty of butter or margarine.

ROAST PHEASANT

Prepare as directed above. Fill with dry-moist savory, cereal or fruit stuffing, and pressure-roast according to the recipe for chicken given in this book allowing 9 minutes to the pound (page 170).

Serve with a gravy made from the liquid in the cooker. Three tablespoons of dry white wine may be added if desired.

PHEASANT IN TOMATO SAUCE
20 minutes

1. Clean and disjoint the pheasant.
2. Brown-heat all over in butter or margarine; then place in the pressure-cooker.
3. Add 1 pint tomato sauce, either homemade or canned, one section of peeled garlic crushed, and ¼ teaspoon thyme.
4. Bring the cooker to 15 pounds pressure and process 20 minutes.

WILD DUCK

Duck should be preferably dry-picked. Pull out the pinfeathers with tweezers. Singe, clean and wash inside and out with salted water. Be sure all shot is removed.

Some gourmets recommend roasting duck with the head and feet on. I personally prefer to remove them, and truss the duck according to the directions for trussing poultry (page 165).

ROAST WILD DUCK

Prepare according to directions for pressure-roasting chicken (page 169). If desired, stuff with dry-moist savory, cereal or fruit stuffing. Pressure-roast 6 minutes to the pound for ducklings, and 7 minutes to the pound for full-sized birds.

Serve with orange sauce (page 240), or with a gravy made from the liquid in the pressure-cooker; serve with hominy grits or wild rice and tart jelly.

SMALL BIRDS

Small birds such as partridge, quail or grouse can be broiled, panned, barbecued, fried or cooked in any of the ways given in this book for preparing young ducklings, frying or broiling chickens, pigeons or squab.

CHAPTER XI

INTERESTING ACCOMPANIMENTS TO MEAT AND POULTRY

IT IS SURPRISING HOW GOOD AND HOW DIFFERENT MEAT and poultry dishes look and taste when served in new ways. Even a sprinkle of crisp fried croutons works wonders with a platter stew or ragout. As to roast beef, we all know how good Yorkshire pudding tastes with that. The English also have another interesting accompaniment to roast or boiled meat, the famous English suet pudding which not only tastes grand but makes the meat go farther. However, there's one thing to keep in mind when you plan to serve it. Be sure to provide plenty of gravy. By the regulation method a suet pudding takes from two to four hours to steam; but in the pressure-cooker it is ready to eat in a fraction of this time.

Recipes proportioned to serve four to six.
All measurements are level.
Timings are minutes required for pre-steaming and actual pressure-ing.
Cool cooker as soon as processing is done.

SAVORY ENGLISH SUET PUDDING
25 minutes pre-steaming—40 minutes at 15 pounds pressure

⅔ cup minced beef suet or raw beef fat

1½ teaspoons poultry seasoning

2 cups all-purpose flour

½ teaspoon salt

4 teaspoons baking powder

¾ cup cold water

1. Mix together the suet, flour, baking powder and poultry seasoning. Stir in the cold water.

2. Rub a quart-size metal mold (or use two pint-sized cans) with suet. (Be sure this mold will fit loosely into the pressure-cooker.) Put in the suet pudding mixture, filling ⅔ full. Tie waxed paper over the top.

3. Put the rack in the cooker. Put in pudding mold. Pour in 5 cups boiling water; close the cooker. Cook 25 minutes without bringing up the pressure at all; merely be sure that steam flows freely through the vent-pipe during this time. Then bring the pressure up to 15 pounds and process 40 minutes.

4. Slice and use as a garnish to a hot meat platter; pass plenty of gravy.

Quick Meat Tarts and Pies

Then there are interesting meat tarts and pies that can be quickly put together after the meat or poultry has been cooked. These are not the old-fashioned type of pie, when the meat or poultry mixture was put into a baking dish lined with pastry and baked slowly for two hours. Instead plain pie-crust shells or tart shells are baked, and kept on hand ready to re-heat and use when needed. Any of the platter stews, fricassees, ragouts or à la king dishes suggested in this book may be used as a filling. Just be sure the meat or poultry is cut in medium-sized "bites." The crispness of the pie-crust is a pleasant contrast to the gravy-rich meat or poultry filling, and is well worth the effort of making.

For not more than four people a full-sized pie shell makes an interesting service. But if serving buffet style, or for a little luncheon or supper party, individual tart shells are smart and dainty.

Or try deep-dish pie service. For this put the bubbling hot pressured stew, ragout or whatnot in a hot pottery dish and top with rich pie-crust, previously cut to fit and baked. Very nice! And the same idea can be applied to individual deep-dish meat pies.

RICH PIE-CRUST
(For all kinds of pie)

2 cups all-purpose flour
¼ teaspoon salt

¾ cup shortening (vegetable fat or lard)
6 tablespoons cold water

1. Sift together the flour and salt.
2. Add the shortening and chop in with a pastry blender or knife until the mixture looks mealy.

3. Add the cold water; mix in with a fork. Another tablespoon of water may be necessary to make the dough stick together, but do not use if it can be avoided.

4. Put the pastry on a large piece of waxed paper. Fold up and pat it together. Chill if convenient.

5. Roll to ⅛ inch in thickness and use as desired.

Pie-Crust Shells: Make rich pie-crust according to preceding recipe. Roll to ⅛-inch thickness. Invert a 9-inch pie plate or glass pie plate, and fit the rolled pastry over it. Prick several times with a fork to let any air escape. Bake in a hot oven, 400–425 degrees F. about 15 minutes.

Pie-Crust Tart Shells: Follow the preceding routine using inverted large shallow muffin pans instead of a single pie-plate.

READY-MIXED PIE PASTRY

Commercial pie-crust mix may be obtained in packaged or frozen form. Both give good results when used according to the directions given by the manufacturer.

DECORATING OPEN MEAT PIES OR TARTS

Reserve all small pieces of dough left after rolling. Fold together and roll out again. Cut into rounds, squares, diamonds or strips; bake and use as a topping for open pies.

About Spoon Bread

In the South spoon bread and ham are traditionally served together. Spoon bread can be pressured with the meat if the pressure-cooker has a compartment. If not, it may be pressured separately in custard cups, or it may be quickly baked while the meat is pressuring.

Spoon bread is good not only with ham, but with all forms of pork and with chicken and smoked tongue.

SPOON BREAD (Pressured)
6 minutes

1 cup white or yellow corn-meal	2 teaspoons baking powder
2 cups boiling water	2 tablespoons butter or margarine
1 teaspoon salt	1½ cups hot milk
	2 eggs

1. Stir the cornmeal into the boiling water.

2. Add the salt, baking powder and butter. Then the hot milk.

3. Pour into the eggs beaten light and transfer to 6 buttered good-sized custard cups. Tie waxed paper over the tops.

4. Place the rack in the cooker. Pour in ½ cup water. Place the custard cups on the rack. If there are too many to fit into the cooker, put in as many as possible, then place a round perforated rack or trivet on top of the custard cups. Stand the remaining custard cups on this. Close the cooker; steam without pressure 2 minutes; then bring slowly to 15 pounds and process 6 minutes.

5. Serve plain, or dusted with cinnamon or paprika, or butter-fried coarse bread crumbs.

Spoon Bread (baked): Make spoon bread mixture according to the preceding recipe using 2½ cups milk. Transfer to a buttered large shallow pie plate or a low baking dish. Bake about 35 minutes or until firm and golden on the top, in a moderate oven, 375 degrees F.

Green Corn Spoon Bread: Follow either recipe for spoon bread, adding to the batter 1 cup kernels of fresh green corn cut from the cob; or substitute ¾ cup well drained canned corn kernels.

Rice, Barley or Potato Rings or Borders

Any fricassee, curry, ragout or platter stew can be prettied up by serving in a rice, barley, or potato border or ring. But to be really attractive the service must be very neat and the platter should be deep and large. Big, colorful, Mexican pottery platters are suitable and glamorous.

Ways to make rice and barley rings are described in detail on page 310 of this book, so look them up if you wish to carry out any of the following suggestions:

Persian Rice Ring: Nice with chicken, duck or game birds.

Yellow Rice Ring: Good with any meat or poultry and some fish dishes.

Spanish Rice Ring: Suited to any plain cooked meat in gravy, such as lamb, veal or chicken fricassee.

Curried Rice Ring: Use with meat or poultry of any kind that is not highly seasoned.

Potato Borders or Rings: Are made with Duchesse potato. This is nothing more than very smooth mashed potato enriched with egg yolks, and made sufficiently moist with hot milk or cream to press easily through a pastry tube. However, if you do not have a pastry tube and bag, or a pastry tube gadget, you can form the mashed potato into a ring or border on the serving platter by heaping it up in shape with a tablespoon; but do not try to make it smooth. It should have interesting little peaks and indentations. In either case the border is put into a hot oven or under a low broiler and cooked a few minutes to firm and lightly brown the potato. To fashion a Duchesse potato border sounds like more work than it really is. But it is often worth while, for it is one of those inexpensive luxury touches that lifts a simple inexpensive service of meat or poultry into the gourmet class.

DUCHESSE POTATO

12 minutes

8 peeled medium-sized white potatoes	1 teaspoon salt
⅓ cup hot milk	¼ teaspoon pepper
2 tablespoons butter or margarine	2 beaten egg yolks
	1 extra egg yolk

1. Pressure-cook the potatoes and put them through a potato ricer, food mill or purée sieve directly into the hot milk mixed with the butter and seasonings. Beat thoroughly.

2. Then beat in the 2 egg yolks.

3. With a tablespoon form into a border on a fire-proof platter, or make the border by forcing the Duchesse potatoes through a large pastry tube. In working with a large amount of material like this it is preferable to use the old-fashioned pastry tube and bag.

4. Last brush over with the extra egg slightly beaten and mixed with ½ tablespoon milk. A nylon pastry brush is good for this purpose.

5. Then brown lightly and fill with the prepared meat or poultry.

Macaroni, Spaghetti and Noodles

COOKED AL DENTE

All meat and poultry dishes harmonize with these members of the paste family. But if they are made with gravy or a sauce, choose macaroni, spaghetti or noodles prepared al dente; that is, plain-cooked, not until soft, but so there is a little resistance to the teeth, al dente, when you bite through. This is especially good when seasoned with a little melted butter or margarine and minced chives or parsley.

Any ragout, fricassee or platter stew can be poured over macaroni, spaghetti or noodles al dente. However, to make serving easy, better break the long sticks into inch lengths before cooking.

Hamburgers, plain or cooked with wine, Veal Balls Italian Style, or crisp sausage may be served with macaroni, spaghetti or noodles al dente in spaghetti sauce (page 239).

CHAPTER XII

TOP-FLIGHT FISH AND SEA FOOD DISHES

Can all kinds of fish be pressure-cooked? Yes, they can. And pressure cooking is a big saver of flavor, kitchen hours and nutrients.

Like all fine foods, fish must be chosen with care, and prepared with intelligence. Then if you put aside prejudices and pre-conceived notions, you will discover that fish in its infinite varieties, pays big dividends in high nutrition and good eating.

In Scandinavia—land of the fisher folk—they serve a delicate fish pudding which you can pressure-cook.

In the Mediterranean countries, housewives are adept in fish cookery, and a fish stew often serves as the main dish with plain bread and a simple green salad. For instance, bouillabaisse (pronounced boo-ya-base) which is the famous fish chowder of Southern France.

In Russia, jellied marinated fish is a favorite dish, as well as fish boiled and served hot with a savory gravy.

The economical and clever Chinese have an ingenious way of steaming sea bass, pike, or butter fish, and serving it with soy sauce and vegetables.

Of course if fish are large, they must be filletted or cut into sections that will fit into the pressure-cooker. Whenever possible it is better to use filletted fish, as most of the bones are removed. However, the super-heated steam inside the pressure-cooker has a tendency to soften and cook small bones, making them edible, as when salmon is commercially canned. So even if a few bones are left in the fish don't worry. Just buy a set of "fish-pics"; those glorified tweezers for table use; put one at each person's place, and removing fish bones becomes neat and easy. But as the hostess you'd better start to use the "fish-pic" first, for they are not at all well known, although they distinctly belong in the Social Register of smart service.

Small fish may be cleaned and pressured whole. Some larger fish may be bent into a circle and trussed with tooth-picks to fit loosely the space in the cooker.

Shell fish are steamed in the shell without being allowed to come into contact with the water in the cooker.

Because of its delicate structure, fish should be kept cold until cooking. If possible cook the same day it is purchased.

Pointers on Buying Fish

In buying fresh fish, see that the *flesh* is *firm* and *elastic,* the *eyes bright.*

Fillets are boneless solid slices of meat with no waste, cut away from the sides of the fish, virtually ready for cooking. Ask to have the skin left on fillets; when cooked they will be juicier and have more flavor. One pound of fillets provides 3 servings.

Fish steaks are cross section cuts of fish. They are ready for cooking as bought and have few bones. Allow 2 to 3 servings to each pound for fish steaks.

"Dressed" is the term used to mean a whole fish from which the fins, entrails, tail and scales (if there are any) have been removed. The head of the fish is left on or not as requested. The heads are excellent to use in making fish-stock for chowders, sauces or molded sea food salads. Allow ½ pound per person for a whole fish weighed before dressing.

Tips on Handling Fish

If fish must be washed, do it quickly, using a strong salt solution (4 tablespoons salt to a quart of water). Do not sprinkle fish with salt and let it stand, as salt draws out the juices. The bloodline under the center backbone should always be removed before storing or cooking. The fish dealer will do this for you if requested.

How to Remove Fish Odors

Rub hands and utensils well with moistened salt before applying any soap.

Rinse dishes in salted warm water before putting them into dishwater.

Save that used squeezed-out lemon to rub over the hands after the cooking is finished.

Starring Fish

Like any stage star, a fish dish "performs" best in the right setting. If most of the menu is planned to harmonize with it, and one or two tart foods are chosen to accent the fish, ten to one the meal will be a success. Four short sentences sum up the salient points.

Include vegetables that are of contrasting color and not over-cooked.

Serve a plain tossed salad or vegetable relish.

For dessert plan fruit or a fruit dessert, or provide a fruit bowl.

If serving wine, choose Chablis or dry Sauterne.

Three Fish Dinners

Starred Recipes are in this Book

A SEA SHORE DINNER

Clam Chowder Manhattan

*Baked Fish   *Savory Stuffing   *Fish Gravy
*String Beans with Carrots   Bowl Salad
Grape Fruit Cocktail
Coffee

JUST TWO COURSES

*Steam Boiled Salmon   *Caper and Egg Sauce
Parslied Potatoes   *Tomato Platter
*Custards with Crushed Strawberries
Coffee

DINNER FOR GUESTS

*Shrimp Cocktail   *Fresh Relish Tray
*Mushroom Soup   Croutons
*Baked Fish Fillets   *Rich Gravy
*Broccoli with *Sauce Vinaigrette
*Peaches Stewed in Wine   Coffee

General Methods of Pressure Cooking Fish and Sea Foods

Recipes are proportioned to serve four to six.
All measurements are level.
Timings are minutes required for actual pressuring.
Cool cooker as soon as processing is done.

PANNED FISH

Use for fish fillets, fish steaks and small whole fish
6 minutes to the pound for one-inch thickness
5 minutes to the pound for thinner cuts

1. Cut the fish in portions for serving. Melt 2 table-spoons butter or margarine in the pressure-cooker and lightly sauté the fish fillets or steaks in this on both sides. Lift out the fish; put the rack into the cooker.

2. Pour in ½ cup hot water, or use the liquid drained from cooked vegetables; or use tomato or vegetable cocktail juice; or ¼ cup water and ¼ cup dry white wine.

3. Place the fish on the rack and season as desired. If there is more than enough fish for a single layer, cover with a piece of parchment paper after seasoning, put a second layer of fish on top of the parchment paper and season.

4. Close the cooker; bring to 15 pounds pressure and process 6 minutes to the pound for fillets of fish 1-inch thick. If thinner, 5 minutes to the pound is sufficient.

5. Transfer the fish to a platter and serve with a gravy or sauce made from the liquid in the cooker (page 215). Or serve with tomato or Spanish sauce, rarebit sauce, almond butter sauce or sauce vinaigrette (Chapter XIII).

Seasonings for Panned Fish: The seasonings may vary

with the fish. Salt and pepper are "musts." Paprika lends attractive color to white or light colored fish. A little lemon or lime juice squeezed over the fish before pressuring adds a pleasant flavor, and the fish may be dotted also with a little butter or margarine; minced fresh herbs or dried herbs (rubbed to a powder) lend variety, such as minced chives and parsley mixed, tarragon or dill.

PRESSURE-POACHED FISH FILLETS AND SMALL FISH

Fish fillets or steaks of all kinds may be pressure-poached. This method is also excellent for smelts, and all types of small fish that may be boiled or simmered. If fish fillets or steaks are used, cut in serving portions before pressuring.

1. Clean the fish unless fillets are used.

2. In the pressure-cooker put liquid to the depth of ½ inch. Use plain salted water; or salted water and dry white wine in equal parts; or the liquid drained from cooked vegetables; or chicken or veal-stock; or a little fish-stock to which one-fourth teaspoon mixed pickle spice has been added. Bring to boiling point.

3. Put the fish or fillets directly into the cooker. Close the cooker, bring to 15 pounds pressure and process 3 minutes for small fish, such as smelts, 5 minutes for fillets cut ½-inch thick, 6 minutes for fillets cut 1-inch thick.

4. Serve hot or cold with a sauce made with the liquid remaining in the pressure-cooker. Or serve as follows:

Hot Pressure-Poached Fish: Arrange on a heated platter and pour over and around a sauce of contrasting color. For instance—with poached salmon fillets use Danish or caper sauce; with poached halibut fillets, use creole, Chausseur or curry sauce. With smelts or other small fish, use sauce vinaigrette, sour cucumber sauce or fish cocktail sauce.

Cold Pressure-Poached Fish Platter: Arrange for service on a very cold platter, leaving ample room for a garnish.

Pour over the fish a suitable cold sauce of contrasting color, such as dill sauce with poached shad fillets, or soured cream or horse-radish sauce with poached salmon fillets. Or mask, that is spread cold fillets of fish with sauce tartare, and decorate further with sliced stuffed olives. Garnish with finely shredded coleslaw, plain, or made of red and white cabbage. Or use halved hollowed tomatoes filled with minced vegetable salad, cucumbers in soured cream dressing, or molds of jellied relish salad. Decorate further with parsley, chicory or water cress.

PRESSURE-BAKED WHOLE FISH OR FILLETS

This method can be used for medium-sized plain baked or stuffed fish of all kinds, or it can be used for thin fillets of fish put together with stuffing in sandwich fashion. If whole fish are to be used, they must not be too large. Consider the size of the cooker when purchasing the fish. If the head and tail are removed and the cleaned fish is gashed in 2 or 3 places on the back so it can be bent and tied into a circle, it can be fitted into the cooker and be removed without breaking, if the cooker has straight sides. If the cooker does not have straight sides, that is, no incurve at the top, a good-sized fish should be cut in halves or thirds before pressure-baking. In any case, to give the baked flavor and appearance, the fish should first be lightly brown-heated exactly as meat is brown-heated before putting in the cooker. If the fish is to be bent into a circle do this before brown-heating.

UNSTUFFED PRESSURE-BAKED FISH

1. Lightly brown-heat the fish on both sides in butter, vegetable or bacon fat. Season with a little salt and pepper and lemon or lime juice.

2. Place the rack in the cooker and pour in ½ cup hot water or enough to barely cover the bottom. It should not come up above the rack. Wrap the fish in a piece of parchment paper (first rinsed with cold water, pressed dry and then rubbed with oil), so it can be easily removed without breaking after cooking. Put in the fish. Close the cooker, bring to 15 pounds pressure and process 5 minutes to the pound.

3. If a slightly crisp finish is desired, remove the parchment paper; put the fish on a fireproof platter, brush with a little butter or margarine and brown further under a low broiler heat or in a hot oven until the fish is dried out. But do not overcook.

4. Serve with a garnish of water cress, parsley, grilled tomatoes, whole string beans in vinaigrette sauce, whole baby carrots in sweet-sour sauce, or molds of chopped spinach or beet greens and chopped beets mixed (first seasoned with lime juice or wine vinegar). Pour around the fish a suitable sauce or serve the sauce separately.

STUFFED PRESSURE-BAKED FISH

Follow the preceding recipe with this exception: First stuff the fish half-full of dry-moist savory stuffing, celery stuffing, vegetabilized or Mexican stuffing (page 88). Fasten the opening together with toothpicks and lace with white string.

BAKED STUFFED FILLETS OF FISH

1. Brown-heat the fish fillets as described, and cut each fillet into 2 sections. Season with salt and pepper.

2. On one section spread 1 tablespoonful of the desired stuffing almost to the edge. Top with the second piece of fillet and press together sandwich fashion.

3. Put the rack in the cooker; pour in ½ cup hot water.

4. Place the stuffed fillets on this; close the cooker, bring to 15 pounds pressure and process 7 minutes. Lift out the fillets with a broad spatula.

Sauces for Pressure-Baked Whole Fish or Fillets: Swedish mustard sauce; caper or dill sauce; tomato sauce (Chapter XIII).

If desired the fish may be well moistened with barbecue sauce before pressure-baking and served with extra barbecue sauce.

PRESSURE STEAM-BOILED FISH

For steam-boiling fish should not weigh more than 3 pounds. They may include blue fish, cod, haddock, carp, bass, sea trout, white fish, weak fish, etc. Or use solid pieces of fish weighing from 1 to 3 pounds, such as salmon, fresh tuna, halibut, cod or tile fish.

1. Put 1½ cups of boiling water into the cooker. Add 2 tablespoons diced celery, 1 tablespoon diced onion, ¼ teaspoon pickle spice, 1 teaspoon minced parsley and the juice of ½ lemon.

2. Season the fish with salt, pepper and a little lemon juice; wrap it in parchment paper first moistened with cold water. Place the fish directly in the cooker; bring to 15 pounds pressure and process 6 minutes to the pound.

3. Serve with fish gravy or sauce made from the liquid in the cooker, but be sure to add ingredients to make it of contrasting color. Or use caper or dill sauce, tomato sauce, creole sauce, spaghetti mushroom sauce (meatless type), Danish or Swedish mustard sauce (page 232). Small parslied pressured white potatoes and a green or yellow vegetable may be served on the same platter.

Pressured Steam-Boiled Shell Fish

SHRIMP, OYSTERS, CLAMS OR MUSSELS

1. Clean the shell fish thoroughly. This means to scrub the shells of oysters, clams, and mussels with a brush and well salted water. If there is plenty of time let clams stand in a pan of cold water containing ½ cup corn meal to 2 quarts of water. They will then open their shells to eat the corn meal and obligingly spit out the sand.

2. Put one cup water in the cooker or enough to barely come over the top of the rack. Put in the shell fish.

3. Close the cooker, bring to 15 pounds pressure and process as follows:

Small shrimp—2½ minutes

Large shrimp—5 minutes (Add 1 teaspoon tarragon or lemon juice)

Oysters—2½ minutes

Mussels—2½ minutes

Clams—5 minutes

Reserve the liquid in the cooker to use in making a sauce to serve with the shell fish, or to use as a basis for a cream of fish soup, a sauce for plain boiled or baked fish, or to use in combination with tomato juice to make a chilled Tomato Fish Cocktail, or hot Tomato Fish Bouillon.

Tomato Fish Cocktail: Combine equal parts of tomato juice and liquid drained from pressure-boiling shrimp, clams, oysters or mussels. Season highly with Worcestershire sauce, celery salt, a touch of tabasco or cayenne pepper, and lemon or lime juice. Or add a little dry sherry, dry white wine, a dash of basil or tarragon wine vinegar, or use both.

Pressure-Cooked Smoked and Salted Fish

FINNAN HADDIE, SMOKED CARP, SALT CODFISH, ETC.

7 minutes

1. Pour boiling water over the fish to cover. Let stand 20 minutes—longer if very salty. Then drain.

2. Place the rack in the pressure-cooker; cover with boiling water; add the juice of one-half lemon and ¼ teaspoon pickle spice if the flavor is desired. Put in the fish.

3. Close the cooker; bring the pressure to 15 pounds and process 7 minutes for fish 1-inch thick.

4. When done, remove the skin and any brown surfaces and serve the fish with a sauce of contrasting color. Tomato, Spanish or Creole sauce are suitable; or use curry, caper cream sauce, Danish sauce, or à la king sauce (see Chapter XIII, pages 231 to 244).

Fish Gravies Made from Liquid in the Cooker

FISH GRAVY NO. 1

2 tablespoons butter or margarine
2 tablespoons flour
¾ cup fish-stock
½ cup water
½ tablespoon minced parsley

1 tablespoon minced chives, grated onion, or chopped scallion
¼ teaspoon powdered tarragon or dill (optional)
2 egg yolks

1. Melt the butter or margarine; add the flour; gradually stir in the fish-stock from the cooker; add the water. Cook and stir until boiling. Add the parsley, chives and scallion, tarragon or dill; simmer 2 minutes.

2. Meanwhile beat the egg yolks with one tablespoon water, or use sherry or dry white wine. Carefully stir into the fish gravy, stirring and cooking all the time. Serve at once.

RICH FISH GRAVY NO. 2

Follow the preceding recipe substituting for the water an equivalent amount of thin sweet cream. Add to the sauce the grated rind of ¼ lemon and the juice of ½ lemon.

Garnishes for Fish

No matter when fish is served it always tastes better if it looks attractive. A successfully garnished fish is really a study in contrast. Light colored fish call for garnishes of vivid and darker colors. Dark fish need the highlights of light colors or gleaming white.

When well-chosen the vegetables, relishes or the sauce itself can become part of the garnish.

For the everyday service of plainly cooked fish we can garnish with wedges of lime or lemon; sprigs of parsley, chervil, water cress, tarragon or leaves of chicory; or we can use various salad relishes such as pickled beets or pickled carrots arranged in lettuce cups.

Vegetables Offer a Wide Selection as Garnishes: There are thin whole or halved slices of tomatoes; sweet or sour pickles; pickled beets, well-drained on paper towels; scallions cut relish style. Strips of scallions, or raw green or red sweet peppers. Coleslaw, chopped fine and piled in lettuce cups. Scooped out halved tomatoes, filled with minced vegetables put together with sauce tartare. Cups made from halving and scooping out lemons or limes for individual service and filled with sauce tartare or a soured cream sauce. Or use tiny patty-pan squash pressured and filled with sauce tartare, chutney, Chinese plum sauce or a relish.

Arranging Fish Platters

Nothing is more appetizing looking than a well-arranged fish platter. It can be made to look positively delectable, whether it consists of an important looking pressure-baked whole fish; or whether it stars baked stuffed fillets of fish, poached fish fillets or steaks, or is based on a large piece of pressure-boiled fish with a tantalizing sauce.

The platter itself must be very large. If the fish is flat in appearance or small, or if fillets are being used, raise them on thick slices of toast placed in the center of the platter; this helps immeasurably the appearance of the finished dish.

Large whole fish which still look very flat can be raised by placing on long toasted bread croustades made by cutting the crust and ends from a loaf of bread, slicing the bread in halves or thirds lengthwise, spreading with butter or margarine and toasting or baking until golden brown. In other words, the fish is best displayed if raised on a pedestal. And that pedestal of course must be edible.

But if the fish itself stands up rather high, try covering the platter with shredded lettuce to make an attractive background and bordering the edge with lettuce leaves, parsley or cress.

Whenever possible arrange the vegetables for the meal on the same platter with the fish, and serve the gravy or sauce separately.

Garnish the top of the fish itself with a smart row of halved slices of lemon or lime; with strips of red and white sweet green peppers; or with mushroom caps, or stuffed olives. Or use merely a little parsley, cress, fresh tarragon or sliced cucumber or mint for an interesting touch.

Fish-Stock

See page 43.

Fish Specials

FISH BOWLS
4 minutes

1 quart cleared fish-stock	¼ cup shredded seeded green pepper (optional)
½ cup shredded celery	
½ cup shredded carrot	
	8 small cleaned smelt or other very small fish

1. Put the fish-stock in the pressure-cooker and bring to a boil. Add the vegetables and the whole fish.

2. Bring to 15 pounds pressure and process 4 minutes.

3. Serve in small deep bowls or soup plates, glass if possible. In each put 1 or 2 fish and a little of the vegetable; strain over the liquid, which acts as a soup. Garnish with water cress. This can be used as a main course at a light luncheon or supper; or as a combination soup and fish course at a more elaborate luncheon or formal dinner.

BOUILLABAISSE (Americanized)
2 quarts

This delectable specialty of Mediterranean France, consists of a savory rich sauce which is poured over the assorted fish always characteristic of bouillabaisse. In spite of its formidable name, you will find this fish dish a rare treat.

Part I
Making the Bouillabaisse Sauce
4 minutes

½ cup peeled shallots or button onions
2 leeks (white portion)
1 peeled carrot
4 tablespoons salad oil
3 cups fish-stock (page 43)
¼ teaspoon fresh black pepper

½ teaspoon powdered thyme
1 peeled section garlic crushed
½ teaspoon saffron
½ teaspoon paprika
½ tablespoon butter
1½ cups dry white wine

1. Chop the shallots, leeks and carrot fine; then cook very slowly in the oil for 10 minutes (no pressure). Do not brown.

2. Add the fish-stock, and the spices except the paprika. Bring to 15 pounds pressure and process 4 minutes.

3. Cool and open the cooker. Heat the paprika in the butter. Add to the sauce. Stir in the wine, and salt sparingly to taste. Pour into a sauce-pan.

Part II
Finishing the Dish
6 minutes

1 fillet fresh water pike cut in four pieces
1 pound halibut steak cut in four pieces
1 porgy, boned and cut in four pieces
8 scrubbed little neck clams in the shell

8 scrubbed mussels in the shell
8 scallops (shelled)
4 lobster claws
4 or more pieces cooked lobster-tail meat
The bouillabaisse sauce

1. Put the prepared fish in layers in the pressure-cooker, the lobster, clams and mussels on top. Pour in the bouillabaisse sauce.

2. Close the cooker; bring to 15 pounds pressure and process 6 minutes.

3. Remove the fish and lobster meat carefully to individual heated shallow casseroles. Set aside the lobster claws and shell fish for garnishing; but leave the clams in the shells; remove the dark "beards" from the mussels.

4. Pour in the sauce. Top each serving with 2 mussels and 2 clams, with a lobster claw in the center for a touch of color.

SCANDINAVIAN FISH PUDDING

8 minutes for custard cups
12 minutes for single mold

1½ pounds fresh or frozen fish fillets	½ teaspoon salt
	¼ teaspoon paprika
2 tablespoons butter or margarine	1 tablespoon lemon juice
	Grated rind ¼ lemon
¾ cup hot milk	3 eggs
1 cup fine soft white bread crumbs	

1. Remove all bones and skin from the fish. Then put the fish through the food chopper twice using the medium-sized blade.

2. Add the butter to the milk; pour over the bread crumbs; add the salt, paprika, lemon juice and rind and combine with the fish.

3. Separate the eggs; beat the whites stiff and the yolks until creamy. Add the yolks to the fish mixture and stir thoroughly. Fold in the whites.

4. Turn into oiled custard cups, or a single mold that fits loosely into the pressure-cooker; tie waxed or parchment paper over the top. Before putting the cups into the pressure-cooker, put in the rack, then add 1¼ cups hot water. If the custard cups will not fit entirely in one layer, put in as many as possible; then place a perforated aluminum rack or ceramic inset on top, and stand the remaining custard cups on this.

5. Close the cooker; bring to 15 pounds pressure and process 8 minutes for custard cups; 12 minutes if a mold is used.

6. To serve hot, unmold and surround with Danish sauce, cream sauce containing oysters, or diced lobster meat, or use caper sauce or tomato sauce. Or serve the fish pudding very cold. In this case, spread lightly with sauce tartare and top with stuffed olives. Garnish with water cress or chicory and border with alternating slices of tomato and cucumber.

FISHBURGERS
4 minutes

1. Prepare the mixture for Scandinavian Fish Pudding. Shape into patties ½-inch thick and about 3 inches in diameter. Roll in flour and quickly brown-heat lightly on each side in butter or margarine.

2. Put one-half cup hot water or fish-stock into the pressure-cooker, but do not let it come up over the rack. Put the fish patties on this. If there are enough to more than cover the bottom, fit in a round piece of parchment paper to within an inch of the edge, and put a second layer on this. Close the cooker; bring to 15 pounds pressure and process 4 minutes.

3. Serve on halved hot toasted rolls, with fish gravy, catsup, or with tomato, creole or barbecue sauce (page 237); or serve on large slices of grilled or fried tomato and pass horse-radish sauce.

MUSSELS MARINIÈRE

2½ minutes

4 dozen mussels
½ cup dry white wine
3 tablespoons chopped on-
    ion
Few grains cayenne

⅛ teaspoon thyme
Bit of bay leaf
¼ cup butter
2 tablespoons minced pars-
    ley

1. Thoroughly scrub and wash the mussels. Remove all small shells.

2. Pour the wine into the pressure-cooker. Add the onion and seasonings; put in the rack.

3. Pile the mussels on top of the rack. Close the cooker, bring to 15 pounds pressure and process 2½ minutes when the shells will be opened. Cool and open the cooker. Remove the mussels and drain any liquid back into the pressure-cooker.

4. Remove the dark "beards" from the mussels, but leave the mussels in the shells. Add the butter to the liquid in the pressure-cooker and heat. Then strain. Add the parsley.

5. Serve the mussels piled in soup plates with the juice in small bowls or glasses in the center of each plate. Dip the mussels into this sauce. The proper eating utensil is a fish cocktail fork.

FINNAN HADDIE NEWBURGH

1½ pounds finnan haddie   Newburgh sauce

Pressure-cook the finnan haddie as described on page 215. Remove any brown outside bits and flake the fish coarse. Heat in Newburgh sauce (page 238). Serve on buttered toast or hollowed out crusty toasted rolls, in pastry tart shells or patty shells. Decorate with parsley or bits of canned pimiento.

SWEET-SOUR FISH CHINESE
4 minutes for fish ½-inch thick
6 minutes if 1 to 1½-inches thick

2 pounds pike, bass, mullet, or 4 small porgies

2 cups water or fish-stock

1 tablespoon cooking oil

2 scallions cut in inch lengths

½ cup diced firm portion cucumber

⅓ cup shredded white turnip

3 tablespoons sugar

¼ cup mild vinegar

2 tablespoons diced preserved ginger

2 tablespoons dry sherry

2 tablespoons cornstarch

1. Clean the fish; remove head, tail and fins. If too large to go into the cooker, cut in sections. Wrap in parchment paper which has been thoroughly moistened with cold water.

2. Put in the rack. Pour the water or fish-stock into the cooker; put the fish on the rack; close the cooker, bring to 15 pounds pressure and process 4 minutes for fish ½-inch thick, 6 minutes if 1 to 1½-inches thick.

3. Meantime heat the oil in an open pan; add the scallions and vegetables, and cook one minute. Then add the sugar, vinegar, ginger and sherry, and cook 1 minute longer.

4. Remove the fish from the cooker; place on a platter. Add the vegetable mixture to the liquid in the cooker. Then stir the cornstarch into 2 tablespoons cold water. Add to the fish liquid stirring constantly. Bring to a rapid boil and boil 2 minutes. Pour over the fish.

5. Accompany by pressured rice and a salad bowl or sliced tomato platter.

CURRIED SHRIMP
5 minutes

2 pounds large raw shrimp
2 tablespoons butter or margarine
⅓ cup chopped onion
2½ tablespoons flour
¼ teaspoon salt
⅛ teaspoon pepper
1 cup top milk or light cream

¾ cup shrimp liquid
1 teaspoon lemon juice
Pressure-cooked rice
1½ teaspoons curry powder
1 scallion (with tops)
Chutney sauce (optional)
Heated potato chips

1. Wash and pressure-cook the shrimp (page 214). Cool shrimp and remove the shells.

2. Then make the curry sauce. Melt the butter; add the onion and curry powder and fry 1 minute. Then stir in the flour and seasonings; gradually add the milk and the liquid drained from the pressured shrimp. Add the lemon juice and shrimp, and heat.

3. To serve, pile the rice in the center of a deep platter. Pour over the curried shrimp and garnish with the scallion minced fine. Pass chutney sauce and heated potato chips.

YUGOSLAVIAN CODFISH AND POTATO

1 pound salt codfish
8 white potatoes
½ cup olive or salad oil
2 tablespoons minced parsley

1 peeled section garlic crushed
2 teaspoons Worcestershire sauce
Salt and pepper to taste

1. Pressure-cook the salt codfish (page 215). Flake into bits.

2. Pressure-cook the potatoes in their jackets, then peel and mash. Add the codfish and mash; continue to mash and beat, adding the oil, parsley, garlic and Worcestershire sauce; season cautiously with salt and pepper.

3. Heat through a moment, and serve piled on a heated deep platter; top with a bit of parsley, and accompany with plain white or red and white cabbage slaw made with French dressing and a little minced green pepper; or pass a fresh relish tray.

Pressure Cooking Quick-Frozen Fish

Quick-frozen fish fillets, shellfish and frog's legs can all be pressure-cooked without de-frosting. The fine flavor is indescribably delicious, the timesaving incredible and there is no fish cooking odor.

General Directions for Pressure Cooking Quick-Frozen Fish without De-Frosting

1. Put seasonings and ¼ cup hot water (or other designated liquid) in the cooker.

2. Rub the rack with fat and put in the cooker.

3. Rinse the fish with cold water. If very thick, or too long to fit in, cut in halves with a heavy sharp knife. Place on the rack. Dust with salt, and any other seasoning desired.

4. Close the cooker. Bring to 15 pounds pressure and process the required time—from 5 to 8 minutes according to the thickness and texture of the fish.

5. Cool cooker at once.

6. Remove by means of tongs or a wide spatula so the fish will not break.

For that Browned Taste: Stop the pressuring 1 minute in advance. Arrange the fish on a fire-proof serving platter, dot with butter or margarine, and place under a pre-heated broiler for about 2 minutes, to brown lightly and finish cooking. Garnish or complete as any fish platter (see page 217).

Using the Liquid in the Cooker: There will be twice as much liquid in the cooker as when starting cookery, because the fish thaws in pressure-ing, releasing both water and juices. This liquid should be used as the basis for a fish gravy (see page 215). Or it may be chilled and combined with tomato juice for a fish cocktail, or an equal amount of milk may be added to make a cream fish broth, or a cream of fish soup with vegetables.

QUICK-FROZEN FILLETS OF COD OR HADDOCK
7 minutes

Do not de-frost. Rinse with cold water. Cut fillets crosswise in 4 sections. Follow the general directions adding a bay leaf to the water. Process 7 minutes. Serve with fish gravy, à la king sauce, or creole, caper, dill or Spanish sauce; see Chapter XIII.

Mackerel with Potatoes: Pressure halved, peeled potatoes with the mackerel, and serve New England style with cream sauce.

QUICK-FROZEN FILLET OF FLOUNDER OR SOLE
7 minutes

If the fillets are long, cut in 4 sections for individual servings.

Do not de-frost. Follow the general directions, seasoning

the flounder before cooking with salt and a little lemon juice if desired. Process 7 minutes.

Serve with fish gravy, tomato, creole, almond butter or rarebit sauce (see Chapter XIII).

Fillet of Flounder in Wine: Substitute ¼ cup dry sauterne or chablis for the water in the preceding recipe.

With Potatoes Quartered: White potatoes may be pressured with the flounder or sole.

POACHED QUICK-FROZEN RAINBOW TROUT
5 *minutes*

Do not de-frost. Rinse with cold water. Then carefully separate the fish leaving them whole. Place directly in the cooker with ¼ teaspoon salt, ¼ cup hot water, ¼ cup each sliced carrot, diced celery and a slice of onion if desired. Add ¼ teaspoon marjoram. Finish according to the general directions, processing 5 minutes. Serve in soup plates with the liquid, or with a fish gravy. (See page 215.)

Wine-Poached Rainbow Trout: Substitute dry sauterne or chablis for water; process as directed, and serve ice cold as a first course at dinner, or for the main course at supper or a summer luncheon. Garnish with slices of lemon and water cress. Accompany with a tossed green salad.

QUICK-FROZEN LOBSTER TAILS
7 *minutes*

Do not de-frost. Rinse with cold water. Pressure according to the general directions, processing at 15 pounds pressure for 7 minutes. With scissors cut out the thin shell from the tail. Serve hot "as is" with melted butter, and lemon wedges.

Almond Lobster: Cut lobster meat from the tails, dice and heat in almond-butter sauce, with or without 1 tablespoon of dry sherry. Serve in nests of rice, plain or pressured.

Lobster Newburgh: Dice pressured lobster tails. Heat in sauce Newburgh. Serve in pâté shells or on toast.

QUICK-FROZEN FILLETS OF OCEAN PERCH
8 minutes

Do not de-frost. Rinse with cold water. Cut fillets crosswise in halves. Follow the general directions. Process 8 minutes.

Small peeled white potatoes may be pressured at the same time.

Serve with fish gravy, with savory white sauce or cream curry sauce; see Chapter XIII.

Perch with Tomato: Substitute well-seasoned tomato juice for water; add ¼ teaspoon marjoram and use the liquid in making tomato sauce to serve with the perch.

QUICK-FROZEN FILLETS OF MACKEREL
6 minutes

Do not de-frost. Rinse in cold water. Cut fillets in halves crosswise; follow the general directions, adding ½ tablespoon lemon juice or wine vinegar to the water if a tart flavor is desired. Process 6 minutes. Serve with a gravy made from the liquid in the cooker or with tomato, Danish, caper or dill sauce.

USING PLAIN PRESSURED QUICK-FROZEN FILLETS OF FLOUNDER, COD, HADDOCK OR PERCH

Creamed: Cool, flake and combine with cream or Danish sauce. Serve in a ring of Duchesse potato.

Escalloped: Flake coarse, and combine with cream

sauce, and a little minced parsley. Cover with equal parts of bread crumbs and grated cheese, moistened with melted butter or margarine; brown in a hot oven.

Fish Salad: Cool and flake the fish. Add ¼ as much diced celery and several sliced red radishes; season with French dressing, blend with wine mayonnaise, and serve garnished with lettuce or water cress.

QUICK-FROZEN SHRIMP
5 minutes

Do not de-frost. Rinse with cold water. Pressure according to the general directions, processing 5 minutes at 15 pounds. Add ½ tablespoon lemon juice and ½ bay leaf to the water. Use for shrimp cocktail, shrimp cocktail salad plate (page 378), Swiss shrimp and egg salad (page 379), grapefruit shrimp salad (page 382), curried shrimp or in any way desired.

QUICK-FROZEN SCALLOPS
6 minutes (small)—8 minutes (large)

Do not de-frost. Wash scallops in cold water. Then process according to general directions. Use in any of the following ways:

Devilled Scallops: Cut pressured scallops into small dice. To 1½ cups add 1 cup Danish sauce, and season highly with ½ teaspoon each mustard and Worcestershire, and a little cayenne. Spread in scallop shells; cover with buttered crumbs and brown in the broiler.

Scallops Chausseur: Dice 1½ cups pressured scallops. Add to Chausseur sauce, heat and serve on pressured brown or white rice.

Scallops Creole: Dice 1½ cups pressured scallops. Add to creole sauce, heat and serve on white rice.

QUICK-FROZEN FROG'S LEGS
8 minutes

Allow 2 pairs of frog's legs to a serving. Do not de-frost. Rinse with cold water, dust with salt and add ¼ teaspoon thyme and ½ tablespoon lemon juice. Process according to general directions. For liquid use water, chicken stock or tomato juice. Drain, and serve in any of the following ways:

Broiled Frog's Legs: Drain on absorbent paper. Brush with melted butter, brown under the broiler, and serve with fish gravy made from the liquid.

Fried Frog's Legs: Brush with sweet or soured cream or slightly beaten egg; roll in fine dry crumbs; sauté in butter or margarine, and serve with mushroom sauce (page 233).

Frog's Leg Omelette: Lightly sauté 4 pairs of pressured frog's legs in ¼ cup butter. Add ½ teaspoon garlic salt, ⅛ teaspoon pepper and ¼ teaspoon nutmeg for seasoning. Prepare a plain omelette mixture; pour this over the frog's legs, and cook slowly until the omelette is set. Garnish with sautéd mushroom caps, and parsley or cress.

ABALONE CALIFORNIA STYLE

Slice abalone and sauté lightly. Measure ¼ cup California white table wine, such as Sauterne or Rhine Wine, into the pressure-cooker; put in the rack; place the abalone slices on it, bring to 15 lbs. pressure, and process 6 minutes. Serve with a sauce made from the wine in the cooker to which has been added ¼ cup sliced California almonds sautéed in 2 tablespoons butter.

Abalone Club Sandwiches: Pressure-cook abalone slices sautéed in butter and arrange as follows: Cover buttered toast with lettuce and thin slices of tomato; top with abalone; spread with Russian dressing; top with more tomato, minced scallions, and a slice of crisp bacon.

CHAPTER XIII

SAUCES AND GRAVIES WITH THAT PIQUANT TASTE

THE SAUCE MAKES THE DISH." WHETHER OR NOT THE preceding statement is true depends to a large extent upon how good a cook you are. In fact, in pressure cooking fewer sauces are needed, for all pressured foods retain their own full flavors, and if a discreet amount of seasoning is added before pressuring, the finished dish will be tops in taste without adding a sauce.

But if a plain-cooked food is being prepared, such as steam-boiled beef or fish, or a plain vegetable, certain quickly prepared sauces improve the dish or really are part of it.

Sauces for Sale

A number of excellent ready-to-use basic sauces are to be found in the stores, such as sauce tartare, mushroom, tomato and barbecue sauce; even reasonable facsimiles of true Bordelaise and Hollandaise. There is also canned Welsh rarebit to double for cheese sauce, and several brands of spaghetti sauce are good. If you are counting kitchen hours, such sauces will prove helpful. Just personalize them—make them individually yours—by adding some little unexpected touch, such as paprika to the Welsh rarebit, a squeeze of lime to the barbecue sauce, or chopped canned mushrooms and their liquid to the spaghetti sauce. And try putting ¼ teaspoon of fresh or dried herbs in canned tomato sauce and let stand a few minutes before heating. (That's to allow time to release the flavor of the herbs.)

But it's fascinating fun to turn out your own saucy sauce. Let's start with that useful old stand-by called white sauce when it is made with milk; cream sauce when made with light cream. This can be varied in many ways to use with vegetables, meats or fish, whether they are served as soon as pressured, or at a subsequent meal in the form of oddments—which is high-hat for leftovers.

Saucy Sauces

Recipes proportioned to serve four to six.
All measurements are level.

WHITE SAUCE

1 ½ tablespoons butter or margarine
1 ½ tablespoons flour

1 ½ cups milk
⅓ teaspoon salt
Few grains pepper

Melt the butter; remove the pan from the heat and stir in the flour and seasonings. Gradually add the milk, stirring continuously. A wire whisk is best for this purpose. Bring to a boil, simmer 2 minutes and use as desired.

Cream Sauce: Follow the preceding recipe substituting 1 ½ cups light cream for the milk.

Swedish Mustard Sauce: Make white or cream sauce and season with 1 ½ teaspoons prepared mustard.

Danish Sauce: Prepare white or cream sauce and beat in ¼ cup mayonnaise and one tablespoon lemon juice.

Savory White or Cream Sauce: Prepare white or cream sauce, beat in 2 hard-cooked egg yolks blended with 1 tablespoon minced parsley, and ½ tablespoon lemon juice.

CHEESE OR RAREBIT SAUCE

Prepare white or cream sauce. Add ¾ cup grated sharp Cheddar cheese, and cook and stir slowly until the cheese melts. Season with ½ teaspoon prepared mustard and ½ teaspoon Worcestershire sauce.

À LA KING SAUCE

Prepare white or cream sauce. Add ½ cup mushrooms and 2 tablespoons each, diced red and green sweet peppers, which have been sautéd together for 5 minutes in 2 tablespoons butter. Then stir into the sauce 2 egg yolks beaten light with one tablespoon sherry wine. Use at once.

WHITE OR CREAM CURRY SAUCE

In making white or cream sauce, add 1 teaspoon curry powder directly to the butter and let it bubble a moment before adding the flour. This brings out the flavor. Then finish according to the directions for white sauce. A little grated onion may be added if desired. Or try some minced chives.

SOURED CREAM MUSHROOM SAUCE

1 tablespoon flour
⅛ teaspoon dry mustard
⅓ teaspoon salt
¼ cup liquid from canned mushrooms

1 cup soured cream
½ tablespoon lemon juice
¾ cup mushroom stems and pieces (a 4 oz. can)

In a double-boiler top combine the flour, mustard, and salt. Stir in the mushroom liquid, and when smooth, the soured cream. Add the lemon juice. Cook and stir over hot water until the sauce thickens. Then add the mushrooms, and heat thoroughly.

BROWNED BUTTER

In a small thick frying pan melt the required amount of butter. Cook and stir slowly until the butter turns color and becomes a medium-brown. Use in seasoning vegetables and cereals doubling as a vegetable.

ALMOND BUTTER

4 tablespoons butter	1 teaspoon lemon juice
1 ounce blanched almonds sliced lengthwise	

Melt the butter in a small heavy frying pan. Add the almonds and sauté very slowly until they are a light brown. (Do not let the butter turn dark.) Then add the lemon juice.

CAPER SAUCE

2 tablespoons butter or margarine	1½ cups hot water
	¼ cup capers
¼ teaspoon salt	1 tablespoon vinegar from caper bottle
⅛ teaspoon pepper	
2 tablespoons flour	1 teaspoon minced parsley
1 teaspoon lemon juice	

Melt the butter; add the seasonings and flour and stir until smooth. Then gradually stir in the hot water and let come to a rapid boil. Add the capers, the caper vinegar, parsley and lemon juice and simmer for a minute.

Caper Cream Sauce: Follow the recipe for caper sauce using only 1 cup hot water. When the sauce is made, beat in ½ cup soured cream.

Dill Sauce: Follow the recipe for caper sauce, omitting the capers and caper vinegar. Instead add 1 tablespoon minced, chopped fresh dill or ¼ cup chopped dill pickles

BRIGHTENING UP TOMATO SAUCE
(Commercially Canned)

Excellent plain tomato sauce may be purchased in canned form. This is rather bland in flavor but can be individualized by seasoning in different ways.

Add ½ teaspoon mixed pickle spice to the canned tomato sauce while heating. Then strain before serving.

Add to plain tomato sauce while heating any of the following: chopped fresh herbs, 1 tablespoon minced parsley, 1 teaspoon minced dill, ½ teaspoon minced basil, or 1 tablespoon minced chives. Or use instead ¼ teaspoon dry powdered marjoram, thyme or mixed dried herbs.

Or season plain canned tomato sauce with a meat condiment, or with celery, garlic or onion salt, or a dash of herb-flavored vinegar.

TOMATO SAUCE

3 tablespoons butter or margarine
4 tablespoons flour
½ teaspoon mixed pickle spice
½ teaspoon sugar

1 cup sieved canned tomatoes or purée
1 cup brown soup-stock or 1 cup water and a bouillon cube
Salt and pepper to taste

Melt the butter; stir in the flour; add the seasoning, and gradually stir in the tomato and stock. Bring to boiling point, simmer 2 minutes; rub through a purée sieve. Use with meat, fish, eggs, vegetables or savory cereals.

Creole Sauce: Follow the recipe for tomato sauce with this exception: Sauté in the fat 2 tablespoons each chopped onion, chopped mushrooms and chopped green peppers. When done, stir in 6 sliced stuffed olives. If convenient season with filé powder (the famous creole seasoning made from powdered sassafras leaves).

QUICK SPANISH SAUCE

To make a quick Spanish sauce: sauté in 1 tablespoon butter, 1 peeled sliced onion, 1 crushed section of garlic, ½ diced sweet green pepper and 1 small bay leaf. Add 1 can tomato sauce. When hot remove the bay leaf and stir in 6 sliced stuffed olives.

CHAUSSEUR SAUCE

2 tablespoons butter or margarine	2 (4 oz. cans) tomato sauce
2 tablespoons minced onion	1 teaspoon meat extract
1 cup sliced fresh or canned mushrooms	½ cup any dry white wine
	2 tablespoons brandy

1. Melt the butter and cook the onion in it until yellowed. Strain out the onion. Add the mushrooms to the remaining butter and sauté slowly for 3 minutes. Stir in the tomato sauce and meat extract.

2. Add the wine and simmer until the sauce becomes thick, about 15 minutes. Season to taste with salt and pepper. Stir in the brandy.

3. Use with beef, poultry, veal, eggs or special vegetable dishes, such as pressured broccoli, whole cauliflower, or braised whole tomatoes filled with risotto, shrimp or chopped ham in dry-moist stuffing.

BARBECUE SAUCE

½ cup butter or margarine
2 tablespoons minced onion
½ section garlic crushed
¾ teaspoon prepared mustard
¾ teaspoon salt

1 tablespoon chili powder
¾ cup tomato juice
¼ teaspoon sugar
2 tablespoons lemon juice
¼ cup water

Melt the butter; add the onion and garlic and simmer until the onion is tender but not brown. Add remaining ingredients and boil 10 minutes.

WINE BARBECUE SAUCE

⅓ cup salad oil
1 peeled section garlic crushed
2 tablespoons grated onion
½ teaspoon salt
½ teaspoon pepper

¼ teaspoon thyme and marjoram
½ cup dry white wine for poultry or
½ cup dry red wine for dark meat or game

Combine in a jar, cover, let stand at least 2 hours. Shake well before using.

MINT SAUCE

1½ tablespoons sugar
⅓ cup minced fresh mint leaves or 2 tablespoons dry mint

½ cup mild plain or wine vinegar
¼ teaspoon salt
Few grains pepper
1 teaspoon onion juice

Combine sugar and mint and stand at room temperature for 30 minutes; then add remaining ingredients and mix well.

This sauce can be made in advance in a jar and kept refrigerated for 2 or 3 weeks.

HOLLANDAISE SAUCE
(A Reasonable Facsimile)

½ cup butter or margarine   1½ tablespoons lemon juice
2 teaspoons flour   ⅛ teaspoon paprika
4 egg yolks   ¼ teaspoon salt
                 ½ cup boiling water

1. Cream together the butter and flour and gradually work in the egg yolks, one at a time.

2. Stir in the lemon juice and seasonings and add the boiling water. Cook and stir over hot water until the sauce is thick and smooth.

3. This sauce will not separate and can stand before serving. Use with fish, or vegetables such as broccoli or asparagus.

NEWBURGH SAUCE

2 tablespoons butter   3 tablespoons dry sherry or
2 tablespoons flour   2 tablespoons sherry
⅓ teaspoon salt   and   1   tablespoon
¼ teaspoon dry mustard   brandy
1½ cups light cream   1 cup diced cooked shrimp
2 egg yolks   or lobster or a mixture
                                                    of diced shell fish

1. Melt the butter and stir in the flour and seasonings. Gradually add the cream, stirring constantly. Bring to boiling point.

2. At this point add the fish.

3. Let stand to become very hot. Beat the egg yolks light and add the sherry and brandy.

4. Stir into the hot Newburgh sauce; heat a few seconds and serve at once.

BUTTER SAUCE FOR STEAMED CLAMS OR MUSSELS

Melt the desired amount of butter in a double-boiler. Add to 1 cup of melted butter, 1 tablespoon lemon juice, ¼ teaspoon Worcestershire sauce, and if the flavor is liked. a little minced tarragon or basil.

RELISH SAUCE

Melt ¼ cup butter; add ¼ cup pickle relish (not too sweet), and re-heat.

SPAGHETTI MUSHROOM SAUCE (MEATLESS)

¼ cup butter or margarine
¼ cup diced onion
½ section garlic peeled and sliced
2 tablespoons flour
⅛ teaspoon powdered ginger
¼ teaspoon powdered oregano

1 (4 oz.) can tomato sauce or use 2 tablespoons tomato purée and ½ cup water
1 cup beef bouillon or 1 cup water and 1 bouillon cube
¼ cup liquid from canned mushrooms
¾ cup mushroom stems and pieces in 1 (4-oz.) can

1. Melt the butter or margarine in a small heavy saucepan. Add the onion and garlic and sauté slowly until golden.

2. Stir in the flour and spices. When smooth and bubbling add the tomato sauce (or the purée mixed with the water).

3. Gradually stir in the beef bouillon and mushroom liquid. Cook and stir over a low heat until the sauce thickens. Then add the mushrooms and re-heat.

Spaghetti Mushroom Sauce (with Meat): Follow the preceding recipe with this exception: Add ¼ pound chopped, fresh beef to the butter, onion and garlic, and sauté slowly for 4 minutes. Then finish as directed. If the sauce seems too thick. thin with a little tomato juice or beef bouillon.

SAUCE VINAIGRETTE

½ cup salad oil
⅓ teaspoon salt
1 tablespoon minced sour pickles
1 tablespoon minced green pepper

⅙ teaspoon ground peppercorns
1 tablespoon minced parsley
⅔ teaspoon scraped onion
3 tablespoons plain or mixed herb vinegar

Add the various flavorings and seasonings to the oil and set aside to marinate or ripen at least 1 hour. Beat in the vinegar and serve cold.

This sauce can be served cold on cold vegetables, chilled fillets of fish, fish loaves or stuffed eggs; or it can be stirred directly into pressured vegetables such as greens, string beans, carrots, turnips or broccoli which are to be served hot.

ORANGE-CURRANT-MINT SAUCE

1 glass currant jelly
Grated rind ¼ orange

Juice of 1 large orange
1 tablespoon minced mint

Slightly melt the jelly in the top of a double-boiler. Beat in the remaining ingredients. Serve warm or cold.

Soured Cream Sauces

Many interesting sauces have been developed recently with soured cream as a base, and they are delicious. They are cold or hot, and are used with vegetables, either cooked or raw; with lean meat such as tongue or veal loaf; or with broiled or boiled fish or fish loaves; or with potato, tomato, or cucumber salad. Be sure to use commercially cultured soured cream rather than cream that has been allowed to stand in the room and become sour by natural methods, for cream of that type is likely to develop a bitter taste. If you must sour sweet cream quickly, this is the best way to do it:

To Sour Sweet Cream: Add 1 tablespoon lemon juice to ½ pint of sweet light or heavy cream. Stand at room temperature about 30 minutes.

SOURED CREAM HORSE-RADISH SAUCE

1 cup soured cream
1 tablespoon sugar
¼ cup prepared horse-radish

½ tablespoon plain or herb-flavored vinegar
¼ teaspoon salt

Combine and use.

SOURED CREAM CURRY SAUCE

1 cup soured cream
¼ teaspoon salt

1 tablespoon lime juice
1½ teaspoons curry powder

Combine the soured cream and salt. Blend the curry powder with the lime juice and add. This is especially good with cold chicken or chopped ham loaf, or with jellied chicken or veal loaf.

SOURED CREAM CUCUMBER SAUCE

1 cup soured cream
¼ teaspoon sugar
¼ teaspoon salt
⅛ teaspoon pepper

1 tablespoon lemon juice or
   herb-seasoned vinegar
½ cup grated firm portion
   cucumber

Combine the ingredients in the order given and serve. This is especially good with any type of cold meat or fish loaf, with hot or cold fish fillets, or with a cold meat platter.

FISH COCKTAIL SAUCE

½ cup tomato catsup or
   chili sauce
2 tablespoons lemon juice
6 drops tabasco sauce

1½ teaspoons meat condi-
   ment sauce
6 tablespoons minced celery
3 tablespoons horse-radish
Salt and pepper to taste

Combine, chill and serve.

RED WINE GRAVY

⅓ cup brown soup-stock
1 cup dry red wine
1 tablespoon lemon juice
1 teaspoon sugar

½ tablespoon prepared
   horse-radish
⅛ teaspoon paprika
Salt and pepper to taste

Combine the ingredients and heat gradually to boiling point. Use at once as unthickened platter gravy with any red or dark smoked meat.

CATSUP SAUCE

⅓ cup melted butter or margarine

1 tablespoon lemon juice
¾ cup tomato catsup

Combine, heat and serve. Use with steamed clams, fish, or smoked meat.

MADEIRA WINE SAUCE

2 tablespoons butter
3 tablespoons flour
1½ cups well seasoned brown soup stock or 1 teaspoon meat extract dissolved in 1½ cups hot water

¼ teaspoon paprika
2 tablespoons minced celery
¼ cup Madeira wine

Melt the butter and let it slightly brown. Stir in the flour and cook until lightly browned, stirring frequently. Gradually add the soup stock, paprika and celery; simmer 10 minutes. Just before serving stir in the Madeira.

CHINESE PLUM SAUCE

Pressure 5 minutes—Simmer about 40 minutes

1 quart sour plums, stones removed
½ cup raisins
½ cup vinegar
1 cup water

1¼ cups brown sugar
1 teaspoon mixed spices
1 teaspoon salt
½ teaspoon ginger
Paprika and cayenne pepper to taste

1. Combine the ingredients in the pressure-cooker. Bring to 15 pounds pressure and process 5 minutes. Cool the cooker.

2. Rub the plum mixture through a coarse sieve; then simmer in an open utensil until thick like marmalade, about 40 minutes. Use cold with pork, poultry or fish.

SAUCE TARTARE

1 cup mayonnaise
2 tablespoons minced sour pickles
½ tablespoon minced chives or scallions

1 tablespoon minced sweet pickle relish
½ tablespoon minced parsley
1 teaspoon lime juice (optional)

The mayonnaise should be well chilled. Beat in the various ingredients just before serving. For a flavor "exotique" grate in the skin of one-fourth of a lime.

Making Gravy

Pan Gravy: The liquid remaining after meat or poultry has been pressure-roasted is highly concentrated, and may be used "as is" for pan gravy; or it is an excellent foundation for thickened gravy. If the meat has been well trimmed before cooking this liquid will rarely contain too much fat; but if it looks as though more than 2 tablespoons of fat are floating on the top, remove the excess before using, by blotting it off with a twisted piece of a paper towel.

Thickened Gravy: Remove the meat, poultry or game and make the gravy in the pressure-cooker. For approximately a pint of gravy, stir 3 tablespoons wheat flour smooth in ¼ cup cold vegetable liquid or water. Stir into the boiling meat liquid in the pressure-cooker; then gradually stir in sufficient additional liquid to make 2 cups of gravy, or 1 pint; 1½ cupfuls of liquid is about the right amount. Boil and stir slowly without pressure for 2 minutes. Scrape up all residue from the bottom of the cooker at this time. The liquid chosen will give the desired flavor. Season to taste. Gravy made by this method should not be lumpy. But if lumps are present put it through a sieve, for lumpy gravy is a cookery unforgivable!

Brown Gravy: Make thickened gravy as described using *browned flour,* that is dry flour baked light brown in a hot oven. Do this in a pie plate, a cupful at a time. Stir occasionally. Browned flour improves both color and flavor. Always keep 2 or 3 cupfuls in a covered glass jar ready to use. To give gravy a very rich dark brown color add a little commercial liquid gravy-seasoning. And to strengthen the meat flavor, add a little dissolved meat extract or a bouillon cube.

Tomato Gravy: Make thickened gravy as described using tomato juice as the liquid. Add one-fourth teaspoon sugar.

Vegetable Gravy: Make thickened gravy as described using, instead of water, the liquid drained from cooked vegetables; or use equal parts plain or potato water and vegetable juice cocktail. Liquids drained from cooked potatoes and all bland vegetables are suitable to use. Do not use liquid drained from "strong" flavored vegetables such as turnips, spinach, beet tops or dandelions, and use onion water only when an onion flavor is desired.

Onion Gravy: Chop enough raw onion to make 1 cupful, and steam-fry by cooking a few minutes in 1 tablespoon each water and meat drippings, margarine or vegetable fat. When pale yellow in color add to the meat liquid in the pressure-cooker, and follow the directions for making thickened gravy.

Mushroom Gravy: Substitute chopped mushrooms for onions in the preceding recipe. Season with a trace of nutmeg.

Milk Gravy: Make thickened gravy as described using as the additional liquid, fluid milk or equal parts of water and evaporated (unsweetened) canned milk.

Soured Cream Gravy: Follow directions for making thickened gravy, using 1 cup water or vegetable liquid, smoothly blended with ½ cup soured cream.

Seasoning Gravy

It might be said that the gravy often makes the meat, especially when the meat itself is naturally bland in flavor, such as veal, boiled beef, and in case of poultry, young birds such as baby broilers or ducklings. With whatever food the gravy is to be served, it should be pleasantly and suitably seasoned. But subtly, please, so that the flavor of the seasoning does not overpower the taste of the meat. To season enough and not too much, is an art, but it is one that can be cultivated, and one you should master if you aspire to become famous as a cook. Much depends upon imagination. Add experience, through the time-tested, trial-and-error method, and you will soon become a good seasoner! The following suggestions will prove helpful in making gravies that are lickin' good.

Beef Gravy: Season with a choice of garlic salt, or crushed fresh garlic; or a little prepared mustard, Worcestershire or other meat condiment sauce, or marjoram.

Lamb Gravy: Season with capers and a tablespoon of the caper vinegar in the bottle; with chopped fresh or dried mint, dill or rosemary, or with crushed fresh garlic or garlic salt. Or to be truly epicurean add a mere sprinkle of crushed juniper berries.

Veal Gravy: Season with onion juice, crushed fresh garlic or garlic salt; with oregano, dried or fresh minced thyme; or with minced fresh or powdered dried celery leaves, or parsley; or add a touch of garlic vinegar, or lemon or lime juice. Soured cream is also especially good.

Pork Gravy: Use fresh minced or dried thyme or sage. But go easy on the latter. A very little poultry seasoning is good, so is a dash (about 1 teaspoon) of basil or garlic vinegar.

Chicken or Rabbit Gravy: Season with fresh minced or powdered dried celery leaves; with capers and 1 tablespoon of vinegar from the caper bottle; or with fresh minced or dried thyme, savory, tarragon or marjoram. Or add chopped sautéed mushrooms, fresh or canned, and their liquor.

Turkey Gravy: Season with dried thyme or marjoram, a little tomato-herb blend, or with chopped sautéed fresh or canned mushrooms and their liquor.

Duck or Goose Gravy: Add a choice of a little basil, marjoram, savory, thyme, tarragon or poultry seasoning.

CHAPTER XIV

PRESSURE COOKING FRESH AND FROZEN VEGETABLES

Y<small>OU HAVE NEVER KNOWN THE TASTE OF FRESH VEGE-</small>tables unless you have eaten them pressure-cooked, for every morsel of deliciousness is retained. This means full food values have been conserved, including the precious minerals, the delicate vegetable sugars, and soluble proteins, and a high quota of vitalizing vitamins. There is no "wash out" of these valuable nutrients. Not a whit is lost in steam, for none escapes. None need be lost in cooking, for the amount of water needed in pressure cooking is so small it may be served with the vegetables as a sauce. There's not a bit of oxidation—that destroyer of vitamins —because air is entirely driven out in pressure cooking and consequently does not come in contact with the food. And in addition to all this, the vegetables are cooked in a fraction of the usual time and have finer color and texture.

Choice of Vegetables

Be sure to start with vegetables as near garden-fresh as possible. When purchasing, choose crisp vegetables, with fresh-looking tops or leaves. Vegetables that are water-sprayed, iced, or encased in cellophane and kept cool have higher nutritional value. And vegetables flown by air-freight, even from distant places, have garden-fresh nutrition.

Preparation of Vegetables for Pressure Cooking

As a general rule, prepare the vegetable in the form in which it is to be served. Dice, slice, shred, schnitzel or julienne to your heart's content as long as you pressure-cook immediately; otherwise cook whole, for oxidation of the vitamins starts while the prepared vegetables stand exposed to air anywhere. And "oxidation" means that the vitality of the vitamins is decreased or entirely destroyed. When oxidation is taking place, the food turns dark or rusty-looking when cut or peeled and exposed to the air; and some foods begin to discolor almost at once. For example, peeled Jerusalem artichokes or oyster plant, sliced bananas or diced apples.

When cooked by ordinary methods the likelihood of oxidation is increased, for the many cut sides of the vegetables act as increased surfaces for oxidation. When pressure-cooked, as just explained, there is no air in the cooker and consequently there is no oxygen present to cause oxidation.

If vegetables are to be peeled, keep the peeling thin. A good vegetable peeler is much easier to use than a knife, and insures thin peeling. If a vegetable is to be pressured with the skin on, as is often the case with beets, white or sweet potatoes and yams, it should first be well scrubbed.

To Julienne Vegetables: Trim and peel if necessary; slice, place on a vegetable board and with a sharp knife cut into match-like strips.

To Shred Vegetables: Place the vegetable on a board and shred with a sharp knife. Or use the "shredder" on one side of a four-sided grater; or better still purchase a commercial shredder, which is easy and quick to use, and not expensive.

To Purée Vegetables: Pressure-cook; remove the skin if not already done; then put through a food-mill or purée sieve with the necessary seasonings.

To Cook Vegetables Separately from Other Foods

When vegetables are to be pressured with meat or fish and the flavors are to be kept separate, prepare as desired, and use a divider if you have one; or before pressuring tie each vegetable in a sheet of parchment cooking paper first wet with cold water, then pressed as dry as possible. This does not lengthen the time needed to cook the vegetables. The parchment paper may be rinsed with warm water, dried and used again and again.

If you are fortunate enough to own a cooker with compartments for cooking foods separately, put the prepared vegetable in one of these with 1 tablespoon of hot water. In this case the parchment paper is not needed.

Seasoning Vegetables

Sprinkle sparingly with salt before pressuring. If special spices or herbs are to be used add before cooking. When ready to serve add a dash of freshly ground black pepper if desired, and ½ tablespoon of butter or fortified margarine (or equal parts of each) to 2 cups (1 pint) of the cooked vegetable. If there are members of the family who do not like butter or margarine, or who are on a diet and cannot eat them, melt and serve it in a small pitcher. Each person then can butter his own.

Brown Butter: This may be used in seasoning any vegetable that is not light colored for in this case it causes unattractive discoloration. When butter is browned, a richer, fuller taste results, and the flavor is extended, so less is needed.

To brown butter put it in a small heavy sauce-pan, melt and brown slowly until it is the color of maple syrup.

Special Butters

Suitable seasonings are sometimes creamed into butter or fortified margarine, or a combination of both, and used to dress vegetables; or they are made into "butter" balls, and served with them, as with green corn, and stalks of asparagus.

Lemon Butter: Cream 1 teaspoon lemon juice into ¼ cup butter or fortified margarine.

Parsley Butter: Cream 2 tablespoons minced parsley into ¼ cup butter or fortified margarine.

Chives Butter: Cream 2 tablespoons minced chives into ¼ cup butter or fortified margarine.

Herb Butter: Cream 1 teaspoon minced tarragon or basil into ¼ cup butter or fortified margarine.

Soured Cream: Commercially soured cream may be used plain for seasoning all kinds of vegetables. Merely add salt and pepper.

Soured Cream with Lemon or Lime Juice, added to taste (with or without a few grains of sugar), may be used to season any vegetable that is slightly sweet, such as carrots, parsnips or beets.

Soured Cream Mixed with Chopped Chives, or a trace

of minced tarragon, may be used with white potatoes, cucumbers, string beans or braised whole tomatoes.

Tart Butter-Lime Dressing is made by barely melting 2 tablespoons butter or margarine, and stirring in 2 tablespoons lime juice. This is especially good with string beans, beets, carrots, cabbage, cauliflower, brussels sprouts and broccoli, especially when they are to be served with fish or smoked meats.

French Dressing is an excellent seasoning instead of butter or margarine for all types of hot greens, for cooked diced or shredded carrots, turnips, beets or string beans, or for cooked shredded cabbage. Use 1 tablespoon to a pint (2 cups) of the prepared vegetable. Drain the vegetable after pressuring, add the French dressing and keep warm for a few minutes until absorbed. Any kind of French dressing may be used. But for epicurean service I suggest Lime French Dressing (see page 381).

Salt Pork, Fat Back or Canadian or American Bacon are old-fashioned seasonings used in cooking greens, string beans, kale and cabbage. In pressure cooking, cut the meat into dice, and sauté in the cooker till crisp and done (no pressure). Remove the cooked meat but leave in 3 tablespoons of the fat. Add the required amount of water. Put the greens into the cooker and pressure the required length of time. Serve garnished with cooked meat. Or use fat drained from cooking bacon as a seasoning. In this case always cook the fat with the greens.

SWEET AND SOUR VEGETABLES

This method of seasoning may be used for pressured beets, turnips, carrots or parsnips. Pressure-cook as described in the timetable, peeling and leaving them whole; or slice, quarter or dice, according to the vegetable and how it is to be served.

While pressuring prepare the sauce as follows:

Sweet-Sour Sauce

1. Combine ½ cup cider vinegar and ½ cup sugar (scant). Bring to boiling point.

2. Stir in ½ tablespoon cornstarch blended smooth with 1 tablespoon cold water. Cook and stir 2 minutes. Add to the vegetable and let stand to season for 5 minutes in a warm place.

3. Just before serving add 1 tablespoon butter to a pint of vegetable. A little minced parsley, mint or dill may be sprinkled in if desired.

Spices or Herbs to Season Vegetables

All dried herbs should be rubbed to a powder before using

Baked or Boiled Dried Beans of All Kinds: Pepper, mustard, all-spice.

Beets: Clove, bay leaf, mint.

Cabbage: Black pepper, caraway or celery seeds, curry powder, tomato sauce.

Carrots: Minced mint, basil, parsley, tarragon, trace of garlic, or use powdered dried mint or tarragon.

Red Cabbage: All-spice and chopped apple.

Cauliflower: Poppy or celery seed, minced parsley or chervil.

Egg Plant: All-spice, sage, mint.

Corn (fresh): Paprika, pepper.

Greens: Marjoram, basil, thyme, garlic salt, trace of prepared mustard, or smoked or salt meat.

Kidney Beans (fresh or dried): Chili powder or bay leaves.

Lima Beans: Parsley or summer savory, cayenne pepper, celery or onion salt.

Mushrooms: Nutmeg, marjoram, tarragon vinegar.

Onions: Celery seed, or brown butter with curry.

Spinach: Nutmeg, almost any herb, lemon or lime juice or tomato.

Sweet Potatoes and Yams: Nutmeg, clove, cinnamon with or without honey, and butter or fortified margarine.

Swiss Chard: Onion salt.

Summer Squash and Zucchini: Chopped chives, paprika, fried onions.

Succotash: Nutmeg.

String Beans: Bay leaf, whole cloves, garlic.

White Potatoes: Paprika, nutmeg.

Winter Squash: Cinnamon and honey or brown sugar; minced dill and a little herb vinegar.

Tomatoes (stewed or braised): Add a bit of bay leaf or small cheese-cloth bag of mixed pickling spice. Or try a little powdered clove, basil, all-spice, thyme, dill, or garlic or celery salt.

Herb-Flavored Vinegars with Vegetables

Try a little herb-flavored wine vinegar if you like a tart pungent taste with cooked greens, with sweet-tasting vegetables such as carrots, beets or parsnips, or with string beans, cabbage, Brussels sprouts, broccoli, kale or sliced turnips. It's different, and transforms the vegetable into a new kind of hot salad. There is quite a selection of these flavored vinegars available, including basil, garlic, mixed herb, tarragon and herb-'n-spice.

The best way to add the vinegar is to heat a little with the melted butter or margarine. Use as much as your fancy dictates. I'd suggest starting with a small amount—from ½ to 1 tablespoonful to a pint of the prepared vegetable. Then next time use less or add more to suit your taste.

Vegetable Juices and Broths

Various vegetable juices and broths can be prepared in the pressure-cooker. They do not have as much sparkle and vitality as freshly prepared raw vegetable juices, but they are appetizing, wholesome and rich in minerals as well as a large proportion of natural vitamins. Serve as an appetizer at any meal or between times as a "pick-me-up."

TOMATO JUICE COCKTAIL
4 minutes

1 (No. 3) can tomatoes
1 medium-sized sweet green pepper seeded and chopped
1 chopped onion
1½ cups diced outer stalks celery and celery leaves

½ tablespoon sugar
1 teaspoon salt
⅛ teaspoon pepper
1 small bay leaf
2 whole cloves
4 peppercorns

1. Combine all ingredients in the pressure-cooker. Close the cooker, bring to 15 pounds pressure and process 4 minutes.

2. Then strain through a fine sieve or cheesecloth and chill.

3. Serve in small glasses with or without a further seasoning of Worcestershire sauce or a little dry sherry.

Tomato Cucumber Cocktail: Prepare tomato juice cocktail as described and serve ice cold with 2 tablespoons grated raw, firm portion of cucumber in each glass.

Tomato Martinis: Serve chilled tomato juice in cocktail glasses, with a stuffed olive in each.

CARROT JUICE COCKTAIL
2½ minutes

2 pounds washed, unpeeled carrots
1 pint diced celery and leaves

2 sprigs fresh mint or ½ teaspoon dry mint
2½ cups water
⅓ teaspoon salt

Lemon or lime juice to taste

1. Put the carrots through the coarse knife of a food-chopper.
2. Combine with all ingredients in the pressure-cooker, except lemon or lime juice.
3. Close the cooker, bring to 15 pounds pressure and process 2 minutes. Cool the cooker. Strain liquid through cheesecloth or a fine sieve. Rub through the pulp if desired.
4. Serve well chilled, seasoned with lime or lemon juice.

BEET-PINEAPPLE COCKTAIL
3 minutes

1 quart scrubbed chopped young beets
4 slices fresh or canned pineapple chopped

2½ cups water
Lemon or lime juice to taste

1. Put beets through the coarse knife of the food-chopper.
2. Combine with the pineapple and water in the pressure-cooker.
3. Close the cooker, bring to 15 pounds pressure and

process 3 minutes. Cool the cooker. Then strain through a fine sieve or cheesecloth. Do not rub through pulp.

4. Serve ice cold with lemon or lime juice to taste.

GARDEN BROTH
3 minutes

1½ cups chopped outer stalks celery and celery leaves

1 chopped raw carrot and carrot tops

¼ cup chopped parsley

1¼ cups shredded spinach, lettuce or any mild-flavored green

2 tablespoons chopped onion

1 cup mushrooms and their stems chopped fine

3½ cups cold water

Plain or vegetable salt to taste

¾ cup chopped water cress

1. Put all the ingredients into the pressure-cooker except the water cress.

2. Add the water; close the cooker; bring to 15 pounds pressure and process 3 minutes.

3. Strain and serve in cups; sprinkle with the water cress.

Do's for Pressure Cooking Fresh Vegetables

Prepare the vegetables for cooking as directed in the Timetable Chart, page 259. Add just enough boiling water to the pressure-cooker to barely cover the bottom; the water *should not come over the rack;* in other words it should not touch the vegetables unless indicated on the chart. If ½ cup of water seems too much, decrease the quantity. However, if the diameter of the cooker base is unusually large, a little more water will be needed to barely cover the bottom.

If vegetables are over-mature, or old, or if root vegetables, such as carrots have been stored for some time, they will be somewhat dehydrated or dried out. *In this case pressure 1 minute longer than the time given in the vegetable chart to insure adequate cooking.*

If pressuring solid vegetables such as potatoes, beets, carrots, onions or turnips, and they are of uneven size, cut the large vegetables into pieces the size of the small vegetables, to insure complete cooking.

Do be careful not to overcook vegetables as this has a tendency to darken potatoes, cauliflower and other light-colored varieties.

Whenever possible serve the liquid with the vegetable. The old-fashioned custom of serving vegetables and their juice in side dishes should be revived. *All* vegetable liquids should be used, including that from potatoes. This book constantly lists them as an ingredient in many dishes. They may also be used in other ways.

How to Use Liquid from Pressured Vegetables

Vegetable Cocktail: Chill, season with lemon or meat condiment sauce and use as a cocktail; or combine with tomato juice.

Vegetable Bouillon: Heat and serve in bouillon cups with a slice of lemon or thick sprinkling of minced parsley or water cress. A combination of juices may be used. Or combine with tomato juice, meat or fish-stock.

Vegetable Cream Sauce: Make with equal parts of vegetable juice, top milk or cream. or undiluted evaporated milk, and thicken each cup of liquid with 2 tablespoons flour and butter or margarine blended smooth.

In Soups: Add to soup in place of part of the liquid before or after pressuring.

In Gravies: Use instead of water. Potato liquid is especially good for this purpose.

Vegetable Liquid from Oddments

Gather, clean, wash and shred oddments of raw vegetables, such as celery tops, lettuce or salad leaves, asparagus ends, carrot tops and any stray vegetables. Add a pint of hot water to a pint of this mixture. Pressure 3 minutes. Cool and open the cooker, strain, pour into a jar, refrigerate and use in pressure-ing savory meat, poultry or meat dishes. Adds flavor and those minerals!

TIMETABLE CHART FOR PRESSURE COOKING FRESH VEGETABLES
Cool cooker as soon as pressure-ing is completed

Vegetable	Preparation	Hot Water	15 Pounds Pressure
ARTICHOKES (Globe)	Cut stems level. Cut off top 1½ inches.	½ cup	Small 6 minutes Large 10 minutes
ARTICHOKES (Jerusalem)	Scrape off skin.	½ cup	Medium-sized 4 minutes
ASPARAGUS (Whole stalks)	Wash, brushing out sand. Cut off tough ends. If old, peel.	½ cup	2 minutes
ASPARAGUS (Cut)	Wash, brushing out sand. Cut in two-inch lengths.	½ cup	2 minutes

NOTE: Allow 1 to 2 minutes longer for vegetables grown in dry regions with little irrigation.

Vegetable	Preparation	Hot Water	15 Pounds Pressure
ASPARAGUS ENDS	Wash.	1 cup	4 minutes
BEANS (Whole green or yellow)	Wash, remove ends.	½ cup	4 to 5 minutes
BEANS (Cut)	Wash, remove ends. Shred or cut in inch lengths.	½ cup	3 to 4 minutes
BEANS (Lima fresh)	Remove from pod. Rinse in cold water.	½ cup	1 minute
BEETS (Young, whole)	Wash, cut off tops to cook as greens.	½ cup	10 minutes
BEET-TOP GREENS	Wash, clean, rinse in tepid water, and shred coarse. Use stems.	½ cup	3 minutes
BEETS (Young, sliced, diced or shredded)	Wash, cut off tops to cook as greens. Peel. Slice ⅛-inch thick or cut in dice.	½ cup	4 minutes
BEETS (Old whole)	Wash, cut off tops.	¾ cup	Medium-size 18 minutes Large 20 minutes
BROCCOLI (Whole stalks)	Wash in well-salted water. Cut off tough ends. If old, peel. Slash ends up two inches for even cooking.	½ cup	2 minutes
BRUSSELS SPROUTS	Wash in well-salted water. Remove yellowed leaves. Slash half open for even cooking.	½ cup	1½ minutes

Vegetable	Preparation	Hot Water	15 Pounds Pressure
CABBAGE — White, Savoy or Red (Chopped or shredded coarse)	Rinse well.	½ cup	3 minutes
CABBAGE — White, Savoy or Red (Wedges 1-inch thick)	Wash in well-salted water. Remove part of core.	½ cup	3 to 5 minutes depending whether head is solid or loose.
CABBAGE—White or Savoy (Quartered)	Wash in well-salted water. Remove part of core.	½ cup	5 minutes
CHINESE CABBAGE	Wash in well-salted water. Cut crosswise in 2-inch slices.	½ cup	3 minutes
CARROTS (Baby whole)	Scrape or peel. Slash ends. Pressure plain or dusted with dried mint.	½ cup	4 minutes
CARROTS (Large)	Scrape or peel. Cut in halves lengthwise.	½ cup	4 minutes
CARROTS (Diced small or julienne)	Scrape or peel. Slice, dice or julienne.	½ cup	2 minutes
CAULIFLOWER (Whole, medium-sized)	Wash in well-salted water. Leave on tender green leaves. Tunnel out core in V-shape to insure even cooking.	½ cup	5 minutes

Vegetable	Preparation	Hot Water	15 Pounds Pressure
CAULIFLOWER-ETTES	Wash in well-salted water. Remove leaves and core. Separate into sections.	½ cup or use tomato juice	1½ minutes
CELERIAC	Cut off tops to use in soup. Peel, and slice ¼-inch thick.	½ cup	2 minutes
CELERY (Cut in inch pieces)	Scrub with salted water; then cut. Save tops for vegetable broth.	½ cup	2 minutes
CORN (On cob)	Remove all husks. Brush out silk. Place corn on rack.	¾ cup	3 to 5 minutes according to maturity
CORN (Kernels)	Remove husks. Brush out silk. Cut kernels from cob.	½ cup	½ minute
CUCUMBER	Peel thin. Cut in quarters. Remove seeds; then cut into dice.	½ cup	1 minute
DANDELIONS	Use before they flower to prevent bitterness. Clean. Cut off roots and white ends. Wash, pour boiling water through.	½ cup	3 minutes
EGGPLANT (Mashed)	Slice crosswise in ¼-inch pieces. Don't peel.	½ cup	1 minute
EGGPLANT (Diced)	Peel thin. Cut in inch slices, then into coarse dice.	½ cup tomato juice; no water	½ minute

Vegetable	Preparation	Hot Water	15 Pounds Pressure
GREENS (Mixed)	Clean, wash and rinse in salted tepid water. Shred coarse. Combine any types desired as spinach, tender celery tops and mustard greens.	½ cup	2 minutes
GREENS (Strong flavored)	Clean, wash and pour salted boiling water through greens of strong flavor. Then pressure as directed.	1 cup	1 minute
KALE	Clean, remove roots and tough edges of leaves; wash and shred coarse.	½ cup	2 minutes
KOHLRABI (Sliced)	Cut off tops. Peel and slice ¼-inch thick.	½ cup	4 minutes
LEEKS	Cut off green tops to three inches of root. Cut off root ends and wash.	½ cup	3 minutes
MUSHROOM CAPS (Large)	Wash, cut off stems, and use these for soup or sauce. Do not peel, nor remove black portion under cap.	½ cup	5 minutes
MUSHROOM CAPS (Small)	See above.	½ cup	3 minutes
OKRA (Whole)	Wash, remove stem ends; cut out imperfections.	½ cup	3 minutes

Vegetable	Preparation	Hot Water	15 Pounds Pressure
OKRA (Cut)	Wash, cut crosswise in ¼-inch slices.	½ cup	1½ minutes
ONIONS (Sliced)	Peel and slice ¼-inch thick.	½ cup	2 minutes
ONIONS (Whole)	Choose medium-sized onions and peel.	½ cup	5 minutes
ONIONS SAUTÉED (For steak, liver, fish, etc.)	Peel, slice ¼-inch and slightly sauté in butter or margarine.	½ cup	2 minutes
PARSNIPS (Halved)	Peel, cut in halves lengthwise, slash large ends.	½ cup	8 minutes
PARSNIPS (Sliced)	Peel, cut crosswise in ⅛-inch slices.	½ cup	3 minutes
PEAS (Fresh)	Pod the peas.	½ cup	Small—1 minute Large — 1½ minutes
POTATOES (White-medium Whole)	Scrub, remove an inch of skin around potato.	½ cup	10 minutes
POTATOES (White large)	See above.	½ cup	12 minutes
POTATOES (Quartered)	Peel, quarter lengthwise.	½ cup	4 minutes
POTATOES — BAKED STYLE (Medium— Idaho)	Cook alone in cooker. Scrub. Cut a half inch strip of skin from middle; place on rack in cooker.	¼ cup	20 minutes. Dry out in open cooker by standing over a low heat a minute after pressureing.

Vegetable	Preparation	Hot Water	15 Pounds Pressure
POTATOES— (Sweet-medium-sized)	Scrub, cut off ends.	½ cup	8 minutes
POTATOES Sweet (Large)	Scrub, cut in halves lengthwise. Peel after processing.	½ cup	8 minutes
POTATOES— White or Sweet (To whip)	Scrub, cut in halves. Peel after processing.	½ cup	8 minutes
PUMPKIN (For pies or mashing)	Wash, leave on peel; cut in lengths. Scoop out seeds and strings.	½ cup	15 minutes
RUTABAGAS (Cubed)	Pare, cut in half-inch cubes. Mix in as much sugar as salt before cooking.	½ cup	4 minutes
RUTABAGAS (Sliced 1 inch)	Pare, cut in inch slices. Season with equal amounts of salt and sugar.	½ cup	10 minutes
SALSIFY (Oyster Plant)	Scrape and drop at once into cold water containing a little vinegar to prevent discoloration. Cook whole.	½ cup	5 minutes
SPINACH	Cut off roots and withered leaves. Wash in salted water; rinse in tepid water to remove grit. Shred coarse and place in cooker.	½ cup	2 minutes

Vegetable	Preparation	Hot Water	15 Pounds Pressure
SQUASH (Acorn)	Leave in shell. Cut in halves, lengthwise; scrape out seeds and pulp. Dust with salt, allspice and a little sugar.	½ cup	7 to 10 minutes according to size and maturity
BUTTERCUP SQUASH	Peel and slice.	½ cup	3 minutes
SQUASH (Hubbard or Winter)	Scoop out seeds and pulp. Cut in individual servings and pare, if desired. Dust with salt, cinnamon and sugar.	½ cup	7 minutes
SQUASH (Summer)	Wash crook-neck squash; cut in half-inch slices. Cut turban or "saucer" squash in inch wedges. If very old remove peeling.	½ cup	2½ minutes
SCALLIONS (Young onions)	Cut off roots, and all but two inches of green tops.	½ cup	3 minutes
SOYBEANS (Green)	Remove from pods	½ cup	3 minutes
SWISS CHARD	Wash in salted water. Rinse in tepid water. Shred leaves coarse. Cut stems in half-inch lengths. Pack into inset pan or put direct in cooker.	½ cup	4 minutes
TOMATOES BRAISED (Whole, medium-sized)	Scald, peel, remove cores. Use only firm tomatoes.	½ cup	1 minute

Vegetable	Preparation	Hot Water	15 Pounds Pressure
TOMATOES (Stewed style)	Scald, peel, remove cores, cut in eighths.	½ cup	½ minute
TURNIP—Whole (Young, white, small)	Save tops for greens. Deep pare to remove covering wax. If small and unwaxed, leave whole.	½ cup	5 minutes
TURNIP (White, sliced or diced small)	Peel; slice ¼ inch or cut in dice.	½ cup	3 minutes
VEGETABLE MARROW	Wash; cut crosswise in half-inch slices and peel.	½ cup	2 minutes
YAMS	Wash, cut lengthwise, cut in half-inch slices.	½ cup	6 minutes
ZUCCINI	Wash and cut in fourth-inch slices.	½ cup	1½ minutes

How to Season and Serve Pressured Fresh Vegetables

PREPARED ACCORDING TO DIRECTIONS ON THE TIME-TABLE CHART

Artichokes (Globe): Serve with browned butter and Hollandaise sauce or a "reasonable facsimile."

Artichokes (Jerusalem): Season with parsley butter, (page 251) or with butter and curry powder.

Asparagus Stalks: Serve stalks of asparagus plain or on hot toast with melted butter, real or imitation Hollandaise sauce (page 238), Danish sauce (page 232).

Asparagus (Cut Up): Season with butter or margarine, or combine with cream or Danish sauce (page 232). Or serve combined with ⅓ the quantity of cooked sliced carrots.

Tough Ends of Asparagus: Use the liquid in which they are pressured for a cream soup, or add to vegetable soup, or vegetable juice cocktail.

WHOLE GREEN OR YELLOW BEANS

Add melted butter or margarine, or season with browned butter. If mature add a few grains sugar.

GREEN LIMA BEANS

Season with melted butter or margarine and sprinkle with minced parsley or chives, or very small fried croutons.

BEETS (YOUNG)

Peel after pressure-ing and leave whole. Season with butter or margarine, with or without a little orange, lemon or lime juice. Or serve in Sweet-Sour sauce (page 253).

Or peel the beets; slice, dice or shred, and season with plain or parsley butter, lemon or lime juice; or use Sweet-Sour sauce, or plain butter and a little minced pickle relish.

BEETS (OLD)

Peel and use in making pickled beets, beet soup or beet purée; or serve with relish sauce (page 239).

YOUNG BEET TOP GREENS

Season with melted butter or margarine, and lemon or lime juice. Top with hard-cooked egg or with sliced young beets.

BROCCOLI (WHOLE STALKS)

Serve plain or on toast with melted butter or margarine, imitation Hollandaise, Danish or cheese sauce (page 233).

BROCCOLI RABE

Pressure and serve the same as broccoli.

BRUSSELS SPROUTS

Serve with melted butter or margarine, or with cream, tomato or Danish sauce (page 232).

CABBAGE (WEDGES)

Serve with melted butter or margarine; with hot vinegar sauce, or soured cream seasoned plentifully with chopped chives and a little lemon juice.

Cabbage (Quartered): Serve with melted butter or margarine and/or chopped parsley, mint or water cress.

Cabbage (Chopped or Shredded): Season with melted butter or margarine, or with soured cream and sliced stuffed olives.

Cabbage (Chinese): Season with melted butter or margarine, or serve with diced red and green sweet pepper slightly sautéed in butter.

Cabbage (Red): Season with melted butter or margarine, grated raw apple, fried onion, pickle relish or Sweet-Sour sauce (page 253).

CARROTS (MEDIUM-SIZED)

Serve whole, seasoned with melted butter or margarine; sprinkle with minced parsley; or serve in spiced tomato sauce.

Small Carrots (Julienne, Sliced or Diced): Season with butter or margarine and/or chopped mint, parsley or chives; or serve in cream, Danish or Sweet-Sour sauce (page 253).

WHOLE CAULIFLOWER

Strew with coarse crumbs browned in butter or margarine, or serve with cheese or Danish sauce (page 232); sprinkle with minced parsley. Or serve with a little horse-radish and soured cream mixed.

Caulifleurettes: Season with butter or margarine; or serve with a cream or egg sauce, or parsley, lemon or herb butter (page 251).

CELERIAC

Season with butter or margarine or browned butter and black pepper.

DICED CELERY

Season with soured cream and/or a little tomato catsup; or with melted butter or margarine; or sprinkle with minced chives. Or serve in a cream sauce made with half celery liquid and half milk.

GREEN CORN (ON THE COB)

Serve very hot with melted butter or margarine or herb butter balls. Provide plenty of fresh black pepper.

CUCUMBERS (DICED OR QUARTERED)

Season with minced chives or curry, with melted butter or margarine; or use soured cream, black pepper and chopped red radishes or minced dill.

DANDELION GREENS

Season with butter or margarine, or with vinegar sauce, and strew with chopped hard-cooked egg. Or season with equal parts of bacon fat and wine vinegar heated together, and garnish with squares of crisp bacon.

EGG PLANT (MASHED)

Remove the peel and mash or purée the pulp. Season with salt, pepper, butter or margarine, and minced parsley or a little mint. Beat until very light. Serve very hot as a vegetable or very cold as an hors d'oeuvre. In this case a little diced firm cucumber may be added.

Diced Egg Plant: Serve with a sauce made of the liquid in the cooker; garnish with small croutons and sliced stuffed olives if desired.

MIXED GREENS

Season with butter or margarine; garnish with small croutons fried in bacon or ham fat, or blend with Danish sauce (page 232).

GREENS—STRONG FLAVORED

Season with a little lemon or lime juice and soured cream; or with butter or margarine and a little minced basil, parsley or chives. Or add chopped young onions and their tops sautéed in butter.

KALE

Season with browned butter, or margarine and lemon juice, or with tomato sauce; or soured cream and black pepper.

SLICED KOHLRABI

Serve buttered, or in cream or Danish sauce (page 232).

LEEKS

Arrange on toast, and pour over white or cream sauce which may or may not contain chopped hard-cooked eggs. Or top with poached eggs dusted with paprika. Or serve plain buttered, or with tomato sauce.

MUSHROOM CAPS

Season with browned butter or margarine with or without a little lemon juice or nutmeg. Or serve in a plain brown sauce. Arrange on toast, pour over a little melted butter and serve garnished with crisp bacon or well-browned small sausages.

Mushroom Caps and Stems: Serve with steak or chicken, or chopped meat balls of any kind; add to chicken gravy, or use as a garnish to any à la king dish on toast.

WHOLE OKRA

Serve with plain, melted or browned butter or margarine, with or without further seasoning of minced chives, parsley, or a trace of basil. Or arrange on toast, pour over

Danish or tomato sauce and serve with a garnish of crisp bacon.

Sliced Okra: Add to soup, gumbos, chicken, lamb or veal stews, or vegetable chowders.

Whole Onions: Serve buttered or margarined; in white or cream sauce, with or without hard-cooked egg chopped; or with soured cream and minced parsley. Garnish with small fried croutons.

Sliced Onions: Serve buttered or margarined; with browned butter, cream or Danish sauce.

Sautéed or Steam-Fried Onions: Season with salt and pepper, and serve with steak, meat balls of any kind, or with corned beef hash.

HALVED PARSNIPS

Season with butter or margarine, or soured cream and lemon juice. Or add lime juice and melted butter or margarine. Or sauté in meat fat and serve with gravy. In this case parsnips are nice arranged on toast with a garnish of crisp bacon or sausage.

GREEN PEAS

Serve plain with the cooking liquid seasoned with butter or margarine; or strew with a little minced mint; or serve in white or cream sauce made partly with the cooking liquid.*

WHITE OR SWEET POTATOES

For pressuring be sure to select potatoes of the same average size. Otherwise small potatoes will be overcooked

*For specially interesting flavor, pressure a small quartered onion with the peas, a whole clove stuck into each piece. Season with fortified margarine.

or large potatoes may be undercooked. If uneven in size, cut the large potatoes into pieces about the size of the small potatoes. After pressuring, cool and open the cooker, then shake it over a low heat to dry out the potatoes if necessary. Serve "as is" peeled, whipped, fried or in any other desired way.

White Potatoes (Quartered): Serve buttered or margarined with or without parsley; or in white or cream sauce containing chopped hard-cooked egg and/or minced chives.

Baked Idaho Potatoes: These potatoes will burst and have a flaky effect. Serve popped open with a small slice of butter or margarine in each. Or stir in bits of crisp fried bacon, or minced chives or parsley.

Franconia Type White Potatoes (Pressured with Meat): Peel medium-sized potatoes. Brown-heat meat in the cooker. Then roll and slightly brown the potatoes in the meat drippings. Remove the potatoes. Put the meat in the cooker, and pressure to within 10 minutes of the specified time. Cool and open the cooker; put the potatoes around the meat. Close the cooker again; bring to 15 pounds pressure and process 10 minutes longer.

If a crisp crust is desired put the potatoes under the broiler about 2 minutes after pressure-ing.

Franconia Sweet Potatoes: Follow the preceding directions using sweet potatoes or halved medium-sized yams.

Sweet Potatoes or Yams Plain: Peel the potatoes or yams; pressure and serve rolled in melted butter or margarine with a dusting of cinnamon or nutmeg.

Sweet Potatoes (Large): Follow the preceding directions; or peel, halve, roll in molasses or honey, place in a well-buttered pan, dust with a little salt and cinnamon and bake in a moderate oven about 10 minutes.

Whipped Potatoes, White or Sweet: Pare the potatoes; put through a purée sieve, ricer or food mill; add hot milk and seasonings. Allow ¼ cup milk, ½ tablespoon butter or margarine, ¼ teaspoon salt, and ⅛ teaspoon pepper to 6 medium-sized potatoes. Whip until fluffy with a wire whisk or electric mixer.

Whipped White or Sweet Potatoes with Water Cress: Follow the preceding directions; then beat ½ cup minced water cress and stems into 3 cups whipped potatoes.

Whipped White or Sweet Parslied Potatoes: Follow the preceding recipe, using ⅓ cup minced parsley to 3 cups whipped potatoes. Add 1 teaspoon basil vinegar for superb flavor.

Whipped White Potato with Carrots: Follow the preceding recipe using 2 cups whipped white potatoes, and 1 cup cooked sieved carrots. Add a little onion salt if desired.

Whipped White Potato with Onion: Prepare whipped white or sweet potato and beat in ¾ cup minced sautéed onions (do not brown them).

PUMPKIN PLAIN OR AS A VEGETABLE

Scrape the pumpkin pulp from the shells and put it through a potato ricer, purée sieve or food mill. Use plain for pies or soup. To serve as a vegetable, season with salt, pepper, butter or margarine, and a little brown sugar or honey. Beat until fluffy. Add a little minced mint or basil if desired.

CUBED RUTABAGAS

Serve buttered, margarined, or with browned butter or Sweet-Sour sauce (page 253).

SALSIFY (OYSTER PLANT)

Serve whole, sliced or cubed, with a seasoning of melted butter or margarine; or serve in white or cream sauce with or without chopped hard-cooked egg. Or arrange on buttered toast; pour over a little melted butter or margarine, sprinkle with minced parsley, and serve garnished with crisp bacon, sausage or frizzled ham.

SCALLIONS

Season with melted butter or margarine and serve on toast. Or arrange on toast and pour over a cream, egg or cheese sauce (page 233).

SPINACH

Add a little nutmeg with the salt and pepper. Season further with butter or margarine; a little lemon or lime juice, slightly fried onion or onion tops, or a little canned tomato; or blend with a cream, or Danish sauce. Or use soured cream and minced chives. Or top with small squares of sweet red peppers heated in butter and lemon or lime juice.

SQUASH

Acorn: Loosen the pulp if the squash are small; serve ½ to a person. In this case add a little melted butter or margarine and dust with minced parsley or a trace of mint.

Buttercup Squash: This is usually diced or sliced. Season with melted butter or margarine, or browned butter, and a little nutmeg or cinnamon; serve with or without minced parsley.

Hubbard or Winter Squash: Serve in individual pieces seasoned with melted butter or margarine, cinnamon or nutmeg. Or scrape the squash from the shell and mash; season with salt, pepper, butter and a little cinnamon, or sautéed sliced onion.

Summer Squash: Serve sliced, with melted butter or margarine, or with parsley-herb-lemon-or-lime butter. Or season with soured cream, and add minced parsley.

GREEN SOYBEANS

Season with butter or margarine, plenty of pepper and/or minced chives or parsley, or a little basil; or use herb butter.

SWISS CHARD

Serve buttered or margarined with or without lime or lemon juice; or with a cream or hard-cooked egg or cheese sauce, or tomato sauce (page 235). Or season and garnish with sliced hard-cooked or halved stuffed eggs.

BRAISED TOMATOES

Pour over melted butter or margarine and strew with a very little minced basil or parsley. Or garnish with bits of crisp bacon or fried tiny croutons.

Stewed Tomatoes: Add sugar to taste. But not much, please. Season with butter or margarine; a little sautéed onion or green pepper may be added.

YOUNG TURNIPS

Season small whole turnips with a few grains of sugar, butter or margarine and/or lemon or lime juice, or add Sweet-Sour sauce (page 253). Or serve with White or Cream sauce (page 232).

Diced or Sliced Turnips: Season with a few grains of sugar, butter or margarine, parsley butter, or with Sweet-Sour sauce (page 253).

VEGETABLE MARROW

Season with melted butter or margarine, or with parsley butter; or pour over cheese sauce. Or serve with tomato, Spanish or creole sauce.

ZUCCINI

Serve dressed with melted butter or margarine, and sprinkle with grated Parmesan or sharp Cheddar cheese.

Julienne Vegetables

Almost all kinds of vegetables may be julienned or cut in long, match-like strips, then pressured. The vegetables most commonly used are string beans, carrots or parsnips, white turnip, celery, kohlrabi or beets.

Several of these vegetables may be pressured together to make Julienne Vegetables Jardinière. But they must be vegetables that require the same time to pressure-cook.

Suitable combinations are:
1. String beans with carrots and celery.
2. String beans, white turnips, celery and green pepper.
3. Kohlrabi with carrots and string beans.

PRESSURING JULIENNE VEGETABLES
3 minutes

1. Trim and pare the vegetables; cut in match-length strips.
2. Place in the pressure-cooker with ¼ cup boiling water to 1 pint or more of the prepared vegetables. Add a little salt and pepper.

3. Close the cooker, bring to 15 pounds pressure and process 3 minutes.

4. Season with butter or margarine, and/or a little lime or lemon juice, and minced parsley.

Vegetables Jardinière or Combinations

Many combinations of vegetables may be cooked together jardinière in the pressure-cooker. Success depends upon choosing vegetables that need the same length of time to cook, whether cubed, diced, sliced or coarse-shredded (schnitzled). If using frozen vegetables separate or break them apart (see page 290), and cook a few seconds less.

Use just enough boiling water to barely cover the bottom of the cooker. Season the vegetables with a little salt and pepper, and pressure as indicated. Please note the sizes specified, for unevenness of size affects the pressuring time. Here is a set of interesting combinations:

1. String Beans and Okra: Halved string beans in inch-lengths with okra sliced ½-inch thick. Pressure 4 minutes.

2. Peas and Carrots: Large green peas and young carrots cut in small dice. Pressure 2 minutes.

3. Asparagus and Peas: Tender asparagus cut in half-inch lengths and large green peas. Pressure 2 minutes.

4. Cauliflower and Peas: Separate cauliflower into small flowerets; combine with large peas and pressure 2 minutes.

5. Spinach and Tomato: Shred spinach leaves coarse; add 1 small peeled diced tomato to a quart of prepared spinach. Pressure 1½ to 2 minutes.

6. Brussels Sprouts with Chestnuts: Slash the sprouts

at the stem end. Add peeled quartered chestnuts and pressure 1½ to 2 minutes.

7. Mexican Corn: Cut green corn kernels from the cob or use frozen corn (the kernels separated with a fork). To 1 pint add 2 tablespoons each sweet green and red peppers cut in small squares; pressure ½ minute.

8. Green Beans with Young Onions: Cut or julienne green beans, and pressure with 12 cleaned young onions or button onions to the pound.

9. Mixed Garden Vegetables: Combine good-sized kernels of green corn, good-sized peas, julienned green beans, carrots diced small, tender baby limas and diced celery. Pressure 3 minutes.

Vegetable Specials

Recipes proportioned to serve four to six.
All measurements are level.
Timings are minutes required for actual pressuring.
Cool cooker as soon as pressuring is done.

BRAISED CELERY FRENCH STYLE
2½ minutes

1. Clean and cut stalks of celery into 2-inch strips. If very wide cut in halves lengthwise.

2. Place in the pressure-cooker with ½ cup canned tomatoes or peeled diced fresh tomatoes, to 3 cups prepared celery. Add salt and pepper.

3. Close the cooker, bring to 15 pounds pressure and process 2½ minutes.

4. Cool and open the cooker; add a little soured cream and a bit of onion salt if desired.

VEGETABLE CHOP SUEY
2 minutes

1 cup diced celery
¾ cup peeled carrots diced small
1 medium-sized onion peeled and diced
1 cup bean sprouts
¼ cup each diced seeded sweet green and red peppers
1 cup Chinese cabbage or celtuce shredded coarse

½ cup shredded white turnip
½ cup soup-stock (any kind)
1 tomato peeled and diced small
1 teaspoon soy sauce
2 teaspoons cornstarch
Pressured rice

1. Combine all the vegetables in the pressure-cooker. Add the soup-stock and soy sauce. Close the cooker, bring to 15 pounds pressure and process 2 minutes.

2. Cool and open the cooker; add the tomato, and the cornstarch dissolved in 1 tablespoon water or stock. Cook and stir until boiling. Add salt and pepper to taste.

3. Serve poured over the rice, with or without a garnish of shredded raw green onions or Chinese shredded egg.

STRING BEANS WITH NOODLES
4 minutes

2 tablespoons butter or margarine
1 peeled good-sized onion sliced
1 pound string beans
3 cups diced peeled tomatoes

1 teaspoon sugar
1 teaspoon salt
¼ teaspoon pepper
½ pound broad noodles
¾ cup fried croutons
1 pound cottage cheese plain or sage-flavored

1. Melt the margarine or butter in the pressure-cooker; sauté the onion in it until soft and yellowed.

2. Trim the beans and shred lengthwise; wash, drain and put into the cooker. Add the tomato, sugar, salt and pepper. Close the cooker, bring to 15 pounds pressure and process 4 minutes.

3. Meanwhile cook the noodles until tender in salted water, plain or seasoned with a little basil; or use water saved from cooking vegetables. Then drain the noodles as dry as possible.

4. To serve, add the butter to the noodles and put them in a deep pottery dish. Cover with the beans and tomato; sprinkle with the croutons and serve with generous portions of the cottage cheese.

Cottage Cheese with Sage: Steep 1 teaspoon minced fresh sage or ½ teaspoon dry sage 5 minutes in 2 tablespoons cream or top milk. Stir into 1 pound of cottage cheese together with salt and pepper to taste. Chill well before serving.

COLCANNON
5 *minutes*

This is an Irish method of cooking potatoes and cabbage together which may be carried out as follows:

1. In the pressure-cooker combine peeled, quartered, medium-sized white potatoes and slices of white or green cabbage, cut one-inch thick. Add ¼ to ½ cup boiling water, or enough to barely cover the bottom of the cooker; sprinkle vegetables with ½ teaspoon salt and a little pepper.

2. Close the cooker, bring to 15 pounds pressure and process 5 minutes.

3. Serve seasoned with butter or margarine and a little minced parsley. Serve with any smoked or salt meat, or with poached or stuffed eggs.

SWEET-AND-SOUR CABBAGE

Savoy cabbage may be used. Cut it in thin slices and pressure-cook according to directions on the timetable; drain, add Sweet-Sour sauce (page 253). Let stand a few minutes to season.

Cabbage with Soured Cream and Olives: Cut white cabbage into 4-inch lengths about ½ inch wide, and pressure according to directions for shredded cabbage given on the timetable. Drain, season with soured cream, plenty of pepper and sliced stuffed olives; re-heat.

ALL-IN-ONE VEGETABLE DINNER
5 *minutes*

8 small white potatoes peeled and halved	½ cup boiling water
	¼ teaspoon salt
8 medium-sized onions peeled	⅛ teaspoon pepper
	Browned butter
8 small carrots peeled	Parsley or cress
2 cups outer stalks celery cut in inch pieces	

1. Put the vegetables in layers in the pressure-cooker, first the potatoes, next the onions, then the carrots and the celery. Add the seasonings to the water and pour in.

2. Close the cooker, bring to 15 pounds pressure and process 5 minutes.

3. Serve the vegetables arranged neatly on a platter and pour over the browned butter. Garnish with the parsley or cress.

If desired a substantial food may be arranged in the center of the platter such as hot stuffed hard-cooked eggs on toast, vegetable custards turned out on toast, or mushrooms on toast. In this case moisten the toast with the

liquid remaining in the cooker. Otherwise use it as suggested on page 258.

MUSHROOMS ON TOAST
4 minutes

1 pound fresh mushrooms
3 tablespoons butter or mar-
    garine
2 tablespoons flour
⅛ teaspoon nutmeg

1½ cups any kind meat-
    stock or broth
Toast, wild rice, buttered
    noodles or small whole
    boiled potatoes

1. Wash but do not peel the mushrooms. Remove the
stems from the caps and cut the stems across in rounds.

2. Melt the butter or margarine in the cooker. Sauté
the mushrooms in it 3 minutes. Stir in the flour and nutmeg and gradually the soup-stock.

3. Close the cooker, bring to 15 pounds pressure and
process 4 minutes.

4. Serve on the toast, or pour over the rice, noodles or
potatoes.

Mushrooms with Chicken, Turkey, Duck or Game: Pressure-cook the mushrooms as described in the preceding
recipe. Add bits of left-over chicken, duck or game and 2
tablespoons of dry sherry. Re-heat and serve in pastry
shells. A few sliced stuffed olives may be added.

Savory Vegetable Custards for Meatless Meals

If using frozen vegetables, separate or break them apart (page 290).

STRING BEAN CUSTARD
6 minutes

½ pound finely shredded string beans
3 eggs
1¾ cups heated milk
1 cup soft white bread crumbs

¾ teaspoon salt
⅛ teaspoon pepper
Few grains nutmeg
1 tablespoon butter or margarine
1 cup hot milk

1. Put the string beans in a bowl. Beat and add the eggs, milk, crumbs, salt, pepper, nutmeg and butter.

2. Transfer to buttered custard cups filling ¾ full; tie waxed paper over the tops. Put the rack in the cooker and set in the custard cups. If necessary make 2 layers by putting a wire rack or perforated aluminum or ceramic inset over the first layer of cups to make a base on which to stand the remaining custards. Pour in the hot water.

3. Close the cooker, bring to 15 pounds and process 6 minutes.

4. To serve, unmold on buttered toast, which may or may not be spread with potted meat of any kind. Or serve with tomato, Spanish or creole sauce (page 236). Dust custards with paprika, or garnish tops with parsley, pimiento dots, or red radish slices for color.

Asparagus Custard: Follow the recipe for string bean custard, using 1 cup chopped, raw tender asparagus (fresh or frozen) instead of string beans, and ¾ cup minced celery.

Celery Custard: Prepare according to the recipe for string bean custard, using chopped celery in place of string beans.

Onion Custard: Follow the recipe for string bean custard, using ¾ cup chopped mild onion instead of the string beans.

Carrot Custard: Follow the recipe for string bean custard, using ¾ cup coarse grated raw carrot instead of string beans.

Green Corn Custard: Follow the recipe for string bean custard, using 1½ cups fresh or frozen green corn instead of string beans.

Mixed Vegetable Custard: Follow the recipe for string bean custard, substituting for string beans a mixture of 1½ cups finely shredded tender string beans and carrot, corn kernels and diced celery. Or use frozen mixed vegetables, well broken apart and process 7 minutes.

YAM OR SWEET POTATO PINEAPPLE PUDDING
12 minutes

3 tablespoons butter or margarine
1 cup pineapple juice
3 cups peeled yams or sweet
  potatoes sliced thin
1 cup chopped canned
  pineapple
½ cup chopped nuts (any
  kind)
1 tablespoon flour
½ cup hot water

This must be cooked in a metal dish that will fit loosely into the cooker.

1. Melt the butter; add the pineapple juice. Butter the dish. Put in a layer of the yams or sweet potatoes; sprinkle with ⅓ of the pineapple and nuts and about 1 teaspoon flour. Repeat, making 2 more layers of the ingredients. Pour in the pineapple juice.

2. Pour the water into the pressure-cooker; put in the rack, set the pudding on it; close the cooker, bring to 15 pounds pressure and process 12 minutes.

3. Garnish with cubes of pineapple; dot with a little butter and place under the broiler to brown slightly.

STUFFED VEGETABLES

These are useful when a light, yet substantial dish is needed for luncheon, a dinner in which meat must be "stretched," or to reinforce a garden platter meal. Made the pressure-cooked way they will be ready to serve in the time it takes to pressure the whole vegetable—from 4 to 8 minutes according to the kind selected. Any whole vegetable that can be scooped out to form a container, may be stuffed and pressured. Large whole onions, firm tomatoes, halved egg-plant, hollowed out cabbage, firm sweet green peppers, sections of marrow, squash, cucumbers may all be used. Be sure the stuffing is made of ingredients that should pressure the same time, and don't *overcook,* or the vegetables will become soft and mushy. Tomatoes will retain their shape while pressuring if put in buttered custard cups. Remove vegetables by means of a broad spatula.

CHICKEN-STUFFED TURBAN SQUASH
6 minutes

4 small turban summer squash
1 cup minced cooked chicken in thick cream sauce
1 cup chopped sautéed mushrooms
½ cup small croutons
½ cup hot water

1. Hollow the squash to within ½ inch of the edge to form cups. Dust inside and out with salt and pepper; fill with the chicken and mushrooms mixed.

2. Pour the water into the cooker; put in the rack, place the squash on it; close the cooker, bring to 15 pounds pressure and process 6 minutes.

3. Sprinkle with croutons and serve with thin tomato sauce. Or cover with grated cheese, dot with butter and brown quickly under the broiler.

Veal, ham, or canned luncheon meat may be used instead of chicken.

STUFFED EGGPLANT
6 minutes

2 small eggplants	¾ cup coarse white bread
Dry-moist stuffing or meat	crumbs
stuffing	2 tablespoons butter or mar-
¾ cup tomato juice	garine
Mint	

1. Wash the eggplant and cut in halves lengthwise, ½ for each person. Hollow out within 1 inch of the edge to form shallow bowls. Dust with salt and pepper. Fill level with the desired stuffing. Put it in loosely as the stuffing swells in pressuring.

2. Pour the tomato juice into the pressure-cooker. Put in the rack. Place the eggplant in the cooker. If space is limited put 2 halves, side by side; cover with waxed paper, and place the remaining eggplant on top. Close the cooker, bring to 15 pounds pressure and process 6 minutes.

3. Serve sprinkled with the crumbs fried in butter with a little minced mint, and with a thin gravy made from the liquid in the cooker.

Meat Stuffing: Prepare half the quantity of dry-moist stuffing (page 86). Add 1 cup minced cooked lamb, chicken, duck, ham or game, and 1 teaspoon minced fresh or ½ teaspoon powdered dried mint.

SHRIMP-STUFFED CUCUMBER
4 minutes

4 small stubby cucumbers
1 cup chopped pressured shrimp

½ cup thick white sauce, or tomato or Spanish sauce
½ cup hot water

1. Peel the cucumbers; cut in halves lengthwise, and scrape out the seeds, forming "boats." Combine the shrimp with the sauce and fill the cucumbers.

2. Pour the water into the cooker; put in the rack; place the cucumbers on the rack, close the cooker; bring to 15 pounds pressure and process 4 minutes. Cool cooker at once.

3. Serve plain or sprinkled with croutons, and accompany with tomato or mushroom sauce. Or cover with grated Swiss cheese, dot with butter, brown under the broiler, and serve with Newburgh sauce containing shrimp instead of lobster (page 238).

MEAT-STUFFED VEGETABLE MARROW
5 minutes

1 long vegetable marrow
Meat stuffing

¾ cup tomato juice or juice drained from cooked vegetables

1. Cut the ends of the marrow so they will be square and even. Then cut the marrow itself into 6-inch lengths; remove the seeds by means of an apple-corer.

2. Fill with the meat stuffing; plug up the ends with

bits of bread to keep the stuffing from cooking out. Dust
with salt and pepper.

3. Put the juice in the pressure-cooker. Put in the rack
and fit the pieces of marrow close together on it. If there
are too many for a single layer, put a piece of parchment
paper over them and fit the remaining marrow on top.

4. Close the cooker; bring to 15 pounds and process 5
minutes. Serve with a thin gravy made from the liquid in
the cooker.

STUFFED GREEN PEPPERS

4 sweet green peppers   ¼ cup coarse white bread
Meat stuffing (p. 288)   crumbs
¼ cup tomato juice   2 tbs. butter or margarine

1. Wash peppers. Cut a thin slice from the top; remove core and seeds. Boil 2 min. in salted water and drain.

2. Fill with meat stuffing. Dust with salt and pepper.

3. Pour tomato juice into the cooker.

4. Put in the rack. Place peppers on it; cover, bring
to 15 lbs. pressure and process 4 min. Cool cooker at once.

5. Serve sprinkled with the crumbs fried in the butter.
Pour around an 8 oz. can of tomato sauce heated with
the juice from the cooker.

Pressure Cooking Frozen Vegetables

It is not necessary to defrost quick-frozen vegetables before pressuring. However, frozen vegetables must always
be separated before pressuring, otherwise the outer surfaces will be cooked while the center vegetables will remain frozen. So always knock the package against a hard
surface several times to separate small vegetables as peas;
or cut a solid frozen vegetable as spinach, into cubes with
a sharp heavy knife. Measure a scant ½ cup of hot water
into the cooker. Do not add any more as the frozen vegetable contributes liquid as it thaws. Put in the rack. Bring
the water to a boil, then put in the vegetable and pressure
the required time according to the following table.

TIMETABLE CHART FOR PRESSURE COOKING FROZEN VEGETABLES

Count Time When Pressure Reaches 15 Pounds

Vegetable	Time at 15 Pounds Pressure
ASPARAGUS (cut or spears)	1½ minutes
GREEN BEANS	¾ minute
WAX BEANS	¾ minute
BEANS (shredded)	30 seconds
BROCCOLI	1½ minutes
BRUSSELS SPROUTS	1½ minutes
CAULIFOWER	30 seconds
CORN (kernels)	30 seconds
CORN-ON-THE-COB	½ minute
SUCCOTASH	2 minutes
LIMA BEANS (green)	2 minutes
MIXED VEGETABLES	2 minutes
PEAS (green)	45 seconds
PEAS AND CARROTS	2 minutes
SPINACH (cut in cubes)	45 seconds
SUMMER SQUASH	3 minutes

Season and serve in any of the ways suggested in this book.

CHAPTER XV

LEGUMES OR DRIED VEGETABLES IN HURRY-UP TIME

THE LEGUMES, FAMILIAR AS DRIED PEAS, BEANS AND lentils, are our most inexpensive source of protein food. And they can be made epicurean instead of plebeian. The reason they are not used to a greater extent in this country is because ordinary methods of preparation call for overnight soaking and long slow cooking, often a twenty-hour job. But the pressure-cooker has made possible revolutionary time-saving methods in cooking the legumes; two hours from package to table being the maximum cooking time needed.

Legumes for Satisfying Meals

Pressure-cooked dried beans, peas and lentils may be used as the main dish for almost any meal, for they furnish a considerable part of the needed protein. If used in the same meal with animal protein in any form such as milk, or with small portions of meat, fish, cheese or eggs, the protein balance of the menu becomes approximately complete.

In some cases these "animal proteins" may be combined in savory dishes with the legumes, which furnish secondary proteins. Good examples are lentil soup garnished with plenty of sliced frankfurters; chili con carne; or dried bean salad served with cottage cheese balls.

What to Serve with the Legumes

Dried peas, beans or lentils in themselves are rather flat in taste. So they need plenty of seasoning; touch them up with herbs, a bit of spice, garlic or onion. With the exception of the soybean, they all lack fat, so a good dose of butter, margarine, vegetable oil, soured cream, savory fat, or fat smoked or cured meat is essential. And they taste much more appetizing when accompanied by a tart food, such as a relish, pickle, coleslaw, a green bowl salad, tomato platter, or a tart fruit salad enlivened with lime juice. Good bread accompaniments are heated rolls or French bread, plain or garlicked; New England toast; bread sticks; thin toasted devilled ham sandwiches, corn bread or muffins. As to Boston Baked Beans, of course they call for Boston Brown Bread (page 233).

Dessert should always be fruit in some form, as a fruit bowl, pears or rosy apples with cheese; a fruit cup, or stewed or canned fruit or a compôte. If it is to be pie, make the deep-dish kind—apple, berry, peach or cherry. Or you could serve a fruit cobbler, if the crust is not thick. The legumes are so substantial in themselves, and, with the exception of soybeans, contain so much starch, that a floury dessert, such as cake, or shortcake, is an anti-climax and a dietetic mistake.

TIMETABLE FOR PRESSURE COOKING DRIED VEGETABLES

Pick over, wash and pre-soak vegetables for 1 hour before pressure cooking by adding boiling water to cover and covering tight. Discard water before pressuring. *Do not add any baking soda.* One cup beans or lentils yields about 2⅓ cups when cooked. C—cup, t—teaspoon, T—tablespoon.

Dried Vegetables	Quantity	Water	Seasoning	Minutes at 15 lbs. Pressure
BLACK-EYED PEAS	2 C	Add hot water to cover.	½ cup cubed salt pork, 1½ t. salt, ⅛ t. pepper, ½ T. molasses	35
GARBANZA BEANS or CHICK PEAS	2 C	Add hot water to cover.	1½ t. salt, ⅛ t. pepper	35
FRIJOLES (Mexican Beans)	2 C	Add hot water to cover.	1½ t. salt, ¼ t. pepper, 2 T. bacon fat, 2 t. chili powder if desired	35
KIDNEY BEANS (White or Red)	2 C	Add hot water to cover.	1½ t. salt, ¼ t. pepper, 1 small onion chopped, 2 T. bacon or smoked ham fat	35
LENTILS	1½ C	Add hot water to cover.	1½ t. salt, ⅛ t. pepper, 2 crushed cardamom seeds if desired	25
LIMA BEANS	2 C	Add hot water to cover.	1½ t. salt, ⅛ t. pepper, 2 T. minced onion, ⅓ cup minced celery	30

Dried Vegetables	Quantity	Water	Seasoning	Minutes at 15 lbs. Pressure
NAVY BEANS	2 C	Add hot water to cover.	1½ t. salt, ⅛ t. pepper, 2 T. minced onion	35
PEA BEANS	2 C	Add hot water to cover.	1½ t. salt, ⅛ t. pepper, 2 T. minced onion	35
PINTO BEANS	2 C	Add hot water to cover.	1½ t. salt, ¼ t. pepper, 2 T. minced onion, ⅓ cup each minced celery and sweet green pepper	45
SOYBEANS (Savory) Special: Cover with boiling water and soak over night before pressure-ing	2 C	Add hot water to cover.	1½ t. salt, ¼ t. pepper, ½ t. dry mustard, 1 t. onion salt, 1 T. molasses, ½ cup tomato catsup, 2 slices bacon diced and fried	35
SOYBEANS (without fat) Special: Cover with boiling water and soak over night before pressure-ing	2 C	Add hot water to cover.	Drain. Add water and 1½ t. salt, ¼ t. pepper, ½ t. dry mustard, ¼ C chopped onion	35

SPLIT PEAS

Whole or split dried peas make a heavy purée when pressured, which is likely to clog the vent-pipe of the cooker, and cause the safety plug to blow out. Therefore dried pea recipes are omitted from this book.

Ways to Serve the Legumes

Recipes proportioned to serve four to six.
All measurements are level.
Timings are minutes required for actual pressuring.
Cool cooker as soon as pressuring is done.

NAVY BEANS

Serve buttered or margarined. Or stir through minced cooked ham and chopped seeded sweet red or green peppers. Season further with curry.

PEA BEANS

Serve buttered or margarined, with browned butter, or with tomato creole or Spanish sauce (page 236).

PINTO BEANS

Serve buttered or margarined, and seasoned with prepared mustard and pickle relish; or with or without grilled sausages, or frankfurters lightly spread with mustard before grilling.

SOYBEANS (SAVORY)

Serve as the main dish at lunch, supper or dinner, with or without a garnish of crisp bacon or sausage, panned ham or bologna.

SOYBEANS (PLAIN)

Combine plain cooked soybeans with any cooked meat which is of insufficient quantity for service, such as diced lamb, veal, beef or ham. Add gravy, tomato sauce or curry sauce and heat.

BLACK-EYED PEAS

Serve with browned sausage, crisp bacon or frizzled ham. Or stir in sautéed, diced, seeded red or green peppers; or combine with one-third the quantity of cooked brown rice, and a seasoning of sautéed onions or curry powder.

GARBANZA BEANS OR CHICK PEAS

Serve plain buttered or margarined, with or without a garnish of sautéed onions and celery, minced parsley, or mixed minced herbs.

FRIJOLES

Serve buttered or margarined, with or without a garnish of minced parsley or chopped scallions and their tender tops. Accompany if desired with sautéed cervelat or bologna sausage.

KIDNEY BEANS
(White or Red)

Serve plain with crisp sausage, bacon or sautéed cold cuts, or very small meat balls of any kind.

LENTILS

Serve buttered or margarined, with onion, sweet green pepper, or curry sauce; or combine with cooked rice and season with curry and chopped sautéed young onions.

LIMA BEANS

Serve buttered or margarined, in shallow bowls with plenty of "juice"; strew with fried bread crumbs. Or serve in tomato sauce, or sprinkled with sautéed diced onion and green and red peppers.

BEAN SALADS

Armenian Bean Salad: Combine 3 cups drained, pressured navy or pea beans with vinaigrette sauce to season (page 240). Add a little minced fresh or dried mint and chill at least an hour.

Serve on lettuce or sliced tomatoes; garnish with black olives.

Boston Bean Salad: Combine 2½ cups pressured Boston beans with 2 cups hard-cooked eggs; 1 seeded, diced sweet green pepper; ⅓ cup sweet pickle relish and ½ cup boiled salad dressing containing plenty of mustard. Chill at least 1 hour. Serve in nests of lettuce, or use as a filling for stuffed tomato-bean salad.

Lima Bean Salad: Combine 2 cups cooked, drained dry lima beans with 1 cup sliced cooked carrots, ⅓ cup minced seeded red or green pepper and French tomato dressing to moisten. Chill and arrange in a bowl lined with lettuce or romaine. Garnish with sliced sweet pickles.

Lentil Salad: Combine 2 cups cooked green lentils with 1 cup minced tender celery; ¾ cup grated raw carrot, 1 cup cooked black beans; 1½ cups toasted chopped blanched almonds or Brazil nuts; ⅓ cup ripe olives; 1 minced pimiento. Add 2 tablespoons French dressing and chill; then stir through plain or wine mayonnaise barely to blend. Serve in nests of lettuce with a garnish of strips of pimiento and green peppers.

BAKED BEANS BOSTON STYLE
35 *minutes*

1 pound pea beans	2 tablespoons molasses
2 oz. salt pork or 3 table-spoons bacon fat	1½ teaspoons salt
	⅛ teaspoon pepper
1 peeled, chopped medium-sized onion	½ teaspoon mustard
	3½ cups water

1. Pick over the beans. Cover with 4 cups boiling water, put on a lid and let stand 1 hour.

2. Cut the salt pork, if used, in cubes and lightly brown in the pressure-cooker. Drain the beans and put into the cooker with all the remaining ingredients.

3. Close the cooker, bring to 15 pounds pressure and process 35 minutes.

4. If desired brown on top, put the pressured beans into a baking dish or bean pot. Dot with a little butter and brown in a hot oven.

Baked Beans Boston Style with Tomatoes: Omit ½ cup water and add 1 cup canned tomatoes before pressuring.

Beans with Soured Cream: Omit the salt pork or bacon and add ½ cup soured cream.

Beans with Sherry: Add 3 tablespoons dry sherry after pressuring.

BAKED STYLE LIMA BEANS

Substitute dried lima beans for the pea beans in the preceding recipe.

SOYBEANS

Pressure according to directions on the chart. They may be varied as follows:

Tomato-ed Soys: Omit 1 cup water and add 1¼ cups canned or diced fresh tomato.

Chili Soys: Add 1 tablespoon chili powder to the soybeans before pressuring. When done stir through 2 seeded, diced sweet green peppers.

Curried Soys: Add 1½ teaspoons curry powder to the soybeans before pressuring. Serve with rice, and scallions, radishes, sliced tomatoes or cucumbers.

CHAPTER XVI

CEREALS—A REVELATION IN FLAVOR

A BRAND NEW TASTE SENSATION AWAITS THE FORTU-
nate person who pressure-cooks cereals. For they are thoroughly steam-cooked, not only in quick time, so that they
retain their natural deliciousness, but also their valuable
minerals, vitamins and other nutrients. When I speak of
cereals, I mean not only the time-honored three or four
kinds we adults customarily eat or cook for breakfast or
supper for children; I mean all kinds of cereals, served at
all kinds of meals. Good old-fashioned cracked wheat;
Scotch and Irish oatmeal; buckwheat; wild and brown
rice, and white rice in several languages; corn-meal, whole
barley, and the whole family of Italian pastes, from
macaroni, spaghetti and noodles to sea shells and bow
knots.

Serving Cereals

A word about the service. When a generous serving of
pressure-cooked whole grain or fortified cereal and whole
milk is provided for breakfast, it is sufficient for the main
course. When a cereal is served at lunch or dinner, as
barley balls, Persian rice, spaghetti or cracked wheat with
brown butter, potatoes should never be served, and the

amount of bread should be cut down. For bread is classed as a cereal food.

A glance at the chart in this chapter shows that cereals calling for 2 or 3 hours of cooking by regulation methods may be pressure-cooked in a fraction of the time.

Do's for Pressure Cooking Cereals

Do be sure all valves and vents in the cooker are clean.

Never fill cooker more than ½ full of cooking cereal.

Use ⅓ less water than for usual cooking.

Note whether cold water is indicated in the directions.

Use ½ the usual amount of salt.

Mix fine cereals such as corn meal, with cold water to prevent lumping. Count this water as part of that needed in the pressure-cookery. Be sure the cereal bubbles rapidly all over before closing the cooker and pressuring. When this is done it will not stick to the bottom of the cooker.

Then if the cereal seems a bit moist, stand the cooker uncovered on an asbestos mat over a low heat for 2 or 3 minutes to dry out any excess moisture.

If cooking a small amount of cereal, bring it to a rapid boil in a regular sauce-pan and transfer to a deep metal or enameled bowl for pressuring. In doing this put the rack in the cooker and place the bowl on it. The bowl must fit in loosely so it can be removed easily. Pour the cereal into the bowl. Then carefully pour 2 cups of hot water around the bowl; close the cooker, bring the pressure up to 15 pounds and process the time indicated in the cereal chart.

Timetable for Pressure Cooking Cereals

Recipes proportioned to serve four to six.
All measurements are level.
Timings are minutes required for actual pressuring.
Cool cooker as soon as processing is done.

Cereal	Pre-Preparation	Amount	Water	Salt	Minutes at 15 lbs. Pressure
BARLEY (whole Pearl)	Put salt and water in cooker. Stir in barley. Boil rapidly 2 min. and pressure-cook.	1 C	4 C Boiling	¾ t.	30 m.
CORNMEAL (white or yellow)	Put salt and water in cooker. Mix corn meal with 1 C cold water. Stir in. Boil rapidly 2 min. and pressure-cook.	1 C	3 C Boiling	1 t.	10 m.
CRACKED WHEAT	Put salt and water in cooker. Stir in cracked wheat. Boil 2 min. then pressure-cook.	1½ C	4 C Boiling	¾ t.	30 m.

Cereal	Pre-Preparation	Amount	Water	Salt	Minutes at 15 lbs. Pressure
BUCK-WHEAT (whole)	Melt 1½ T. butter in cooker. Turn heat low. Put in buckwheat and slightly sauté until color turns. Add water and salt. Boil 2 min. and pressure-cook.	1 C	3 C Boiling	½ t.	20 m.
FARINA (light)	Put water and salt in cooker and boil. Stir in farina mixed with 1 cup cold water. Boil 1 min. then pressure-cook.	1 C	3 C Boiling	½ t.	3 m.
FARINA-TYPE Fine Dark Whole Wheat Cereals	Put water and salt in cooker. Mix cereal with cold water and stir in. Boil 1 min. then pressure-cook.	1 C	3 C Boiling	½ t.	7 m.

Cereal	Pre-Preparation	Amount	Water	Salt	Minutes at 15 lbs. Pressure
HOMINY (granulated)	Put water and salt in cooker and boil. Mix 1 C cold water with hominy; stir into boiling water. Boil 1 min. and pressure-cook.	1½ C	3 C Boiling	1 t.	20 m.
HOMINY (grits)	See above	1½ C	3 C Boiling	1 t.	25 m.
OATS (rolled)	Put water and salt in cooker. Stir in oats. Boil 1 min. and pressure-cook.	1½ C	3½ C Boiling	¾ t.	5 m.
OATMEAL (steel-cut, Scotch, or Irish type)	Put salt and water in cooker. Stir in oats. Boil slowly 2 min. and pressure-cook.	1½ C	3 C Boiling	½ t.	10 m.
RICE (white) Dry and flaky	Pick over rice. Put in cooker. Pour in water and pressure-cook.	1 C	2 C Cold	none	10 m.

Cereal	Pre-Preparation	Amount	Water	Salt	Minutes at 15 lbs. Pressure
RICE (brown)	See above	1 C	2½ C Cold	none	25 m.
RICE (wild)	Pick over rice. Add water and salt and pressure.	1 C	2½ C Cold	½ t.	25 m.
*MACARONI (in inch lengths)	Put water and salt in cooker. When boiling hard, add macaroni and pressure. Drain.	3 C	4 C Boiling	½ t.	5 m.
*SPAGHETTI (al dente)	Put water and salt in cooker. Bring to boiling point. If spaghetti is to be whole, place ends in water so it will bend, then press under water. Otherwise break in 2-inch lengths. Pressure required time and drain. Do not rinse.	½ lb.	4 C Boiling	½ t.	6 m.

*Stir well before pressuring.

Cereal	Pre-Preparation	Amount	Water	Salt	Minutes at 15 lbs. Pressure
*"Sea Shells"	Put water and salt in cooker. Bring to boiling point; add sea shells; pressure and drain. Do not rinse.	2 C	4 C Boiling	½ t.	5 m.
Noodles (in inch lengths)	Put water and salt in cooker. Add noodles. Pressure required time and drain. Do not rinse.	3 C	4 C Boiling	½ t.	3 to 4 m. according to width

Suggestions for Serving Pressure-Cooked Cereals

Barley: Serve instead of mashed potatoes with meat and gravy, or in the form of balls or molds with meat and gravy, or in soup.

Cornmeal Mush: Serve with honey, brown or maple sugar and cream and top milk. Or serve fried, or as polenta; make into scrapple.

Fried Cornmeal Mush: Transfer the pressure-cooked cornmeal to a long pan or glass refrigerator dish; cover and chill. Slice, dip in beaten egg, then in fine bread crumbs and fry in butter or vegetable fat, if to be used as a sweet; or in savory meat fat, if used as a main course food. Serve in place of potatoes with meat, or accompany with honey or jelly as a sweet.

Cracked Wheat: Serve with sugar, honey or scraped maple sugar and cream or top milk. Or add a little browned butter and minced fines herbes, and serve plain or shaped into balls in place of potatoes.

Hominy: Serve with sugar and top milk; or season with butter and use instead of potatoes at any meal. Or fry and serve plain as a vegetable; or with honey, jelly or syrup as a dessert.

Fried Hominy Slices: See recipe for Fried Cornmeal Mush.

ROLLED OATS

Serve as a cereal with sugar, honey or scraped maple sugar and a little butter, cream or top milk; or serve plain fried as a vegetable; or with jelly, syrup or honey as a dessert.

Fried Rolled Oats: See recipe for Fried Cornmeal Mush.

Steel Cut, Scotch or Irish Oatmeal: Serve as a cereal with brown or maple sugar; with honey and top milk or cream or a little butter. Or use instead of potatoes with meat and gravy.

WHITE OR BROWN RICE

Serve as a cereal with granulated or natural sugar and cinnamon, with maple or brown sugar and top milk or cream. Use plain as a vegetable, or seasoned with plain or browned butter or fines herbes. Or mold individually, chill and serve as a dessert with canned, stewed or fresh fruit and plain or whipped cream.

RICE WITH RAISINS

Serve hot as a cereal with honey and top milk or cream; or use in place of potatoes with chicken, duck, turkey or game. Or mold and chill for a dessert. In this case unmold and serve with sweetened plain or whipped cream and a sprinkle of chopped nuts or coconut.

WILD RICE

Use plain or buttered in place of potatoes. Stir in fines herbes or sautéed mushrooms if desired.

Savory Cereals Good with Meat, Poultry or Fish

White or brown rice, cracked wheat, barley, corn meal, buckwheat, and cracked wheat are suitable to use in this way. The preparation is indicated on the Timetable for Pressure Cooking Cereals with these variations:

Cereals Cooked in Vegetable Liquid: In place of water use liquid drained from cooked vegetables (avoid onions, cabbage or beets; the latter turns the cereal pink). Season with butter or fortified margarine.

Cereals Cooked in Bouillon: Add a bouillon cube or ½ teaspoon meat extract to each cup of water used. Omit salt.

Cereals in Tomato Bouillon: Use equal parts tomato juice and water with 1 bouillon cube or ½ teaspoon meat extract to each cup of water.

CEREAL BALLS OR MOLDS

Pressure-cooked rice, barley, cracked wheat or hominy in any form may be served in individual molds or balls. To make, first rinse demi-tasse cups or small molds or custard cups with hot water. Press in the cereal and unmold. Or shape by means of an ice cream scoop first dipped in hot water.

Cereal Balls or Molds in Soup: Place the ball or mold of cereal in the center of a soup-plate and surround with the soup. A good way to make a plate of soup look and taste substantial.

CEREAL RINGS

Ragouts, platter stews, fish, chicken, ham or eggs à la king, or mixed vegetables taste and look important when served in cereal rings. These may be made of any coarse grain cereal as white, brown or wild rice, barley, cracked wheat, hominy grits, buckwheat, or chopped noodles, whether plain, or made into some special dish such as risotto, Persian, Spanish or curried rice, or polenta. Be sure to choose the correct cereal for the type of filling you are planning to serve. For instance:

Curried Rice Ring: Chicken, poultry, veal or lamb in a plain gravy, or white or cream sauce, or tomato sauce. Mixed vegetables, plain or in tomato sauce.

Wild Rice Ring: Ragout of rabbit, squirrel or poultry.

Spanish Rice Ring: Poultry, beef or veal balls, fried scallops, or shrimp in butter sauce.

Barley Ring: Any réchauffé of meat or poultry in gravy, brown, tomato, creole or Madeira sauce, or use mushrooms in brown sauce.

Yellow Rice: See above. Good with mixed vegetables in tomato or curry sauce.

Persian Rice: Use with poultry or game in plain gravy.

Cracked Wheat Ring: Any réchauffé or ragout of meat or poultry in gravy, Spanish or tomato sauce.

Polenta Ring: See above.

Jambalaya Ring: Fill with buttered shrimp, plain or with oysters (page 214).

INDIVIDUAL CEREAL RINGS

Rinse individual ring molds or Mary Ann pans with hot water. Press in the cereal. Let stand 1 minute in the oven to re-heat and dry out. Then unmold on the plate and fill the center with the selected food.

CEREAL PLATTER RINGS

To make large platter rings for ragouts, stews, fricassees, casserole type dishes, etc., a different technique is needed to keep the ring from breaking when it is unmolded. Here's how: Mix 1 tablespoon of milk with 1 beaten egg and stir into the hot cereal. Rub a ring mold with butter or margarine. Pack in the cereal. Place in a hot oven for 3 minutes. Then loosen the cereal carefully with a spatula and unmold on a large platter. Fill the center with the selected food. If desired minced parsley, fines herbes or chives may be mixed with the cereal before being put into the mold.

YELLOW RICE OR PILAF
9 minutes

1 cup large grain white rice	1 peeled onion sliced
1 tablespoon butter or margarine	½ teaspoon salt
	2 cups hot water

1. Pick over the rice, but do not wash it. Melt the butter in the pressure-cooker. Stir in the rice and onion and sauté and stir slowly until the rice turns golden.

2. Stir in salt and water and bring to boiling point.

3. Close cooker; bring pressure to 15 pounds and process nine minutes. The grains of pressure-cooked rice will be larger than usual, and completely in shape.

CURRIED RICE

Prepare white, brown or wild rice as described in the Timetable for Pressure Cooking Cereals. When done stir in 1 teaspoon curry powder heated for 1 minute in 1 tablespoon melted butter. Do not allow this to brown.

PERSIAN RICE
10 minutes

Prepare white rice according to the directions in the Timetable for Pressure Cooking Cereals. When done, stir in 2 tablespoons butter, ¼ cup soft small raisins and ¼ cup shredded almonds or broken filberts, which have been simmered together until the nuts begin to turn color.

SPANISH RICE
9 minutes

2 tablespoons butter or margarine
⅓ cup minced onion
2 medium-sized sweet green peppers diced
1 pint canned tomatoes
½ cup hot water
½ teaspoon salt
⅛ teaspoon pepper
1 cup white rice

1. Melt the butter or margarine in the pressure-cooker; add the onion and green peppers and cook a moment. Add the tomatoes, water and seasonings and bring to boiling point.

2. Stir in the rice; boil for 1 minute; close the cooker, bring to 15 pounds pressure and process 9 minutes.

JAMBALAYA
9 minutes

2 slices lean bacon	¼ teaspoon pepper
2 tblspoons minced onion	1 cup quartered cooked
1 cup raw white rice	shrimp
2 cups canned tomato	1 cup cooked chicken and
1 cup water	ham combined, or 1
½ teaspoon salt	cup raw oysters

1. Cut the bacon in dice; fry in the pressure-cooker until the fat flows freely. Add the onion and cook for ½ minute.

2. Put in the tomato, water and seasonings; stir in the rice. Bring to boiling point and boil ½ minute.

3. Close the cooker; bring to 15 pounds pressure and process 9 minutes.

4. When done add the shrimp, or chicken and ham together, or a combination of shrimp and ham. Let stand 2 or 3 minutes to heat through.

5. If the oysters are used, stir them into the hot mixture, cover, and heat without pressure for 3 minutes.

Almost any mixture of meat or shell fish with tomatoes can be used in jambalaya. It is served as a main dish at lunch or supper, and is often accompanied with grated cheese.

RISOTTO
9 minutes

1 peeled onion sliced	1½ cups white rice
3 tablespoons salad oil (ol-	3 cups soup-stock or bouil-
ive oil preferred)	lon
3 tablespoons butter	Grated Parmesan cheese

1. Fry the onion 30 seconds in the oil; add the butter and let it melt. Stir in the rice, which should be picked over but not washed. Sauté until yellowed, stirring constantly. Stir in the soup stock, or bouillon made by adding 3 bouillon cubes or 2 teaspoons beef extract to 3 cups water. Bring to boiling point.

2. Close the cooker, bring to 15 pounds pressure and process 9 minutes. Serve with grated Parmesan cheese.

Risotto with Sausage: Any kind of cooked sausage, from sliced skinless frankfurters to cervelat, may be stirred into plain risotto after it has been cooked. Heat 1 minute before serving.

Risotto with Fish: Prepare risotto. Liquid used in boiling fish may be used instead of water if desired. Serve with cooked fish in any form, or combine with fish as a special luncheon dish. To prepare this add to the cooked risotto, diced cooked shrimp, oysters sautéed in a little butter until the edges curl; or flaked cooked or canned fish of any kind.

FRIED RICE CHINESE STYLE

1 egg	1 scallion chopped with the green top
½ tablespoon butter or salad oil	3 cups pressured white or brown rice
½ cup diced roast or barbecued pork	1 teaspoon soy sauce
Black pepper	

Beat the egg, scramble lightly in the butter or oil. Add the pork, scallion and rice and sauté gently for 2 minutes. Do not let the mixture brown. Then stir in the soy sauce and pepper. Slowly cook 1 minute longer to blend the seasonings, and serve very hot with a garnish of extra chopped scallions.

Fried Rice with Ham: Follow the preceding recipe using diced smoked ham in place of pork.

Fried Rice with Chicken, Turkey or Duck: Follow the preceding recipe for fried rice using diced chicken, turkey or duck in place of the pork. Add 2 tablespoons minced celery if convenient.

Fried Rice with Crab or Lobster: Follow the preceding recipe for preparing fried rice, using ⅔ cup diced lobster or crab meat in place of the pork.

Fried Rice with Mushrooms Sauté: Follow the preceding recipe for fried rice, using ⅔ cup chopped sautéed canned or fresh mushrooms in place of the pork. Garnish with sautéed mushroom caps and water cress or parsley. This is particularly good served with grilled or sautéed sliced tomatoes.

POLENTA
10 minutes

Cook white or yellow corn meal according to directions on the Timetable for Pressure Cooking Cereals. Transfer to a lightly oiled bread pan and bake in a hot oven 15 minutes. Then unmold on a platter, slice and sprinkle thickly with grated cheese. Serve with tomato, Spanish or creole sauce; or as a whole course with boiled ham; bacon; mushrooms in brown sauce; sautéed fish fillets; or with mixed vegetables in tomato sauce.

Fried Polenta: Chill the baked polenta. Slice, dip in flour and brown in vegetable fat.

QUICK SCRAPPLE
10 minutes

1. Prepare corn meal mush as described on the Timetable for Pressure Cooking Cereals.

2. Stir in ½ teaspoon minced powdered sage and ¼ teaspoon thyme. Add 1½ cups bits of cooked fresh pork, smoked ham, or pork and ham mixed.

3. Transfer to a slightly oiled bread pan or oblong glass dish with a cover; cool and chill. It may be stored in the refrigerator for a week if closely covered.

4. To serve, slice, dip in flour or fine bread crumbs and fry in vegetable fat or meat drippings. This is an excellent breakfast or luncheon dish.

CRACKED WHEAT WITH FIGS
25 minutes

Prepare cracked wheat according to directions on the Timetable for Pressure Cooking Cereals with this exception. When the water begins to boil add 1 cup of quartered well-washed figs from which the stem ends have been removed.

BUTTERED MACARONI

Any form of macaroni may be used. Tiny macaroni squares or small bow knots are especially good. Pressure-cook the macaroni as directed on the Timetable. Drain (do not rinse with cold water) and season with a little browned butter.

Macaroni with Rarebit Sauce (5 minutes) : Cook macaroni according to directions given on the Timetable for Pressure Cooking Cereals. Drain (but do not rinse with cold water). Combine with rarebit sauce (page 233) and re-heat. This is appetizing served in small deep plates with a garnish of grilled tomato, minced chives and a topping of crisp bacon.

SPAGHETTI ITALIENNE
6 minutes

Cook ¾ pound of spaghetti in 4 cups water according to directions given in the Timetable for Pressure Cooking

Cereals. Drain thoroughly, but do not rinse in cold water. Mix for serving with either of the spaghetti sauces on page 239. Pass grated cheese, Parmesan preferred. If a meatless sauce is used the spaghetti may be accompanied by small meat balls, thin slices of grilled ham, or crisp bacon.

BUTTERED NOODLES
4 minutes

Pressure noodles according to directions given in the Timetable for Pressure Cooking Cereals. Drain, but do not rinse with cold water. Season with lightly browned butter, and serve sprinkled with small croutons fried in butter and mixed with minced chives or parsley.

HERB-FLAVORED MACARONI, SPAGHETTI AND NOODLES

Before pressuring add 2 teaspoons powdered savory to the liquid in the cooker.

HERB-FLAVORED RICE

Add ¼ teaspoon powdered savory, thyme, bay leaf or basil, or ½ teaspoon saffron to the liquid in the cooker.

CHAPTER XVII

PRESSURE-STEAMED DESSERTS, PUDDINGS AND BREADS

THE PRESSURE-COOKER CAN PRODUCE DELECTABLE steamed desserts, those old-time delicacies seldom served today in most homes because of the length of time involved in cooking and the amount of gas or electricity needed to steam them. But pressure-steaming is as speedy in dessert making as in many other departments of cookery. So it brings back these desserts in all their glory, making meals more nourishing and glamorous; yes, and thrifty, too. Many a meal that seems a bit scant of meat, poultry or fish, really supplies full nutriment. However, it often seems unsubstantial. But climax it with a luscious steamed dessert, and "all's well that ends well."

You are familiar with the excellent commercially canned rice and Indian puddings, and the steamed fig and plum puddings. You are delighted with the Boston brown bread and fruit and nut bread sold in cans. All these delicious foods plus many more can be easily prepared at home in the pressure-cooker, for all of them are commercially pressure-steamed. Up to the advent of the pressure-cooker the preparation of steamed foods took hours of top-of-the-stove boiling, and careful watching; but they now can be pressure-steamed in a brief fraction of the regulation old-fashioned cooking time. Moreover, remember you can make these desserts whether or not an oven is available. You may be cooking in an improvised kitchenette or in a trailer, but you can still end dinner with the grand flourish of a homemade dessert.

What Desserts Can Be Pressure-Cooked?

Briefly desserts that may be pressure-cooked include:
>Custards (firm type, as cup custards)
>Bread or Crumb Puddings
>Baking Powder Biscuit Type Puddings
>Puddings with a Cereal Base
>Steamed Molded Puddings
>Fruit Betties
>Bread and Fruit Charlottes

To these should be added steamed breads that give enjoyment when eaten throughout a meal, or which are so delicious and nutritious in themselves that a dessert is not needed when they are provided.

Steaming desserts in the pressure-cooker corresponds to the regulation top-of-the-stove method when the mold, filled with the uncooked dessert mixture and closely covered, is placed in a steamer, or surrounded with boiling water in a kettle, covered, and steamed for a long time; or when it is placed in a pan of hot water in the oven—as cup custards—and slowly steam-baked.

However, there are two marked differences between the regulation and pressure-ing methods. In regulation steaming, the mold of pudding is closely covered, or even sealed with adhesive tape to keep in all possible heat. In pressure-steaming an open top mold should be used— covered only with two thicknesses of waxed paper which is tied on to keep a film from forming on the surface, and to keep a pudding that cooks too rapidly from spattering and clogging the vent pipe.

What—No Cover on the Mold?

Yes,—no cover. Raised desserts cannot be steamed in the pressure-cooker if the mold is covered with a lid, unless the lid is perforated to allow the escape of excess air and gases released by the leavening agent. Moreover, no leavened dessert can be pressure-steamed unless it is first allowed to cook without pressure until the action of the leavening (called rising) has taken place, so the dessert has risen almost the required extent before the pressure is brought up to 15 pounds. It cannot rise if the mold is closely covered with a lid as in the regulation method. The exact time each specific pudding or bread needs for proper rising and the subsequent processing, depends on the quantity of basic ingredients, the leavening agent and the size of the mold or utensil used. Obviously individual-sized puddings or breads call for less pressuring time than those prepared in pint or quart-sized molds.

Choice of Molds

For individual-sized steamed custards or other desserts, use aluminum custard cups or molds.

For pint-sized puddings or breads two types of molds may be used. First a small metal or enamelware bowl that fits loosely into the cooker. There should be at least 1-inch space at the edge. Do not use glass or earthenware as they take up too much space and may crack from the high internal heat to which they are subjected. As an alternate, which I prefer by the way, use quart-sized molds or pint-sized tin cans without the lids. The cans produce a pudding or bread uniformly round in diameter which slices neatly and without waste. They may be used in most four-quart

cookers, but be *sure* they clear the top by at least 1 inch
Otherwise use lower cans, or a bowl.

However, with cookers of small diameter, smaller can
must always be used in place of bowls, which usually fi
too tight, or regulation molds which are too tall. If the
size of the cooker permits, it is advisable to use 2 or 3 small
molds or cans rather than 1 large mold or bowl, as pressure-
ing time is speeded up; besides, instead of having frag-
ments of a large pudding or bread left over you have a
whole one, which may be re-heated for a subsequent meal
by steaming without pressure for 10 minutes in the covered cooker.

However, if making a gorgeous plum pudding to present
"flaming" as the climax to a holiday dinner, better use a
large mold (without the cover) if it fits loosely into the
cooker; or choose a metal or enamelware bowl. If you do
not own a mold you may be able to find one of suitable
size at a house-furnishing store, which can be used without
the cover. If possible, buy a mold with a tube in the center;
this allows the steam to penetrate the interior of the dessert
more quickly for more rapid pressure-ing. A small tube
angel cake pan can be used if it fits loosely into the cooker.

Do's in Pressure-Steaming Raised Desserts or Breads

1. Place the rack in the cooker.

2. Thoroughly butter or oil the bowl, mold or cans and
fill ⅔ with the batter.

3. Tie 2 thicknesses of waxed paper over the top of each
container. Keep the ends of the string short.

4. Place the containers in the cooker.

5. Pour in enough boiling water to come halfway of the
depth of the mold, *and no more.*

6. Adjust the cover of the pressure-cooker and *steam without pressure* as long as directed in the recipe; then bring the pressure to 15 pounds and process the required length of time.

Steaming without Pressure

The pressure-cooker is an excellent utensil to use for steaming foods without pressure in the regulation way, as there is very little escape of steam.

Pressure-Steaming Unleavened Desserts

These include all puddings that are made without leavening, and so do not call for baking powder, baking soda, or cream of tartar and baking soda. They include custards, cereal and bread puddings, and fruit betties. Follow the preceding routine with this exception: Omit the preliminary steaming without pressure. Instead, bring the pressure up to 15 pounds at once, and process the directed time.

Adapting Favorite Home Pudding and Bread Recipes to Pressure-Steaming

Make the batter as usual. The exact length of time to be allowed for the preliminary steaming, and for pressuring depends on the density and quantity of the batter and the size of the mold. Count the pre-steaming time from the point when the steam flows freely through the vent pipe. The following will prove a helpful guide.

1. Desserts or Breads Which Steam Normally in 30 Minutes.

Pre-steam 5 minutes without pressure, and process 15 minutes at 15 pounds.

2. Desserts or Breads Which Steam Normally in 45 Minutes.

Pre-steam 15 minutes without pressure, and process 20 minutes at 15 pounds.

3. Desserts or Breads Which Steam Normally in 1 to 1 ½ Hours.

Pre-steam 30 minutes without pressure, and process 30 minutes at 15 pounds.

4. Desserts or Breads Which Steam Normally in 2 Hours.

Pre-steam 30 minutes without pressure, and process 50 minutes at 15 pounds.

5. Desserts Which Steam Normally from 3 to 4 Hours.

Pre-steam 30 minutes without pressure, and process 50 minutes at 15 pounds.

Pressure-Steamed Desserts

Recipes proportioned to serve four to six.
All measurements are level.
Minutes are those required for actual pressuring
and for pre-steaming if required.
Cool cooker as soon as processing is done.

CUP CUSTARDS
5 minutes

2 large or 3 small eggs
2 tablespoons granulated sugar
⅛ teaspoon salt

⅓ teaspoon vanilla or lemon extract
2 cups heated milk
½ cup hot water

1. Beat the eggs, sugar and salt together until well-mixed. Add milk.

2. Pour into aluminum custard cups. Put the rack in the cooker. Add hot water. Stand the custards on the rack. Close cooker.

3. Bring pressure to fifteen pounds and process five minutes. *Cool cooker at once* and remove custards.

4. Chill, unmold and serve plain, with cream, with sweetened fresh or defrosted frozen fruit, or with chocolatina sauce.

Honey Custards: Substitute mild flavored honey for sugar in the preceding recipe, and use 2 tablespoons less milk.

Custards de Luxe: Unmold, pour over ½ tablespoon Curaçao or any sweet liqueur, top with whipped cream and garnish with shredded toasted almonds.

French Custards: Caramelize ½ cup granulated sugar (that is, slowly melt in a heavy pan until light brown); and pour it into custard cups. Rotate them to make a thin coating. Pour in a plain custard mixture, and pressure as directed. When unmolded the caramelized sugar lining will have melted, forming a sauce. Serve plain, with whipped cream and strewn with chopped nuts.

Macaroon Custards: Prepare plain or honey custard; add 6 crumbled medium-sized plain or coconut macaroons Transfer to custard cups and process as directed. Serve ice-cold with whipped cream or bing cherries.

CHOCOLATE CUSTARD
5 minutes

1½ squares (ounces) bitter chocolate
⅛ teaspoon salt
2 cups heated milk
2 large or 3 small eggs
⅓ cup granulated sugar
⅓ teaspoon vanilla
½ cup hot water

1. Shave the chocolate; add to the milk and slowly heat until the chocolate melts.

2. Combine the sugar, salt, eggs and vanilla and beat until well-mixed. Add the milk and stir well. Transfer to aluminum custard cups.

3. Place rack in cooker. Add water. Put in custard cups. Close cooker. Bring to 15 pounds pressure and process 5 minutes. Cool cooker at once and remove custards.

4. Chill, unmold and serve with plain cream, or chocolatina sauce and a topping of whipped cream.

LEMON RICE CUSTARD

5 minutes in cups—15 minutes in bowl

1 cup cooked rice	Juice and grated rind ½
1 egg beaten	lemon
6 tablespoons granulated	2 cups heated milk
sugar	½ cup hot water
⅛ teaspoon salt	

1. Mix in the order given; transfer to buttered aluminum custard cups, or a metal bowl, with 2 thicknesses of waxed paper tied over the tops.

2. Put rack in cooker. Add water. Put in custard cups or bowl. Close cooker.

3. Bring pressure to 15 pounds and process 5 minutes in the cups, fifteen minutes in the bowl.

4. Serve hot or cold, with or without cream or stewed fruit, or melted jelly sauce.

To Steam Two Layers of Custards: This can be done by placing a wire rack or trivet, or a perforated aluminum or ceramic inset, on top of the first layer, and setting the remaining custards on this. Process as described.

PINEAPPLE PUDDING

Pre-steam 5 minutes—pressure 10 minutes

5 thick slices day-old white bread

1 cup canned grated pineapple

2 eggs

3 tablespoons granulated sugar

2 cups heated milk

1 cup hot water

1. Butter a metal or enamelware bowl.

2. Remove crusts from the bread and use for croutons. Cut bread in inch-wide strips.

3. Put bread and pineapple in the bowl in alternating layers.

4. Beat eggs and sugar together. Add milk and pour into mold. Leave an inch free space at the top as this pudding swells. Tie 2 thicknesses waxed paper over the top. Let stand 15 minutes.

5. Put rack in cooker. Add water. Put in mold. Close cooker.

6. Steam without pressure 5 minutes. Then bring to 15 pounds and process 15 minutes.

7. Serve hot or cold with cream or with ginger fruit sauce.

CHOCOLATE PUDDING

Pre-steam 30 minutes—pressure 30 minutes

2 cups all-purpose flour

4 teaspoons baking powder

¼ teaspoon salt

½ teaspoon cinnamon

⅔ cup granulated sugar

2 eggs

⅔ cup milk

6 tablespoons shortening melted

3 squares (ounces) bitter chocolate melted

½ teaspoon vanilla

1. Sift together the flour, baking powder, salt, cinnamon and sugar.

2. Beat the egg, add the milk, and stir into the dry mixture.

3. Add the shortening, chocolate and vanilla. Transfer to a buttered quart-sized mold or bowl that fits loosely into the cooker. Cover with 2 layers of waxed paper, tied on. Put in rack. Add 3 cups hot water. Pre-steam pudding 30 minutes, bring to 15 pounds pressure and process 30 minutes.

4. Serve with hard sauce, or chocolatina sauce and whipped cream.

Chocolate Nut Pudding: Follow the preceding recipe, adding ½ cup chopped walnuts, pecans or blanched almonds with the flour.

STEAMED CAKE SLICES

As served on American Overseas Air Lines
Pre-steam 5 minutes—no pressure

Pour ¼ cup water in the cooker. Put in rack. On this place slices of cake to be steamed—pound, sponge, nut or fruit cake. Close cooker and steam without pressure 5 minutes. Serve with Ginger Fruit Sauce (page 235).

This is an excellent method of utilizing cake that may have become a bit dry.

INDIAN PUDDING

Pressure 15 minutes

1 quart milk	2 teaspoons powdered
1 cup yellow corn meal	ginger
½ cup molasses	2 tablespoons butter or
⅓ cup sugar	margarine
½ teaspoon salt	1 cup hot water

1. Scald 3 cups milk in a double-boiler.
2. Mix the cornmeal with the remaining cup of milk. Stir into the scalded milk and cook and stir until thickened. Add the molasses, sugar, salt, ginger and butter. Pour into a buttered metal or enamelware bowl.
3. Put the rack in the cooker. Pour in the hot water. Put in the pudding. Bring pressure to 15 pounds and process 15 minutes.
4. Serve half warm with plain or whipped cream or topped with ice cream.

Indian Fruited Pudding: ½ cup raisins, or raisins and diced dried figs may be added to the mixture for Indian Pudding.

FRUIT PUFFS
Pre-steam 5 minutes—pressure 12 minutes.

½ recipe baking powder biscuit dough (page 62) (made with 7 tablespoons milk) ¾ cup any drained canned or stewed fruit, or 1 cup diced sugared apples, peaches, stoned cherries or sliced strawberries 1 cup hot water

1. Butter aluminum custard cups and sprinkle lightly with sugar and cinnamon.
2. Fill ⅓ with baking powder biscuit dough. Make a hollow in this and put in 1 tablespoon fruit. Add enough dough to fill cup ⅔. Tie over two thicknesses of waxed paper.
3. Place rack in cooker. Add water. Put in pudding. Pre-steam 5 minutes; then bring pressure up to 15 pounds and process 12 minutes.
4. Serve hot with any hot liquid fruit sauce.

APPLE BETTY
Pre-steam 5 minutes—pressure 10 minutes

2 cups soft bread crumbs lightly browned in oven

3 tablespoons melted butter or margarine

½ cup granulated or brown sugar

½ teaspoon cinnamon

¼ teaspoon ground clove

2 cups sliced tart cooking apples

1 cup hot water

1. Combine the crumbs, butter, sugar and spices.

2. Butter a metal or enamelware bowl that will fit loosely into the cooker. Put in alternate layers of the crumb mixture and apples. Leave at least one-inch free at top as this pudding expands. Tie 2 thicknesses of waxed paper over the top.

3. Place the rack in the cooker. Add the hot water. Put in the bowl. Close the cooker. Steam 5 minutes, then bring the pressure to 15 pounds and process 10 minutes.

4. Serve warm with cream or hard sauce.

Peach Betty: Substitute sliced peaches for apples in the preceding recipe.

Cherry Betty: Substitute stoned cherries for apples in the recipe for apple betty.

Cake Crumb Betty: Make any fruit betty using crumbled stale cake or cookie crumbs (plain or mixed) instead of bread crumbs.

BERRY PUDDING

Pre-steam 30 minutes—pressure 25 minutes
Make with blueberries, huckleberries, cranberries
or blackberries

1⅓ cups all-purpose flour
½ teaspoon nutmeg
3 teaspoons baking powder
¾ teaspoon salt
⅓ cup shortening
1 cup quick oats
1 egg

¼ cup molasses
⅔ cup milk
1 cup berries
2 tablespoons sugar
1 tablespoon flour (additional)
Hard sauce

Hot water

1. Measure and sift together the flour, nutmeg, baking powder and salt.

2. Chop in the shortening with a pastry blender until the mixture looks mealy.

3. Add the oats, the egg well-beaten, the molasses and milk; mix well.

4. Mix berries with the flour and sugar.

5. Oil a metal bowl or mold, or use 2 pint-sized cans. Put in a layer of batter. Top with one of berries. Continue until all is used. Tie two thicknesses of waxed paper over the top.

6. Put the rack in the cooker. Set in the molds or cans. Pour in hot water to half the depth of the molds. Close the cooker.

7. Pre-steam 30 minutes. Then bring to 15 pounds pressure and process 25 minutes for cans; 35 minutes for a mold. Cool the cooker.

8. Unmold, slice and serve hot with hard sauce, and stewed berries if desired.

STEAMED CARROT PUDDING

Pre-steam 30 minutes—pressure 50 minutes

½ cup melted shortening
1 cup dry bread crumbs
½ cup brown sugar
½ cup all-purpose flour
2 teaspoons baking powder
½ teaspoon salt
¼ teaspoon nutmeg

Grated rind ½ lemon
1 cup halved, seeded raisins
2 cups grated raw carrots
  (or put through a food
  chopper)
1 egg, slightly beaten
Hot water

1. Combine the ingredients in the order given, and mix till well-blended.

2. Transfer to a buttered metal bowl or mold, or 2 pint-sized cans, filling them ⅔ full. Tie 2 thicknesses of waxed paper over the top.

3. Place the rack in the cooker. Put the pudding on it. Pour in hot water to half the depth of the mold. Close the cooker.

4. Pre-steam 30 minutes. Then bring to 15 pounds and pressure 50 minutes.

5. Slice and serve warm with a liquid fruit sauce, and/or hard sauce.

HOLIDAY FRUIT PUDDING

Pre-steam 30 minutes—process 50 minutes

⅔ cup halved raisins
½ cup dried currants
3 dried figs diced
¼ cup candied peel
½ cup chopped walnut
  meats
1¾ cups all-purpose flour
½ teaspoon cinnamon
½ teaspoon ground clove

½ teaspoon salt
½ cup chopped beef suet
¼ cup brown sugar
¾ teaspoon baking soda
½ cup sour milk or butter-
  milk
¼ cup molasses
1 egg
Hot water

1. Mix together the dried fruits, nuts, flour, salt and spices. Add the suet and sugar.

2. Add the baking soda to the sour milk. Stir and beat into the flour mixture. Add the molasses and egg well beaten.

3. Transfer to buttered pint-sized cans or one metal tube mold that will fit loosely into the cooker. Tie two thicknesses of waxed paper over the top.

4. Place the rack in the cooker. Put in the pudding. Pour in water halfway of the depth of the molds. Close the cooker.

5. Pre-steam for 30 minutes. Then bring pressure to 15 pounds, and process 50 minutes.

6. Slice and serve hot with a liquid fruit or wine sauce and hard sauce.

HOLIDAY PUDDING FLAMBÉE

Turn out the pudding on a round serving-platter. Put rosettes of hard sauce around the edge, and decorate with chopped pistachio nuts and halved candied cherries. Pour 3 tablespoons good brandy carefully over the *pudding*—not the plate! Touch a match to the brandy, and bring flambée (flaming) to the table.

CHRISTMAS PUDDINGS BRAZIL STYLE
Pre-steam 15 minutes—process 30 minutes

1. Make up the mixture for holiday fruit pudding, putting it in individual oiled aluminum custard cups. Tie 2 thicknesses of waxed paper over the top of each.

2. Put 1½ cups hot water into the cooker. Put in the rack. Set the puddings on it. Pre-steam 20 minutes; then bring to 15 pounds pressure and process 30 minutes.

3. To serve, put a small glass dish of rum-flavored hard sauce strewn with toasted sliced Brazil nuts, in the middle of a round glass or silver platter. Surround with the puddings. Insert a whole shelled Brazil nut in each. Light the Brazil nuts and serve.

Steamed Breads

Any steamed bread may be successfully prepared in the pressure-cooker.

Carefully read the instructions for steaming given in this chapter.

BOSTON BROWN BREAD
Pre-steam 30 minutes—process 40 minutes

2 cups sour milk or butter-milk	1 cup coarse entire wheat flour
¾ cup dark molasses	1 cup rye meal
1 teaspoon salt	2 cups granulated corn-meal
1 teaspoon baking soda	
Hot water	

1. Mix together the sour milk and molasses. Add the salt, and the soda dissolved in one tablespoon water.

2. Beat in the entire wheat flour, the rye and cornmeal.

3. Transfer to oiled pint-sized cans or molds. Tie 2 thicknesses of waxed paper over the top.

4. Place the rack in the pressure-cooker. Put in the bread. Pour in hot water halfway the depth of the molds. Close the cooker.

5. Pre-steam 30 minutes and process 40 minutes.

Boston Brown Bread with Raisins: Follow the preceding recipe adding ¾ cup seedless raisins mixed with the meal.

What Pudding Sauce?

Cold Fruit or Cereal Puddings: Use plain cream, whipped cream, soured cream sauce, sunshine sauce, or a sauce of fresh or defrosted frozen fruit, or stewed fruit.

Vanilla Flavored Hot or Cold Desserts: Use sweetened whipped cream, sunshine or chocolatina sauce; use hard sauce for hot puddings if desired.

Hot Steamed Fruit Desserts: Use cream, a liquid fruit sauce, melted jelly, sweet claret or sherried lime juice sauce, or fruit sauce as served on American Overseas Air Lines.

Rich Hot Steamed Desserts: Use two sauces; a hot liquid fruit or wine sauce, and a small serving of hard sauce.

All measurements are level.
Recipes serve four to six.

SWEET CLARET SAUCE

¾ cup granulated sugar   Few grains nutmeg
¾ cup boiling water   ½ cup sweet claret

Combine the sugar and water and boil 5 minutes. Add the nutmeg and claret and serve.

LIME JUICE SAUCE

1 tablespoon cornstarch   1 cup boiling water
⅓ cup sugar   ¼ cup Florida lime juice
Few grains salt   1 teaspoon butter or margarine

1. Combine the cornstarch, sugar and salt in a small sauce-pan and gradually pour in the boiling water. Boil and stir for 2 minutes.

2. Add the lime juice and butter.

3. Serve hot with baked bananas, cottage pudding, gingerbread, fruited bread pudding, steamed puddings, etc.

Sherried Lime Juice Sauce: Prepare as above, using ⅞ cup boiling water. Add 2 tablespoons sherry when done.

GINGER FRUIT SAUCE
(As served on American Overseas Air Lines)

1 tablespoon plain granulated gelatin

2 tablespoons fruit juice (extra)

1½ cups boiling juice from canned fruits

⅔ cup sieved fruit pulp

½ teaspoon powdered ginger

1 tablespoon maraschino cherry juice or grenadine (optional)

Sugar to taste

1. Soften gelatin in the extra fruit juice, then stir into the boiling juice. Cook and stir about 3 minutes.

2. Add the fruit pulp and ginger, and the maraschino juice or grenadine for a red-rose color. Chill till thickened.

Use with steamed sliced left-over cake, custards, or cold rice pudding.

SUNSHINE SAUCE

¼ cup butter or margarine

¼ cup confectioners' sugar

1½ cups light cream or top milk

3 eggs

1 teaspoon vanilla or orange extract

1. Cream the butter and sugar together until light; add the eggs well beaten.

2. Scald the cream or top milk; pour it over the first mixture beating while pouring.

3. Cook over hot water (double-boiler) until thick; cool slightly, and add the flavoring.

4. Serve hot as a sauce for hot puddings, or chill for service with plain ice cream or cold puddings.

HARD SAUCE

⅓ cup butter or margarine 3 teaspoons boiling water
½ teaspoon vanilla Nutmeg or cinnamon
1¾ cups sifted powdered
    sugar

1. Cream the butter; add the vanilla.

2. Alternately cream in the sugar and water.

3. Pile in a dish, dust with nutmeg or cinnamon and chill until firm.

Orange Hard Sauce: Follow the recipe for hard sauce, using 1 tablespoon orange juice and 1 teaspoon lemon juice in place of the water. Omit vanilla.

Rum-Flavored Hard Sauce: Follow the recipe for hard sauce, using rum in place of water. Omit vanilla.

CHOCOLATINA SAUCE

4 tablespoons powdered ½ tablespoon butter
    cocoa 4 tablespoons honey
⅓ cup very strong coffee ⅓ cup white corn syrup
    (or use ½ teaspoon in- ¼ teaspoon vanilla
    stant coffee and ⅓ cup
    hot water)

1. In a small sauce-pan blend the cocoa and coffee. Add the butter. Stir until boiling.

2. Add the honey and corn syrup, and cook and stir until it boils all over. Then add vanilla.

3. Use hot or cold. This sauce is delicious, and keeps indefinitely in a covered jar in the refrigerator.

SPICED SOURED CREAM SAUCE

1 cup soured cream
½ tablespoon lemon juice
¼ teaspoon cinnamon or clove extract

3 tablespoons honey or granulated sugar or more to taste

Combine the ingredients in the order given. Use with fruit betties, gingerbread, Indian pudding or fruit puffs.

CHAPTER XVIII

PRESSURE-COOKED FRESH AND DRIED FRUITS

Aниколай FRUIT MAY BE PRESSURE-COOKED WHETHER FRESH or dried. But as fresh fruits have a very delicate cellular structure, most of them require very little, and in a few cases, no actual pressure-ing, for they cook tender in seconds or a few minutes.

Pulpy fruit sauces as apple or cranberry sauce, are thick and heavy when pressured, and may cause the vent pipe to clog. So better use regulation methods for preparing them.

However, there are times when every moment counts and it is a real asset to prepare stewed fresh fruit quickly. Attractively served in gleaming glass dishes these stewed fruits, which are superb in color and appearance, are suitable for breakfast or dessert at any meal. For a "company" dessert try cooking them in wine (page 341). The following methods will prove practical.

All measurements are level.
Recipes proportioned to serve four.
Timings are minutes required for actual pressuring.
Cool cooker as soon as processing is done.

PRESSURE-STEWED PLUMS

1½ pounds firm plums, any kind
1¼ cups hot water
½ cup sugar
⅛ teaspoon cinnamon (optional)

1. Wash plums and place on rack in cooker. Add sugar and cinnamon.

2. Pour in water. Close cooker. Allow steam to flow from vent pipe for 3 minutes. Bring just to 15 pounds pressure; then *cool cooker at once.*

3. Remove the plums. Boil the liquid 3 minutes and pour over plums.

4. Serve ice cold, plain, or topped with shredded blanched almonds.

Pressure-Stewed Nectarines: Follow the preceding recipe, substituting nectarines.

PRESSURE-STEWED PEACHES
3 to 5 minutes

8 firm ripe peaches
½ cup sugar
1 cup hot water

1. Rub fuzz from peaches with a towel; then wash.

2. Place on rack in cooker. Add water; sprinkle over sugar.

3. Allow steam to flow from vent pipe for 3 minutes.

Bring to 15 pounds pressure and process 4 minutes for small peaches, 5 minutes if large.

4. Cool cooker at once. Remove peaches, slip off skins if desired. Boil the liquid 2 minutes and pour over.

5. Serve plain, or with a slice of plain cake or ice cream.

PRESSURE-STEWED APRICOTS
Steam 3 minutes

1 dozen firm apricots   1 ¼ cups hot water
                    ½ cup sugar

1. Wash apricots. Put directly in cooker. Add water and sugar. Close cooker.

2. Allow steam to flow from vent pipe for 3 minutes. Bring just to 15 pounds pressure; then *cool cooker at once.*

3. Remove the apricots. Boil liquid 2 minutes and pour over.

4. Serve plain or sprinkled with coconut. This is delicious topped with grated canned pineapple. Or accompany with cream cheese and crisp crackers.

PRESSURE-STEWED PEARS
4 to 8 minutes according to size, variety and degree of ripeness

8 firm ripe pears   ½ cup white or brown sugar
1 cup hot water   6 cloves

1. Wash pears but leave on stems. Put on rack in the cooker. Add water and cloves; sprinkle over sugar. Close cooker.

2. Allow steam to flow from vent pipe for 3 minutes. Bring to 15 pounds pressure and process 4 to 8 minutes.

3. Cool cooker at once. Remove pears, slip off skins if desired. Boil liquid 2 minutes and pour over.

4. Serve ice cold, plain, with boiled custard or cream.

FRUITS STEWED WITH WINE

Any of the pressure-stewed fruits described in this book may be prepared with wine. Follow the recipes with this exception: Substitute tokay, muscatel or any sweet wine for half the water specified. Serve ice cold.

STUFFED APPLES BAKED STYLE
2½ to 4 minutes

4 to 6 good-sized cooking apples
4 tablespoons granulated or brown sugar
½ teaspoon cinnamon
Choice of ¼ cup diced dried figs, cranberries, canned grated pineapple or ½ a large banana, diced
½ cup hot water or half water and half sweet wine

1. Wash apples and remove core to within ½ inch of stem-end. Cut a thin strip of peel from the top.

2. Fill with half the sugar mixed with the cinnamon and the chosen fruit. If convenient put ¼ teaspoon butter on top of each one.

3. Put rack in cooker. Pour in water. Put in apples. Sprinkle with remaining sugar. Close cooker.

4. Bring pressure to 15 pounds and process 2½ to 4 minutes according to size. *Cool cooker at once.* Boil liquid 1 minute and pour around apples.

5. Serve hot or cold, or with sweet or soured cream, or cream cheese.

Raisin-d Apples: Follow the preceding recipe, filling

the apples with halved raisins, mixed with a little grated lemon rind.

STUFFED ORANGES
30 minutes

4 large thin-skinned or-
  anges
3 tablespoons sugar
4 tablespoons halved raisins

2 tablespoons chopped preserved ginger
1¼ cups hot water
¼ cup sugar (additional)

1. Wash oranges; cut in halves crosswise; scrape out seeds.

2. Fill centers with the sugar, raisins and ginger mixed.

3. Place on rack in cooker. Pour in water. Sprinkle with remaining sugar. Close cooker.

4. Bring to 15 pounds pressure and process 30 minutes.

5. Serve hot or cold with smoked ham, poultry or game. Eat skin and all.

BANANAS PRESSURE-BAKED IN SKINS
30 seconds

1. Wash firm yellow or green-tipped bananas and cut ends off square.

2. Pour ½ cup hot water in the cooker. Put in rack. Arrange bananas on it. Close cooker.

3. Bring pressure to 15 pounds and process 30 seconds. Cool cooker.

4. Remove a loosened strip of skin from each banana and serve in the "jackets" with butter and salt as a vegetable.

PEELED BANANAS PRESSURE-BAKED
30 seconds

1. Peel firm yellow or green-tipped bananas.

2. Put ½ cup hot water in cooker. Put in rack.

3. Brush bananas with butter and sprinkle with salt. Put on rack. Close cooker.

4. Bring pressure to 15 pounds and process 30 seconds.

5. Lift out bananas with a broad spatula or a pancake turner.

GLAZED BANANAS
30 seconds

1. Peel firm yellow or green-tipped bananas. Brush with butter. Sprinkle with lemon juice and sugar.

2. Pour ½ cup hot water in cooker. Put in rack and place bananas on it. Close the cooker.

3. Bring pressure to 15 pounds and process 30 seconds.

4. Lift bananas from cooker with a broad spatula or pancake turner. Serve as a vegetable.

BANANA COCONUT DESSERT

Prepare glazed bananas. Serve hot, sprinkled with grated coconut and accompanied with lime or fruit sauce. (See page 334.)

DRIED FRUITS
10 minutes

Dried fruits may be quickly pressure-cooked. Always wash thoroughly first. If very dry soak an hour in hot water to cover, and use the same water for pressuring. If moist and fairly soft no pre-soaking is required. Very little if any sugar is needed as pressuring brings out the natural sweetness; and full flavor is retained in the fruit because none escapes during the pressuring process; it is indeed delicious. It is a good plan to pressure enough dried fruit at one time to use at several meals, either as a sauce or compôte, or to have on hand for making mixed fruit cups, deep dish pies, tapiocas, Dutch fruit cake, fruit whips, etc. Be sure the steam vent of the pressure-cooker is thoroughly clean and free.

PRESSURE-STEWED DRIED PRUNES

| 1 pound medium-sized prunes | 2 cups hot water 2 tablespoons sugar (optional) |

1. Wash prunes. Soak if necessary.

2. Place directly in the cooker with the soaking water or the hot water designated. Close the cooker.

3. Bring to 15 pounds pressure. Process 10 minutes. Cool in the cooker. Add sugar if desired.

A few thin slices of orange or lemon may be pressured with the prunes. Or add 3 cloves.

PRESSURE-STEWED DRIED FIGS
10 minutes

1 pound dried figs, any kind   2 cups hot water

1. Wash figs. Soak if very dry as directed. Remove tough ends with scissors.

2. Put directly in cooker. Add water (or use soaking water); close cooker.

3. Bring to 15 pounds pressure and process 10 minutes. Cool in cooker.

PRESSURE-STEWED DRIED APRICOTS
1½ to 2 minutes

1 pound dried apricots   1½ cups hot water
⅓ cup sugar

1. Wash apricots and soak if necessary. Put in cooker with sugar and hot water, or the water in which they are soaked.

2. Close the cooker. Bring to 15 pounds pressure and process 1½ to 2 minutes according to dryness. Cool at once.

DRIED PEARS
10 minutes

1 pound dried pears
6 whole cloves
2 cups hot water

2 tablespoons granulated or
brown sugar or mild-
flavored honey

1. Wash pears and soak if necessary. Put directly in cooker with the cloves and water. Close the cooker.

2. Bring to 15 pounds pressure and process 10 minutes. Cool cooker at once, and add the sweetening.

FRUIT COMPÔTE WALDORF

Use rather large sauce-dishes, glass or china, perhaps with a wide-rimmed green edge. Arrange 3 separate fruits of contrasting color in each dish with a little liquid. For instance:

1. Stewed apricots, prunes, quartered sections of canned pineapple.

2. A stewed peach, orange sections and stewed figs. Add a red cherry or seedless green grapes for a touch of color.

CHAPTER XIX

CANNING DAY BY DAY

Several pressure-cookers, previously designed solely for cooking, have now been adjusted to carry out the double job of pressure cooking and canning. Not canning on the grand scale, but the canning of 3 pint jars of food at a time. If you have your own garden, or can obtain small quantities of fresh vegetables and fruits, this will prove practical, and may be carried on easily while the daily cooking and kitchen work is being done. Persisted in from spring through fall this method will turn out a surprising number and variety of canned foods by the season's end. Vegetables, fruits, relishes, meat, poultry, game and fish may all be canned with safety in the family-size pressure-cooker.

Remember the United States Department of Agriculture recommends pressure-canning as the only safe method for processing non-acid foods.

Home canning is a study and art in itself. So instead of detailing instructions in this book, I am going to refer you to the manufacturer's booklet of canning instructions that may have come with your cooker, and for complete information, to the Superintendent of Documents, Washington, D. C., from whom you can obtain the U.S. government's reliable and most recently published literature on the Home Canning of Fruits, Vegetables, Meats, Poultry and Fish.

CHAPTER XX

MEALS THAT SAVE KITCHEN HOURS

THE TIME-SAVING HELP YOU GET FROM A PRESSURE-cooker depends upon you. It is a fast operating cooking unit, but like other mechanical devices it is started, controlled and stopped by an operator. And in this case the operator is yourself.

Moreover, the pressure-cooker cannot do your thinking and plan your meals. It is up to you to purchase foods that can be pressure-cooked in the time you plan to be in the kitchen. It is up to you to use the cooker not only to assist in preparing dinners, but for every possible cooking operation, such as pressuring cereal ahead for next day's breakfast, preparing dried fruit, cooking potatoes to fry or cream, making soup stock or soup, or cooking beans, meat or poultry in advance. There it stands in your kitchen, ready to go to work to save countless hours of kitchen food watching. All it asks is for you to make its use a habit.

Let the Pressure-Cooker Do It

And it is right here that many owners fail to get the most out of their cookers. Pressure cooking is a new system of cooking. There are new things to learn. The cooker is tried out successfully with an occasional dish, but weeks and months often pass before it is accepted as an active member of the kitchen family. Don't let this happen. From the very first day it comes into the house, the pressure-cooker should be used for every possible cooking process. It will perform so willingly and save so much time, that within a few days its use will become an established habit. And from that point on you can expect to save appreciable amounts of time and energy and turn out foods that are more appetizing, delicious and thrifty than when prepared by old-time procedures.

Starting

Better start your pressure cooking adventure with a single food, such as potatoes. Next try dried fruit or a cereal, and a simple meat dish as a pot roast or a chicken fricassee. By this time you will be a veteran at pressure cooking, with enough experience to know how to operate the cooker, how to take advantage of its speed, and how to plan meals that will be completed when the dish or dishes selected for pressure cooking are ready to serve.

Every homemaker, whether she is an at-home house-wife or a career-housewife, can estimate the amount of time she has to prepare dinner on certain days. This time-unit will vary according to other duties or activities. *For this reason menus should be planned to fit time-budgets.* To help you, I have given with the recipes in this book approximate timings for pressure cooking the foods. And there are hundreds of them—enough to keep the cuisine operating indefinitely on a varied and time-saving basis.

Planning Time-Saving Dinners

First decide how much time you wish to spend in preparing the meal. Then plan a menu made up of foods that can all be made ready to eat in the time allowed. We will assume that the day has been busy and long; perhaps it's the afternoon for the club or PTA meeting, or, if you are a career or business homemaker, it may be the day you always have to work overtime. Perhaps you have only twenty minutes in which to get dinner on the table, and nothing is ready. If you will study the following menus you will find out how to get a hearty dinner ready in those twenty minutes.

Starred recipes are in this book.

SWISS STEAK DINNER
20 minutes

Hot or Chilled Tomato Juice
*Swiss Steak Pressured with Halved White Potatoes
and Carrots
A Tossed Green Salad   Re-heated Rolls
*Lemon Rice Custard   Choice of Beverage

Procedure

1. Brown-heat the Swiss Steak and pressure 16 minutes.

2. Peel the vegetables.

3. Prepare the salad.

4. Put together rice custard ready to pressure.

5. Cool cooker and put in vegetables. Pressure 4 minutes longer.

6. Cool cooker. Put Swiss Steak and vegetables on serving platter and keep hot. Make gravy.

7. Wash cooker. Put in lemon rice custard; and serve dinner while it is pressure-ing.

If you find it hard to get this meal ready in twenty minutes, it is because the kitchen is inefficiently arranged, or because your actual work has been interrupted. This procedure does not include time spent in telephone calls and other interruptions.

Now let's turn fantastic, and assume that the time budget for dinner is only twelve minutes and not a thing ready. What could you have? Try this.

PEPPERED BEEF DINNER
12 minutes

*Chinese Peppered Beef Pressured
with Quartered Potatoes and Onions*
Tomato Platter   Re-heated Rolls
Apple Betty with Cream   Choice of Beverage

Procedure

1. Prepare Chinese peppered beef ready to pressure.

2. On it place quartered peeled white potatoes and halved small onions. Pressure 3 minutes.

3. Prepare tomato platter.

4. Put apple betty together and place in custard cups.

5. Cool cooker; finish cooking the beef and arrange with the vegetables on a deep platter to keep hot.

6. Wash cooker; put in apple betty; serve dinner while it is pressure-ing.

Now don't tell me this can't be done. I've proved it too many times myself. If you are behind schedule it may be because the paring knives are so dull you are slowed up. Many apparently inconsequential things cause inefficiency.

An extra pressure-cooker will pay for itself over and over again if real-time saving is your goal. Suppose you plan to serve baked tenderized ham, a pot roast or some other food that takes up to thirty or forty-five minutes for complete pressure cooking. Two vegetables and a stewed fruit are also on the menu. How could you get the meal ready to serve within forty-five minutes? Let's see.

BAKED HAM DINNER

45 minutes with two pressure-cookers

Grapefruit
Celery   Radishes
*Baked Tenderized Ham   Re-heated Rolls
*Sweet Potato Pineapple Pudding
*Whole Cauliflower with Brown-Buttered Crumbs
*Whole Peaches Stewed in Wine
Choice of Beverage

Procedure

1. Pressure ham in one cooker.
2. Pressure peaches in second cooker and chill.
3. Prepare and chill grapefruit and relishes.
4. Put sweet potatoes into the "peaches" cooker to pressure.
5. Remove ham from cooker; add glaze, and brown in oven.
6. Pressure cauliflower.
7. Serve dinner.

This dinner could start with soup if desired; either pressure-cooked in advance, or canned. A tossed salad might be included. Or the peaches might be accompanied by ice cream, or sliced sponge cake or cookies made in advance, or purchased at a bakery. For an intelligent woman, interested in saving kitchen hours, can and should take advantage of outside commercially prepared foods to a

reasonable extent, *if*—and this is a big IF—these expend-
itures will not upset the food-budget.

I might go on indefinitely suggesting time-saving dinner
menus. But they may not fit your needs, for each family
has its own likes and dislikes. So instead of putting pages
of menus into this book I strongly urge you to devise your
own to suit the family. Consult this book for time-saving
recipes for pressured foods. Think through the menu; then
plan the procedure and cook the meal. Write down the
most successful menus in a notebook, together with the
time-saving routines. You can make a menu-book of your
own and be proud of it.

Kitchenette Cooking

Space limited? Not even an oven? You're cooking in the
parlor? Never mind. You can still produce good meals
without undue muss and cooking odors, if you use a good-
sized pressure-cooker with intelligence. And with only a
two-burner gas or electric unit and a few cooking utensils.

Order all meat or fish trimmed by the dealer. As far as
possible use frozen vegetables and fruits. Buy canned soups,
unless a pressure-cooked soup or chowder is the main dish
of the meal. Let a generous tossed salad containing a variety of raw vegetables take the place of cooked vegetables
two or three times a week. Reserve one burner of the cooking unit for the pressure-cooker. Use the second burner for
heating soup or cooking some other food and for heating
water for coffee or tea-making.

With a little forethought kitchenette dinners like this
can be produced:

KITCHENETTE DINNERS

From a two-burner gas or electric plate.
Starred recipes are in this book.

I

Spinach Soup (Canned)   Crackers
*Panned Chicken with Potatoes (Pressure-Cooker)
Chef's Salad Bowl   Rolls
Half Frozen Apricots   Choice of Beverage

II

Tomato Juice   Cheese Crackers
*Lamb Chops Jardinière (Pressure-Cooker)
Lettuce with Russian Dressing   Rolls
Citrus Fruit Cup   Choice of Beverage

III

Green Pea Soup (Canned)   Toast
*Pressured Fillets of Fish with *Tomato Sauce
Coleslaw   Potato Chips
Fruits in Lemon Gelatin   Choice of Beverage

IV

Grapefruit
*Irish Stew   Toast-at-the-Table
*Tomato Platter
*Custards   Choice of Beverage

Garden Meals

These are so easy to pressure-prepare, so scintillating in taste and so time-saving, we should serve them more often. Garden meals are a wonderful pick-up after too much so-called good eating; too many cocktail parties, or overlong sieges of old-fashioned hard work. (I am not saying anything about the nutritional values of pressured vegetables, as you may think it a bit boresome. However, the real food values are there, plus. And we all like to feel we are getting "plus" values.)

If your pressure-cooker is not equipped with compartments, it will be necessary to do a little planning to cook interesting garden meals. However, this is really very easy. For instance, check through the following menus and directions on pressure-cooking the foods.

Garden Meals

Starred recipes are in this book.

LUNCHEON

Garden Broth
Chicken-Stuffed Squash with Cheese Topping
Tomato Platter　　　　*Crisp Rolls*
Cantaloupe　　　*Choice of Beverage*

The garden broth should be pressured for 3 minutes, strained and kept hot while the squash is pressured the required 6 minutes.

DINNER

Tomato Juice Cocktail
All-in-One Vegetable Dinner   *Corn Custard*
New England Toast
Bowl Salad with Bleu Cheese   Deep Dish Fruit Pie
Choice of Beverage

Pressure and chill the tomato juice at any time and keep it chilled in the refrigerator. Pressure the vegetables 5 minutes and keep them hot, while the corn custard is processing its 6 minutes. Prepare the pie in advance.

COUNTRY SUPPER

Small Salad Bowls with Stuffed Eggs
Asparagus on and with Toast
Fruit Compôte   Gingerbread
Choice of Beverage

Pressure the fruit compôte and bake the gingerbread in advance. Pressure the asparagus and serve on toast with plenty of cream sauce or rarebit sauce (page 233). A really delectable meal.

Cooking Ahead

The pressure-cooker works so rapidly that foods for the next day can often be wholly or partly pressured while the dinner dishes are washed. And correspondingly some foods may be pressured while the breakfast dishes are being dispatched and the kitchen put in order. These jobs, which take from fifteen to thirty minutes, keep you in the kitchen anyway. And most pressure-cooking processes can be completed in that length of time. Stews, fricassees, ragouts and chowders can be pressured ready to re-heat. Or if meat, poultry or game is to be brown-heated, this can be done in advance ready for pressureing even the next day. If the pressure-cooker is allowed to work while *you* are working in the kitchen at other necessary tasks, many kitchen hours will be saved.

FOODS THAT CAN BE PRESSURED AHEAD
To keep, place in jars or refrigerator dishes and cover closely.
Store in an adequate refrigerator—45 degrees F.

Food	Time to Keep
CEREALS COOKED IN WATER	Up to 3 days
SCRAPPLE	Up to a week
SOUPS OF ALL KINDS	Up to 2 days
CLEAR MEAT SOUP-STOCK	Up to 5 days
STEWS, RAGOUTS, FRICASSEES, ETC.	Up to 2 days
TOMATO OR VEGETABLE JUICES	Up to 3 days
VEGETABLES	Up to 3 days
POTATOES (WHITE OR SWEET)	Up to 3 days
ALL LEGUMES	Up to 4 days
SAUCES	Up to 2 days
DRIED FRUITS	Up to 5 days
PRESSURE-STEWED FRUITS OR JUICES	Up to 3 days
PARTLY OR WHOLLY PRESSURED MEAT OR POULTRY	Up to 4 days

The Baby's Food

Babies are exceptionally sensitive to the flavors of food because their "taste-buds" react at once, as they have not been dulled by use. So it is very necessary to prepare baby foods that are not only pure and of the best quality, but that actually taste good in themselves. Any and all forms of puréed foods may be prepared in the pressure-cooker, with little effort and considerable economy. As all foods for young babies with few teeth or none at all, must be puréed, they should be pressured half again as long as for table use. I strongly recommend the purchase of a one- or two-quart pressure-cooker to be used only in preparing baby's food, a food-mill in which to purée it, and small glass jars with tight-fitting covers, in which it may be kept for 24 hours in an adequately cold refrigerator—45 degrees F. Buy the best quality fresh vegetables and pressure-cook them at once. Plan a different vegetable each day for three or four days to furnish variety, and rotate them. Cook a variety of cereals and soups, and an occasional liver or chicken and vegetable combination; or prunes or dried apricots. Use only a trace of salt, and natural sugar or honey. The baby will become accustomed to a wide range of flavors, and a foundation will be laid for good eating habits later on. All foods that are pressure-cooked are automatically sterilized. The baby's diet, of course, should be supervised by the family doctor.

Meals for Children Up to Seven Years

If babies have been fed properly pressured puréed foods in considerable variety, one of the most difficult of child-feeding problems will be painlessly overcome. You know what I mean—that problem, "I don't like it." The child will have formed a liking habit for many puréed foods in little babyhood, and later on will eat solid foods of the same flavor as a matter of course. Children provided with a balanced diet including pressured garden-fresh vegetables, whole grain cereals, all rich in vitamins and minerals, and grade A meats, are eating foods that build strong bodies to house alert minds.

Up to seven years of age doctors and dietitians recommend a substantial noon meal for children, and a light supper. This routine causes considerable extra work in many households, for overconscientious mothers prepare two dinners a day, one for their small children at noon, and an evening meal for the older members of the family. This is not necessary—not when foods are pressured, for almost no nutrients are lost. A portion of the meat and vegetables pressured for the evening meal can be used for the young children's dinner the next noon. Just refrigerate at 45 degrees F. in closely covered heatproof or ceramic casseroles. Ten minutes before serving, place them on the rack in the pressure-cooker. Add a cup of hot water, put on the cover, and steam *without pressure* for 10 minutes. The food will have retained its nutritive value and deliciousness, and many cooking hours will be saved. If the adults' dinner includes a soup, this can be served young children at the evening meal; or substitute an egg or pressured cereal. Add whole grain bread, lettuce, celery or carrot sticks, milk, fresh or pressured fruit, or a fruit compôte, and an appetizing evening meal for the youngsters is ready with little effort.

This same routine will solve the problem of feeding convalescents, or the very elderly who need their substantial meal at noon.

The Pressure-Cooker As a Sterilizer

A four- or six-quart pressure-cooker is an ideal sterilizer for baby bottles, nipples, juicers, small instruments, etc.

How to Sterilize in a Pressure-Cooker: Be sure the cooker and the articles to be sterilized are washed clean. Put the rack in the bottom. **Pour in 1 cup of cold water.** Lay the articles to be sterilized on the rack. Put the nipples in a clean, covered jar. Close the cooker. Turn the heat high until there is a steady flow of steam from the vent pipe. Then bring pressure to 15 pounds and process 15 minutes. Let the articles cool in the cooker. If not needed at once, they will remain sterile and sealed away from air until ready to use a few hours later.

CHAPTER XXI

WHEN YOU ENTERTAIN

ENTERTAINING MAY BE PLEASANT AND ENJOYABLE, OR nerve-racking and difficult. It depends a good deal upon how much and how well you plan, and the quickness and ease with which you prepare the food.

Of course I do not need to suggest to any modern hostess that the day she entertains is *not* the time to choose for a general housecleaning or even for odd jobs, such as polishing silver. All special housekeeping tasks can be done ahead. The marketing should be done the day before. Then with only routine tasks to do, the food in the house, a planned menu and the pressure-cooker to help carry it through with speed and ease, the day you entertain should even present opportunity for a bit of leisure.

The Table

Today's trend toward informal service, with no servants, has simplified table settings. There is still no adequate substitute for a full-sized dinner cloth of gleaming white damask, oyster gray embroidery, or delicate lace. And nothing can take the place of candles after dusk, and a low flower or fruit arrangement on the table. Such a setting dramatizes even the simplest food. We can use lovely dishes, glamorous glass and shining silver, and still keep the menu simple. But if a dinner cloth is too difficult to launder, linen or lace placemats, or table runners are still within the bounds of good taste. However, if possible use linen napkins; paper napkins belong to casual service.

Serving Without a Maid: It is not necessary to be a table-hopper, really, when you both cook and serve a meal —not if you plan to have most of the food served at the table, or if you purchase one of those easy-to-roll buffet carts, on which to push in each course. This should stand at your left during the meal, the top shelf to hold extras, and the lower shelf to be used for soiled dishes. By the way, these buffet carts are also practical and convenient for mixing and serving drinks.

Food Pictures

Given the most charming table setting you can devise, plus good food and radiant YOU, what is the one thing more needed to make the occasion a success? It is delicious glamorous-looking food arranged to present a lovely picture. And making "food pictures" is an art in itself, one which every hostess can and should learn. It does not add especially to the cost of the meal, for food garnishes and decorations are part of the meal itself. It *does* depend, however, upon serving the foods in dishes of the right contrasting or harmonizing color, and upon *not* overgarnishing. Throughout this book many ideas will be found for attractive food presentation. But here are a few additional suggestions.

Arranging Food for Service

Be neat. No gravy or fat spilled on the edge of a plate.
Be careful not to spill coffee into the saucer.

Arrange salads only to within an inch of the edge of a plate.

Serve chef's salad in individual salad bowls.

Place meat and vegetables on the plate so they do not run together.

Add a bit of green garnish to savory foods.

Pass gravy instead of spooning it over meat.

Avoid the use of blue dishes. Blue does not harmonize with the color of most foods.

Supplement the regular set of dishes with a set of glass dishes, as they can be used together to advantage at the same meal.

Remember that the *edge* of the plate, platter or bowl is the frame for the food.

Study food arrangements in the women's magazines and try to carry out the ideas in your own food presentations. It is a fascinating pastime; a hobby that can transform you into an artist with food.

Company Dinners

The following menus for company dinners for four to six guests can be made ready within forty-five minutes the pressure-cooker way. If you are a business woman and are entertaining during the week, better plan a late dinner so there will be time for a shower and fresh make-up. If you do a little beforehand preparation, such as crisping lettuce, preparing relishes, or brown-heating meat ready for pressuring, you can steal enough time to freshen up while dinner is cooking.

The two following company dinners will be ready to eat in forty-five minutes.

All starred recipes are in this book.

*CHICKEN CACCIATORE DINNER
45 minutes complete

Shrimp Cocktail Salad Plates
Chicken Cacciatore   *Spaghetti al Dente*
Peas   Crusty Rolls
Pound Cake à la Mode Chocolatina
Chianti   Coffee

Time-Saving Routine

1. Pressure-cook, cool and shell shrimp for salad plates.
2. Make and cool chocolatina sauce.
3. Set the table.
4. Prepare and pressure-cook chicken cacciatore. Keep hot for service in a covered dish.
5. Assemble salad plates.
6. Pressure-cook spaghetti al dente.
7. Start coffee. Put rolls, butter and relishes on table.
8. Combine spaghetti and chicken for service.
9. Serve dinner.

BEEF À LA MODE DINNER
45 minutes

Tomato Juice Martinis   *Whitefish Canapés*
Olives   Celery Hearts
Beef à la Mode with Gravy
Parslied Potatoes   Chef's Salad Bowl
Citrus Fruit Cup
Burgundy   Coffee

The only preliminary preparation for this hearty dinner is the marinading of the beef which should be done in advance. (See page 97.)

Time-Saving Routine

1. Pressure-cook the beef à la mode.
2. Prepare and chill fruit cups.
3. Prepare and chill tomato juice.
4. Make canapés.
5. Set table.
6. Prepare chef's salad bowl ready to dress.
7. Pressure potatoes.
8. Make gravy.
9. Start coffee.
10. Serve dinner.

Holiday Dinners

Here are two holiday dinner menus. The meat, poultry and game sections of this book contain dozens of further suggestions for appetizing main dishes that will meet both time and money budgets.

Starred recipes are in this book.

TURKEY FRICASSEE DINNER
45 minutes

*Crab Stuffed Avocados   *Heated French Bread
Assorted Olives   Celery Hearts   Radishes
*Brown Turkey Fricassee   *Spanish Rice Ring
*Brussels Sprouts in Brown Butter
Mince Meat Tarts with Ice Cream Topping
Nuts   Fruit
Sauterne   Coffee

TIME-SAVING ROUTINE

1. Buy the tarts or make them using prepared pie-crust mix and packaged mince meat.

2. Pressure-cook the Spanish rice; pack into a ring mold and keep hot.

3. Pressure-cook the turkey fricassee. Do preliminary cooking while the rice is pressure-ing.

4. Prepare relishes.

5. Prepare and chill avocados.

6. Set table.

7. Start coffee.

8. Re-heat mince meat tarts; heat French bread.

9. Pressure-cook Brussels sprouts.

10. Serve dinner.

BAKED HAM DINNER
45 minutes

Tomato Soup with Sour Cream Garnish
Olive Cheese Canapés   *Table Garden Relishes
*Baked Ham with *Grilled Pineapple
*Pressured Halved Sweet Potatoes
*Whole String Beans in Brown Butter
*Macaroon Custards with Frozen Strawberry Sauce
Nuts   Fruit
Burgundy   Coffee

Time-Saving Routine

1. Defrost frozen strawberries at room temperature.

2. Pressure-cook macaroon custards and chill.

3. Pressure-cook ham.

4. Prepare table garden.

5. Make canapés.

6. Prepare sweet potatoes and string beans to pressure-cook together.

7. Set table.

8. Remove ham from cooker, cover with a glaze and heat in oven. Grill pineapple at same time.

9. Pressure vegetables.

10. Start coffee and assemble dessert.

11. Season vegetables.

12. Serve dinner.

Luncheon Parties

Whether big or little, luncheons are always smart and popular—and a very graceful and easy way they are to entertain. Here is a pattern for an adequate three-course luncheon.

Fruit appetizer or soup
Substantial salad or hot dish
An interesting bread
An unusual dessert
Tea or Coffee

For a two-course luncheon omit the appetizer or soup. Here is a group of menus. Use the pressure-cooker for the dish needing longest to cook.

THREE-COURSE LUNCHEONS

Starred recipes are in this book.

*Tomato Madrilene   **Stuffed Roll Slices*
*Raw Relish Plate
*Swiss Egg and Shrimp Salad
*Fruit Compôte   *Coffee*

Honeydew Melon with Lime Wedges
*Hot or Cold Chicken Curry
Rice   *Chutney*   *Vegetable Relishes*
Peach Cake   *Coffee*

TWO-COURSE LUNCHEONS

*Cream of Fresh Pea Soup   **Croutons*
*Fruit Hors d' Oeuvre Plate
Cinnamon Toast Sticks   *Coffee*

*Lobster Bisque
*Heated French Bread   **Fresh Relishes*
*Café Crême   *Coffee*

*Rolled Chicken Pancakes   **Green Peas*
Chef's Salad
*Custards Chocolatina   *Coffee*

Supper Parties

Supper parties are perfect for Sunday entertaining or even for Saturday nights. The menus should be simple, so be sure to provide ample amounts of the foods you serve. If the weather is cold, an informal supper in the living-room before an open fire is delightful. If it is summertime, supper is even more enjoyable when served on the terrace.

The following menus feature one pressure-cooked food. *Starred recipes are in this book.*

In Winter Time

BOUILLABAISSE SUPPER

*Bouillabaisse   **Heated French Bread*
*A Relish Tray
*Four Fruits Cake   *Coffee*

With this menu prepare the relishes, make the cake and assemble all the ingredients for the bouillabaisse in advance. Then pressure-cook it the last minute.

CHICKEN À LA KING SUPPER

Citrus Fruit Cup
*Chicken à la King in *Pastry Shells
Olives   Celery Hearts
*Brownies à la Mode
Sauterne   Coffee

Most of the preparation for this supper may be done in advance. Pressure-cook the chicken; dice and add it to the à la king sauce ready to re-heat. Buy pâté cases or make pastry shells of prepared pie-crust mix. Buy or make the brownies and ice cream.

In Summer Time

SHRIMP COCKTAIL SALAD SUPPER

*Chilled Melon with Wine
*Shrimp Cocktail Salad Plates   Hot Rolls
*Hazel Nut Ice Cream Chocolatina
Hot or Iced Tea or Coffee

Pressure-cook, cool and shell the shrimp for the salad in advance. Prepare and chill the melon ahead of time and make the chocolatina sauce. Buy the ice cream.

COLD FRIED CHICKEN SUPPER

*Chilled Madrilene or a Cream Soup
Assorted Relishes   Potato Chips
*Cold Fried Chicken
Vegetable-Stuffed Tomato Salads   Small Buttered Rolls
*Fruit Cocktail Cake
Hot or Iced Tea or Coffee

Pressure-cook the soup and chicken long enough in advance to be well chilled. Make or buy the sponge cake needed as the basis of the dessert.

"Make Your Own" Parties

These are as enjoyable as they are practical. If the kitchen is roomy and attractive it is a perfect setting. Or the foods can be arranged on a large table in the dining or living room, with small tables here and there where each guest can assemble and enjoy his own food.

Always cook and serve one hot dish in the pressure-cooker such as a pressure-cooked soup, barbecued meat or shrimp creole.

In addition have plenty of raw relishes, pickles and olives; the makings of two or three kinds of sandwiches, including two kinds of bread, a spread and cold meat for sandwich fillings; a bowl of chef's salad, and a second bowl of potato, tomato relish or egg and green pepper salad; a big pie or cake, or fresh fruit and a cheese board, hot or iced coffee or tea, and a fruit or wine punch. An attractive menu might be:

Chinese Won Ton Soup

Olives   *Fresh Vegetable Plate*

The makings for { **Shrimp Creole Sandwiches*
Egg Salad Sandwiches
Olive-nut Sandwiches

*Fruit Cocktail Cake

Hot or Iced Coffee

Barbecues and Picnics

Here the pressure-cooker can be of untold assistance. Pressure-cook the soup, chowder, barbecued meat or baked beans at home. Let out the steam and wrap the cooker in several layers of newspapers. The food will keep hot for an hour or so. Or if the meal is to be cooked outdoors, remember the cooker operates just as quickly over a sheltered outdoor grill as it does at "Home on the Range." So take your pressure-cooker along with the makings for barbecued spare-ribs or lamb riblets, or for clam or fish chowder. And it's wonderful for green corn! You might have:

*Barbecued Spare-ribs   Long Buttered Rolls
Pickles   Scallions   Potato Chips
Minced Coleslaw in Hollowed Tomatoes
Fresh Fruit   Cup Cakes
Coffee

*Pressured Baked Beans
Rolls with Smithfield Ham Spread
Thin Bologna or Ham and Mustard Sandwiches
Pickles   Tomatoes
*Corn-on-Cob
*Four Fruits Cake   Coffee

Hostess Specials

Innumerable letters and telephone calls come to me from career girls and homemakers of all ages, who would like to carry out various menus, but do not know how to prepare all the foods suggested. "Why can't all the recipes be in one book?" they ask.

So to supplement the hundreds of pressure-cooking methods and recipes in this book, and to enable anyone to carry out the menus, I have included this brief section of Hostess Specials—a group of sparkling, easy-to-prepare dishes I hope you and your guests will enjoy.

In passing, I might suggest investigating the many excellent partly prepared packaged, canned and frozen foods on the market. Try them, one at a time; and if they are satisfactory, adopt them into your menu. *But*—remember that every person who uses them "as is" secures the identical flavor or taste you get. So use imagination and personalize them with clever seasoning, combinations with other interesting foods, and new decorative touches. Dare to be deliciously different and you can become a famous cook.

All measurements are level.
Recipes proportioned to serve four to six.

ANCHOVY ROUNDS

3 tablespoons butter	Crisp cheese crackers
1½ tablespoons anchovy paste	Grated yolks 2 hard-cooked eggs
	Water cress or parsley

1. Cream the butter with the anchovy paste.
2. Spread on the crackers.
3. Hold the crackers, buttered side down, and dip into the egg yolk; garnish with water cress or parsley.

SMOKED WHITEFISH CANAPÉS

½ cup minced broiled smoked whitefish	1 teaspoon lemon juice
1 cream cheese	Canapé crackers or strips of crisp toast

1. Combine the smoked whitefish, cream cheese and lemon juice and spread on the canapé crackers or toast.

2. Decorate with a slice of red radish or stuffed olive, or with 3 capers placed clover leaf fashion.

MUSHROOM LIVER PÂTÉ CANAPÉS

2 chicken or duck livers
2 tablespoons butter
3 tablespoons minced fresh or cooked mushrooms

1 minced hard-cooked egg
Onion juice or onion salt to taste

1. Slowly fry the chicken or duck livers in the butter until tender. Then mince fine. Add the mushrooms and fry 1 minute longer.

2. Add the chopped hard-cooked egg; mix and season with the onion juice or onion salt, and salt and pepper to taste. The mixture should be quite smooth.

3. Spread on finger lengths of white or rye bread, or crisp crackers.

CHEESE TURNOVERS

Rich pie pastry (p. 199) or packaged pie-crust mix

1 package Old English cheese spread

Paprika

1. Roll the pastry to one-eighth inch in thickness; cut in three-inch rounds with a cookie cutter.

2. On half of each, place a teaspoonful of the Old English cheese spread.

3. Moisten the edges of the pastry with a little water; then fold turn-over fashion, in the shape of a half moon. Press the edges together with a fork.

4. Brush with melted butter and dust with paprika.

5. Bake twelve minutes in a hot oven, 400 degrees F. Serve at once.

STUFFED ROLL SLICES

6 long, fresh, crisp dinner rolls

1 package cream cheese

2 tablespoons butter or margarine

¼ cup finely minced salted nuts any kind

¼ cup minced olives, or devilled Smithfield ham spread

1. Make an incision at the end of each roll and pull out the soft portion leaving the roll tunnel-shaped.

2. Cream together the cream cheese, butter, nuts and olives or Smithfield ham spread. Pack this into the rolls and chill.

3. To serve cut in ¼-inch slices. This makes about 50 roll slices.

CHILLED MELON WITH WINE

1 medium-sized honeydew melon or 3 honey balls

1 cup Marsala wine—port or sherry

1. Make a round incision about 3 inches in diameter at the stem end of the melon. Remove this section.

2. Scoop out the seeds with a spoon. Pour in the wine. Replace the melon top and chill for several hours in a very cold part of the refrigerator.

3. Serve sliced with a little of the wine poured over each portion. Use as the first course at a summer luncheon or dinner.

CARROT FLOWERS

Scrape large carrots and rinse. Cut thin slices from the large end and notch in four places with the scissors. Let stand in ice water until the "blossoms" curl at the edges.

RADISH TULIPS

Cut the root ends, and all but a single green leaf from the radishes. Cut a thin slice from the bottom end. Slash the 4 sides of the radish down to form "petals," and let the radishes "blossom" in ice water.

SCALLIONS RELISH STYLE

Cut the green tops off to within 2 inches of the root end. Cut off the little roots. Slash the root end crosswise and let "blossom" in ice water—a new type of Bermuda Lily.

FRUIT HORS D'OEUVRE PLATE

½ package cream cheese
2 tablespoons snappy cheese
2 tablespoons minced celery
Paprika
8 sections canned or fresh pineapple
Quartered slices 2 bananas
1 lemon
½ cup chopped salted nuts
Strawberries or blackberries
Powdered sugar
1 can litchi (optional)

1. Make balls by blending together the cream cheese, snappy cheese, and the celery. Sprinkle with the paprika.
2. Place a cheese ball in the center of each salad plate.

3. Around this arrange alternating sections of pineapple, the banana dipped in lemon juice and rolled in chopped nuts, the berries sprinkled with powdered sugar, and the canned litchi (Chinese fruit).

RAW TOMATO RELISH

2 tablespoons chopped parsley
6 chopped green onions with an inch of the top
1 teaspoon minced tarragon, basil or marjoram, or ½ teaspoon if powdered
⅓ cup salad oil
2½ tablespoons tarragon wine vinegar
1 teaspoon sugar
½ teaspoon salt
Black pepper
5 large red tomatoes
1 short stubby cucumber

1. Combine the parsley, young onions, herbs, oil, vinegar and sugar. Add the salt and a generous amount of black pepper.

2. Do not peel the tomatoes. Remove the stem ends. Cut the tomatoes in chunks for easy eating; add the herb sauce.

3. Wash and dry the cucumber. Cut off the ends. Peel half the cucumber lengthwise. Then slice paper-thin, leaving on the remaining green rind. Add to the tomatoes.

4. Stir gently; cover, chill and serve in place of a salad.

Indian Relish: Add ¾ cup grated fresh, or unsweetened frozen coconut to raw tomato relish.

TOMATO PLATTER

Firm, good-sized red, white or yellow tomatoes; or all three kinds
Water cress or parsley
½ cup chopped chives, or green onions, with or without ½ teaspoon minced tarragon, basil or mint

1. The tomatoes should be well chilled. Slice ¼-inch thick. (A saw-toothed knife is best for this purpose.) Arrange the tomatoes in overlapping rows. If all 3 colors are available, make the center row yellow and the outer rows of alternating red and white slices.

2. Sprinkle with salt; grind over a little black pepper, and sprinkle the onions and herbs down the center row.

3. Garnish sparingly with water cress or parsley.

4. Serve "as is," or with plain or wine mayonnaise, soured cream salad dressing or sauce vinaigrette.

Table Vegetable Garden

Star this lovely table garden as a dinner centerpiece. All eyes focus on it. Anticipating fingers pull out tempting morsels. No difficulty coaxing the family to eat their full quota of appetizing raw vegetables when a table garden appears. Everyone munches till dessert when the empty dish makes its exit. Provide plain or herb salt to dust on the vegetables, or serve "dunking style" with small glasses or paper cups half filled with mayonnaise, Russian dressing, or well-seasoned soured cream.

I have seen this table garden served not only at the smartest of dinners, but at buffet suppers, and at cocktail parties, too. At these parties dark bread canapés were served, with toppings of chicken liver pâté or cold scrambled eggs crisscrossed with strips of smoked salmon. In addition to the usual cocktails, sherry, chilled tomato, and grapefruit juice were provided, giving the guests a choice of several beverages.

Raw Relish Plates: Instead of arranging raw relishes in table garden form, interesting arrangements can be made on plates. I like to use big glass plates; or pottery or Mexican plates about 14 inches in diameter.

TABLE VEGETABLE GARDEN

1 whole bunch celery	2 tomatoes
2 long raw carrots	12 red radishes
2 large raw beets	½ bunch water cress
1 tender cucumber	1 small red apple
6 raw young onions	6 caulifleurettes

1. Wash vegetables; trim and wrap them in a damp cloth; crisp in refrigerator.

2. Trim tough branches from celery with scissors; then pull off all the strings.

3. Cut unpeeled cucumber lengthwise into fourths, then into eighths forming sticks.

4. Cut roots and excess tops from onions; slash through white portion and crisp.

5. Peel beets and carrots; cut into sticks; quarter tomatoes; core and slice the apple.

6. Break off and wash the caulifleurettes, which are small raw sections of cauliflower.

7. Stick celery, cucumber and onions into a dish of ice cubes. Add other vegetables, making an attractive "garden" arrangement.

HAM-O-LAS
(Individual Service)

2 wheat cakes	2 tablespoons minced ham
1 plain one-egg omelet	Melted butter

1. Make 2 plain wheat cakes for each person.

2. Butter and put together with a one-egg omelet of the same size as the pancakes and sprinkled with or containing minced ham.

3. Serve with plenty of melted butter poured over. Pass maple or date syrup if desired.

ROLLED CHICKEN OR TURKEY PANCAKES

1 dozen very thin French pancakes
Grated Sbring or Parmesan cheese

1½ cups minced chicken or turkey in thick cream sauce

1. Make pancakes about 6 inches in diameter.

2. On each put a heaping tablespoon of the creamed chicken or turkey.

3. Roll up, and place side by side, fold side down in a buttered pan. Sprinkle thickly with the cheese.

4. Ten minutes before serving time put under the broiler to heat and melt the cheese.

FRENCH PANCAKES

2 eggs
1½ cups milk

1 cup all-purpose flour
¼ teaspoon salt

1. Beat the eggs light; add the milk and beat in the flour and salt.

2. Cook one at a time as follows: heat a six-inch frying-pan and oil it sparingly with butter. Pour in a generous tablespoon of the mixture. It will spread and almost fill the pan; then cook a second one.

3. Continue in this way until the batter is all used.

SHRIMP COCKTAIL SALAD PLATE

3 cups pressure-cooked or canned shrimp
½ cup pickled pearl onions
1½ cups diced celery or cucumber

½ cup sliced stuffed olives
White Wine Mayonnaise
Coleslaw
Tomatoes
Water cress

1. All the ingredients should be very cold. Mix the shrimp with the onions, celery, olives and White Wine Mayonnaise to blend.

2. Heap in the middle of a large round platter; surround with spoonfuls of coleslaw, slices of tomato and cress.

CRAB-STUFFED AVOCADOS

2 chilled medium-sized avocados
1 cup flaked crab meat
1 tablespoon chili sauce
½ tablespoon horseradish
1 tablespoon soured cream

1 tablespoon mayonnaise
½ tablespoon lemon or lime juice
Water cress, chicory or parsley

1. Wash and dry the avocados. Cut in halves crosswise and remove the seeds just before using.

2. Fill with the crab combined with the seasonings. Top with a bit of water cress or other greens.

3. Serve on individual plates with a salad garnish.

Tuna-stuffed Avocados: Substitute flaked tuna fish for crab meat in the preceding recipe, and add half of a chopped hard-cooked egg.

SWISS SHRIMP AND EGG SALAD

4 hard-cooked eggs
2 tablespoons mayonnaise
1 tablespoon minced parsley or herbs
½ pound pressured fresh shrimp or 1 (5 oz.) can shrimp

8 narrow strips green pepper
Lettuce
French dressing

1. Halve the eggs lengthwise. Remove the yolks, mash.

2. Add the mayonnaise, parsley and salt and pepper to taste.

3. Replace in the whites. Stand 2 shrimp upright on each half egg with a strip of green pepper between.

4. Arrange in lettuce nests. Pour over French dressing, plain or curried.

CHICKEN SALAD WITH NUTS

Prepare chicken salad with a little celery, cutting the chicken in flakes rather than dice. Add 2 or 3 tablespoons of crisp salted nuts, chopped coarse. Garnish with whole nut meats. Use wine mayonnaise if possible.

Turkey Salad with Nuts: Substitute turkey for chicken in the preceding recipe.

WALDORF SALAD FLORIDA STYLE

1½ cups diced apple
2 tablespoons lime juice
1 cup diced celery
⅓ cup chopped toasted nut
  meats any kind

Mayonnaise or salad dressing
Lettuce or other salad greens
A few whole nut meats

1. If the apples are red leave on the skin. Add the lime juice to the apple and mix to prevent discoloration. Add the celery and nut meats.

2. Blend and mix with the mayonnaise.

3. Serve in nests of lettuce or other salad greens. Decorate each serving with 1 or more whole nut meats and 2 thin slices of red-skinned apple sprinkled with lime juice.

HORS D'OEUVRE SUPPER PLATTER

On half of a large round pottery platter arrange sliced pressured-potato and green pepper salad. On the second half arrange large canned sardines. Border with wedges of tomato, scallions and hard-cooked eggs, the stuffing seasoned with a little Smithfield ham spread.

LIME FRENCH DRESSING
(For Fruit Salads)

¼ teaspoon salt	½ tablespoon sugar
¼ teaspoon paprika	⅓ cup salad oil

⅓ cup Florida lime juice

Mix the salt, paprika and sugar. Gradually add the salad oil and lime juice; beat constantly until well blended. Chill and re-mix before serving. Use with fruit salads.

Savory Lime French Dressing: For vegetable or fish salads. Follow recipe for lime fruit French dressing omitting the sugar. Instead, add 1 tablespoon prepared mustard and a little onion juice.

WHITE WINE MAYONNAISE
(With any savory meat or salad)

1 cup mayonnaise	3 tablespoons dry Sauterne
½ tablespoon lemon juice	Reisling or any dry white wine

Combine the three ingredients and use.

COTTAGE CHEESE DRESSING

1 cup soured cream   1½ tablespoons lemon juice
1 teaspoon honey   ½ cup cottage cheese
            Salt and pepper to taste

Combine and use with fish, fruit or vegetable salads.

A TRIO OF GRAPEFRUIT SALADS
(*Individual Service*)

1. Arrange alternately sections of fresh or canned grapefruit and whole strawberries in a deep salad plate. Garnish with water cress.

2. Arrange fresh or canned grapefruit sections, in fan shape, on half of a deep salad plate. Place lettuce on the second half and top with pressured jumbo shrimp.

3. Arrange a "wheel" of 6 fresh or canned grapefruit sections in a deep salad plate. Between each place a bing cherry stuffed with a toasted almond. Garnish with dark green lettuce and points of French endive.

Serve these salads with a choice of white wine mayonnaise, lime French dressing or cottage cheese dressing.

FUDGE BROWNIES

¼ cup butter or margarine   1 teaspoon vanilla
¾ cup granulated sugar   ¼ cup milk
2 squares bitter chocolate   ¾ cup cake flour
    melted   ¼ teaspoon salt
1 tablespoon dark corn   ½ teaspoon baking powder
    syrup   1 cup chopped walnut
2 eggs well beaten   meats

1. Cream the butter and sugar together. Add the chocolate, corn syrup, eggs and vanilla. Stir until well mixed. Add milk.

2. Sift together the flour, salt and baking powder; add the nuts. Stir into the first mixture.

3. Oil a shallow pan 8 × 13 inches. Spread the brownie mixture evenly in this. It should be about ¼ of an inch thick.

4. Bake 15 minutes in a moderate oven, 375 degrees F. Cut in 2-inch squares while still warm. These will keep fresh several days if stored in a closed can.

Brownies à la mode: For each person top a brownie with a half scoop of ice cream, and pour over chocolatina sauce.

CAFÉ CRÊME

¾ cup whipping cream
2 tablespoons sugar
1 cup strong well-sweetened coffee
2 tablespoons brandy (optional)

Shaved sweet chocolate
1 package social teas, vanilla and chocolate mixed

1. Whip the cream with the sugar.

2. Combine the coffee and brandy.

3. Butter a quart oblong mold, and sprinkle thickly with shaved sweet chocolate.

4. Dip the social teas in the coffee, and arrange in layers in the mold; spread each layer with the whipped cream. Make the last layer social teas. Cover with waxed paper.

5. Chill overnight. Unmold and serve covered with more shaved chocolate.

FRUIT COCKTAIL CAKE

1 (eight-inch) sponge cake
½ cup tokay wine
¼ pound blanched almonds halved lengthwise

2 cups fresh fruit cocktail mixture in ¼ cup tokay wine

1. Put the sponge cake on the serving plate and pierce it with a fork in a dozen places. Then pour over the tokay which will be immediately absorbed.

2. Make little incisions and stick the almond meats all over the top; chill at least an hour.

3. Serve surrounded with the fruit cocktail mixture.

Note: This can be made individually with sponge cup cakes.

FOUR FRUITS CAKE

½ cup butter or margarine
1 cup granulated sugar
2 eggs
Grated rind ¼ lemon
Grated rind ¼ orange
1 tablespoon lemon juice
½ cup mashed banana

1¾ cups all-purpose flour
1¾ teaspoons baking powder
¼ teaspoon salt
¼ cup orange juice
¼ cup pineapple juice
Fruit icing
Grated coconut

1. Stir butter or margarine until creamy. Add the sugar, the eggs well beaten, the lemon and orange rind, the lemon juice, and the mashed banana.

2. Sift together the dry ingredients and add alternately to the first mixture with the orange and pineapple juice mixed.

3. Transfer to an oiled good-sized cake pan and bake 40

minutes in a moderate oven, 350–375 degrees F. Cover with the icing and sprinkle with grated coconut.

Fruit Icing: Stir ¼ cup butter or margarine until very creamy. Add ½ teaspoon grated lemon rind. Gradually beat in 2 cups sifted confectioner's sugar alternately with one tablespoon each lemon and orange juice.

Note: For further dessert suggestions see Chapters XVII and XVIII of this book.

INDEX